Acclaim for *Italy's Shrines and Wonders*

"In *Italy's Shrines and Wonders*, Teresa Tomeo beautifully describes Italy's rich spiritual heritage and many of its cultural treasures. This very accessible and easy-to-use guide transcends the typical travelogue, inviting readers to embark on a spiritual and cultural pilgrimage through the heart of Italy, a land steeped in faith, history, and beauty. This book is a wonderful resource for those eager to visit Italy and discover the profound connections between faith, history, natural beauty, and the vibrant Italian spirit."

— *Most Reverend Frank J. Caggiano*, Bishop, Diocese of Bridgeport

"Teresa has done it again — thorough research, gorgeous photos, sacred spaces, fantastic sights, and everything in between! Italy is covered by this 'seasoned' Italian from head to toe. Teresa caters to everything you could desire. *Bravissima!*"

— *Susan Tassone*, Author, *New Friends Now and Forever*

"Several things make a book stand out from the rest — engaging content, organized presentation, thoughtful wording, and, in this case, lovely pictures and informative sidebars. But what makes *Italy's Shrines and Wonders* a treasure is Teresa Tomeo's ardent love and enthusiasm, which light up every page. With the expertise of an experienced guide, Teresa invites you to share her favorite adventures and little-known secrets in the land of her ancestors, which she has adopted with a passion. The gorgeous beauty and exquisite culture of Italy draw you in. Italy's palpable Catholic heritage exudes from every page. Join Teresa on a delightfully spiritual and culturally enriching journey through a country that radiates the glory of Christendom."

— *Steve Ray*, Author, filmmaker, Bible teacher,
pilgrimage leader, CatholicConvert.com

"When Teresa says grace before meals, she often adds, 'And thank You, God, for Italy!' Now we have our own thank-you to Teresa for this big, bold, beautiful book — *Italy's Shrines and Wonders*! Her encyclopedic knowledge of 'the Motherland' totally captures the magic of Italy, where churches, piazzas, fountains, and palazzi are old, but the spirit is young! We are drawn by the remarkable yet distinctive beauty of each Italian region. We are endlessly awed by shrines and saints, by incomparable art, by majestic basilicas and elegant bridges, by splendid piazzas with their bubbling fountains. We are seduced by food unmatched this side of Heaven, perhaps as we dine on an ancient square with a church bell accompanying our grace before meals. This and so much more."

— *Joan Lewis*, EWTN Senior Contributor;
Host of *Joan's Rome and Vatican Insider*

"Teresa Tomeo has done it again with this fascinating, faith-based, fact-packed guide to *Italy's Shrines and Wonders*. The fruit of years of study and on-the-ground exploration, this book makes Italy come alive, whetting the appetite for travel all across the "boot," from its celebrated hot spots to its countless hidden treasures. Best of all, the book is laced with love — love for food, love for people, love for travel, love for Italy, and above all, love for God. *Buon viaggio!*"

— *Dr. Thomas D. Williams, Ph.D.*, Theologian,
author, speaker, and consultant

ITALY'S SHRINES AND WONDERS

TERESA TOMEO

FOREWORD BY FR. JOHN RICCARDO

ITALY'S
SHRINES
AND
WONDERS

DISCOVERING SACRED SPACES, FASCINATING PLACES, AND DESTINATIONS OFF THE BEATEN PATH

EWTN Publishing, Inc.
Irondale, Alabama

Cover by LUCAS Art & Design, Jenison, MI.

Cover image: *Shrine of Madonna del Corona*

Interior Design: Perceptions Studios with Emma Helstrom and Charity Walton

Unless otherwise noted, biblical references in this book are taken from the New Revised Standard Version Bible: Catholic Edition, copyright © 1989, 1993 National Council of the Churches of Christ in the United States of America. Used by permission. All rights reserved worldwide.

EWTN Publishing, Inc.
5817 Old Leeds Road, Irondale, AL 35210

Distributed by Sophia Institute Press, Box 5284, Manchester, NH 03108.

paperback ISBN 978-1-68278-425-9

ebook ISBN 978-1-68278-426-6

Library of Congress Control Number: 2024950135

first printing

DEDICATION

To John Hale and the Team at
Corporate Travel Service

Every journey starts with a first step. My initial step bringing me closer and closer to the land of my heritage began in full with the invitation from my dear friend and "little brother" John Hale. Thank you all for your amazing work, a ministry that makes such a difference in the lives of so many as you and your co-workers help travelers experience the true, the beautiful, and the good. And *grazie* for allowing me and Deacon Dom to join you in this effort.

TABLE OF CONTENTS

Foreword — Fr. John Riccardo. ix

Preface — A Pilgrim's Perspective by John Hale, Corporate
Travel Service xiii

Introduction 1

How To Use This Book 7

PART 1: ROME AND THE LAZIO REGION
Marvels of the Vatican and Beyond. 11

PART 2: UMBRIA REGION
The "Green Heart" (Cuore Verde) of Italy. 67

PART 3: CAMPANIA AND PUGLIA REGIONS
Italy Coast to Coast. 127

PART 4: SICILY AND CALABRIA REGIONS
Nautical Neighbors. 181

PART 5: TUSCANY, LIGURIA, AND CINQUE TERRE REGIONS
Delighting by Land and by Sea 221

PART 6: LOMBARDY, PIEDMONT, AND VENETO REGIONS
Northern Lights 275

PART 7: GOING HOME AGAIN
Continuing to Explore. 331

APPENDIX
T's Italy: Your Ultimate Insider Travel Tips 359

Index 369

Acknowledgements. 381

Image Credits 383

About the Author. 395

FOREWORD
BY FR. JOHN RICCARDO
Founder of Acts XXIX Ministry, www.actsxxix.org

— — — — — — —

EXPLORING ITALY: WE WERE BORN FOR THIS

Sit back, pull out your favorite highlighter, and prepare to dog-ear more than a few of the following pages. You are about to dive into a wondrously eclectic book the likes of which I've never come across in Italy or anywhere else for that matter. In her own inimitable style, with both wit and wisdom, Teresa Tomeo has given us a treasure.

Like Teresa, I am also an Italian American, although not full-blooded like she and her husband, Dominick. I have also been blessed to spend a fair amount of time in *Bella Italia*, having lived there for four years in the early 1990s, and I have been a frequent visitor ever since. That said, I found myself constantly repeating, "How did I miss that?" or, "Why did I never go there?" as I eagerly devoured *Italy's Shrines and Wonders: Discovering Sacred Places and Fascinating Places off the Beaten Path*. I simply can't wait to go back. So, what a gift this book is, especially for those headed to Italy for the first time. Teresa calls our attention to places that are simply not to be missed in Rome, Milan, and the Amalfi Coast, but also makes us aware of locations like Spello and Montallegro that we've probably never heard of. In short, if you're planning a trip, read this book first and then decide where you want to go and what you want to do.

What is the enduring appeal of Italy? Rome and the Roman Empire continue to capture the imagination of modern audiences in movies and books. As you walk along the streets near the Forum, maps reveal the steady and extraordinary growth of the city from a small little village to a geographical expanse that boggles the imagination. It's almost unfathomable how one place could have been so dominant. The sheer power of the Roman Empire, then, is one cause of allure.

Ancient Roman buildings continue to impress the minds of modern engineers and architects. I live in Detroit, home of the Detroit Lions. In 1975, the team moved into its massive new stadium, the Pontiac Silverdome. Not only does the team no longer play there, but the stadium doesn't even exist! Compare this with the Roman Colosseum — built in the 70s (not the 1970s) as a home to lions and various other exotic animals. It's still standing, remarkably intact despite barbarian invasions, two world wars, and all sorts of other disasters, both natural and otherwise. Especially for us moderns who often and foolishly consider ourselves intellectually superior to the ancients, Italy serves as a powerful reminder that the ancients were brilliant!

When I lead pilgrimages to Italy, I often subtitle them "Learning to Live." My own experience of late has led me to think that one of the most serious crises facing us nowadays is the simple and crucial truth of what it means to be authentically human. Oh, the Italians, like the rest of humanity, have their issues, but they have much to teach us about what it means to be fully human. Food, for example, isn't just fuel for the body for Italians; it's relational. It's normal in Italy to spend all evening around a table, savoring local table wine, delectable pasta, fresh vegetables and fruit, and of course a little gelato after. Why rush home to bury our heads in a device, when we were created for friendship and communion?

Italy in general, and Rome in particular, is also a place where the saints come alive. Until I moved there, these heroic men and women from ages past were more or less statues, stained glass windows, or mere names of a parish. Italy changes all of that almost in an instant. Within hours of landing at Fiumicino Airport, about twenty miles outside of Rome, you can find yourself not just in but under St. Peter's Basilica, walking first-century streets of an ancient necropolis, and encountering the bones of a man who walked with Jesus around the Sea of Galilee. A short trek brings you to the rooms where St. Ignatius of Loyola lived, the founder of the Society of Jesus. Hop onto a bus or a taxi — if you're up for a little adventure — and you're inside the Basilica of St. Paul Outside the Walls, praying before relics not only of Peter's Cilician contemporary but his student and friend Timothy as well.

Board a train and you find yourself in the enchanted town of Assisi, where you can pray in front of the same San Damiano crucifix from which Francis heard Jesus say, "Go and rebuild My Church, which, as you can see, is obviously in ruins." His tomb, and that of his dear friend Clare is right at hand as well. "The communion of saints" becomes no

Basilica of St. Paul Outside the Walls

longer just a line in the Creed but a reality from the past that calls out to us. The witness of these and other saints reminds us that now we are called to take the baton from them and become saints ourselves.

This land of my paternal grandparents strikes me especially, though, because it reveals the power of the gospel like no other place I know. It's frequently said that history is written by the winners. That's often true. It wasn't true, however, for the early Church. Christianity was an illegal sect in the most powerful empire in the world from the time of Nero in 64 until the early fourth century. According to Roman law, it was not licit for a Christian to exist in the Roman Empire; believers in the Lord Jesus were considered a serious threat to the Empire who worshiped another lord — Caesar. Yet, this grandest of empires — including brilliant architects and artisans — was won to Jesus because of the joyful, charitable, merciful, and convincing witness of those first believers. They serve as a powerful witness to those of us who might be tempted to despair about the state of our country or the world. God changes lives time and time again, and He uses ordinary men and women to do extraordinary things and to change the lives of others.

So, settle in, enjoy, and start planning your trip. As you do, ask the Lord Jesus to use you even as He used Peter, Paul, Clare, Francis, Ignatius, Catherine of Siena, and so many others to change the world. They were born for their times; we were born for this.

PREFACE
A PILGRIM'S PERSPECTIVE

— ■ — ■ — ■ — ■ — ■ —

By John Hale
President of Corporate Travel Service, Southeastern Michigan

EXPERIENCING THE TRUE, BEAUTIFUL, AND GOOD IN ITALY

If pilgrimage is a metaphor for life, nowhere is this metaphor more real and present for me and countless others over the centuries than on a pilgrimage to Italy. This image of pilgrimage is most especially vibrant in the off-the-beaten paths of Italy that my dear friend Teresa introduces us to in this book. Through her many years of research and leading groups to Italy, Teresa introduces us to some of the most spectacular and little-known places of Italy.

On arrival in Italy, pilgrims are often greeted by locals with a poignant sign: "Salve." A derivation of the Latin verb *salvēre*, it means "to be in good health." Italy is truly a place of good health, good food, and good company through Italy's incredible beauty, art, architecture, faith, and food.

And yet, there is another side to Italy as well, almost in opposition to this call to renewed health: it is the witness of the many martyrs you will meet throughout the churches and streets you walk. Everywhere you turn, almost upon arrival, you will encounter otherwise peaceable people who were killed, not for who they were, but for whom the enemy saw in them: Our Lord and Savior, Jesus Christ. These witnesses — in the form of shrines, relics, and other wonders — will be profound, life-changing, and ever-present on any pilgrimage to Italy.

Of course, those who are open to receiving such invitations to faith will have many incredible opportunities to encounter God along the way, often off-the-beaten path. Throughout this book you will encounter several such stories of people who responded to this invitation to faith — representing just a tiny fraction of the total number of lives changed.

GOD IS INVITING YOU . . .

I am convinced that the Holy Spirit calls to each of us, and that every person on a pilgrimage is there — whether they know it or not — by a working of the Holy Spirit. (This is true of other retreats or conferences as well.) This calling can take different forms.

For some, it is a desire that bubbles up from some undefinable source, often combining with a natural interest. Maybe you heard someone talk of their own pilgrimage experiences. Perhaps you have a devotion to a particular Italian saint or artist. Perhaps you have received many subtle points of invitation over many years before receiving an opportunity to act on it, being invited by a friend, parent, child or someone they trust to join them on a pilgrimage.

Other times this invitation comes from an unexpected, even difficult circumstance or experience. Many years ago, I found myself seated next to a man on a bus, and asked how he was enjoying his day. His eyes glistened, and he replied that it was "the best day of his life." It turns out he had been to Confession and Communion for the first time in forty years and felt very close to his deceased wife, whose dying wish was for him to go on a pilgrimage. Not to go back to church, or to meet with a priest. To go on a pilgrimage. Not long after she passed, he happened to hear Teresa talking about this upcoming pilgrimage and remembered his promise to his wife.

And here we were.

How did you come to be here, today, at this moment? We know that God invites; He does not compel. Each day He invites us to take steps of faith — large and small ones. Our lives are essentially determined by how we respond to this series of invitations.

Of course, not all invitations are from God (and not all are good, or to be accepted). We need to prayerfully discern each one. Which of the many invitations we accept each day (and those large ones that come along every so often) determine not only the trajectory of our lives but eternity as well.

MOVE OFF THE BEATEN PATH

When we break with the busyness of our days, the assault of the electronics, and the assault of the media in order to visit the quiet of a lake, meadow, forest, or mountain, we can better hear God and His call. Of course, we can and should discern that call in the quiet presence of the Eucharist, and in reading Sacred Scripture. That is very important!

And yet, when we are on pilgrimage, many well-known "holy sites" can be crowded and noisy, creating a physical barrier to going deeper and experiencing God in a more meaningful way. The crowds and internal pressure to experience something of the transcendent can itself become a barrier to hearing God's voice.

As we move outside our routines and daily paths, both physically and spiritually, we can often hear anew (or for the first time), the voice and will of God in our lives. Once we determine an invitation is from God, we can say yes and move forward with faith. God blesses even the smallest steps, when we "walk by faith, not by sight" (2 Cor. 5:7).

As you embark upon your pilgrimage — whether that means flying to Italy or simply pondering the "shrines and wonders" you will find on these pages in the comfort of your own home — may you experience His grace through the sites, saints, and people you will meet along this journey.

As you will read in the "Pilgrim's Perspective" stories you will find in this book, many did not expect to have their lives dramatically changed so quickly and so positively. But they were open. They took the invitation, even if somewhat reluctantly, and the rest, as they say, is history.

God willing, we have many other exceptional journeys planned. If you would like to join us, please visit www.ctscentral.net.

Pellicano Hotel, Ercole, Tuscany (Deacon Dom, Teresa Tomeo, Kristan Hale, and John Hale)

INTRODUCTION
WHAT IS IT ABOUT THIS PLACE?

I can still remember when my husband Dominick asked me that question. We were celebrating our twentieth anniversary by returning to what we as full-blooded Italian Americans like to call "the Motherland." It was our third trip to Italy, and we had arrived two days early to have some R and R along the Amalfi Coast before our tour began.

Our hotel was perched above the town on a cliff overlooking the dramatic, deep turquoise Mediterranean. But it wasn't just the striking scenery that took our breath away. It was the very strong feeling of familiarity that came over us during our previous visits.

After a quick nap and a nice hot shower, we decided to stroll down to the beaches of Positano. As we made our way down and around a never-ending path of twists and turns, we noticed the locals who reminded us so much of our aunts, uncles, and grandparents. Maybe it was the way they spoke to each other, with so much passion and joy, constantly gesturing with their hands in conversation. Or perhaps it was the warm and welcoming smiles

Positano at night

and greetings. Practically every person we passed as we continued our trek down to Positano's city center greeted us with a hearty ciao or buongiorno. The cordial nature of the local Italians reminded us so much of our affectionate Italian American family and friends. Of course, it probably didn't hurt that my husband and I, with our dark hair and olive skin tone, look very Italian. But these lovely folks were expressing the same kind sentiments to other tourists, including the blond-haired-blue-eyed types as well.

We were also struck by how much time everyone spent outside on park benches, terraces, and small balconies. This reminded us of our family back home, too. My mother's father, for example, loved to spend afternoons feeding the pigeons from the park bench, just across the street from his Jersey City apartment. Both Dominick and I remember sitting on the "stoops" (the small staircases leading into apartment buildings), chatting with friends. We saw all this in Italy as well — including the wrought-iron patio furniture that was so similar to the chairs and tables used so frequently by our relatives, where they drank their morning coffee or dined alfresco during the warmer months. Italy, from the very beginning, felt comfortable and welcoming. Instinctively, we knew we belonged, and those first few trips sparked a lifelong love affair with Italy.

Those early voyages inspired us to learn more about our family history and visit the towns and regions of our heritage. We soon chose Italy first as our annual vacation spot, then as a part-time residence; despite its relatively small size, the boot offered endless beauty and one unique experience after the other, whether it was braving the rather tricky "Walk of the Gods" hike high above the Amalfi Coast or standing for hours along Venice's gorgeous Grand Canal during the annual Regata Storica, not wanting to miss one of the lavishly decorated gondolas. No matter what location we chose, Italy always left us with, as my godmother Jenny Aielli always said, countless "frozen moments": special memories that stay fresh in your mind because they're so magical and meaningful.

The incredible quality of the food was another reason we kept going back, eager to explore another corner of the land of our heritage. Of course, millions of people flock to Italy each year to savor the food and wine as well as the exquisite art, ancient structures, and picturesque landscapes. However, as FBIs (full-blooded Italian Americans), we figured the fascination with Italian food was a result of Americans not growing up the way we did. Our homes were the places our friends wanted to visit, especially on Sunday afternoons. That's when the spaghetti and meatballs or homemade lasagna, with fresh ricotta and the basil-infused tomato sauce or gravy (always made from scratch), were front-and-center on the dinner table. It never occurred to us that the quality and flavor of the meals we would find in Italy would be *even better* than what we'd enjoyed at home on a regular basis. How much better could it be than Aunt Mary's homemade pizza, or my grandmother's stuffed artichokes? Well, may sweet Aunt Mary and Grandma Paolina rest in peace, but as delectable as their dishes were, they could not hold a *forchetta* (fork) to the Italian food served in the Motherland.

This might be a good time to let you in on a couple of little secrets about eating in Italy: First, if you're looking for a plate of spaghetti and meatballs, you won't find it at any decent Italian restaurant's menu — unless you wander into a tourist trap in Rome or Florence. Meatballs (*polpette*) are sometimes served as an appetizer or a secondi (second course).

Another thing that surprised us about our first dining experience in Italy was the amount of time it takes to get the check. We were a bit perturbed at first; it took us a while to understand that, unlike Americans, Italians take their time with their meals. Once you sit down, that table is yours for as long as you decide to linger, even well after the espresso and limoncello. No one will be rushing you from your seat or dropping the check in front of you, hinting that it is time to leave. Meals are meant to be savored with family and friends. What a concept!

A MATTER OF FAITH

So, going back to my husband's original question, What is it about this place? Well, I've mentioned the matter of heritage. Then there is the friendliness or fellowship with Italians. Let's not forget the fantastic food and the gorgeous scenery, a never-ending feast for the eyes. And yet all this combined comes in second on the Italian hit parade, when highlighting the reasons why Dominick and I keep coming back.

Our most important reason is the faith factor. We keep coming back for longer periods of time — just as we ventured here the first time — because we deeply desired to continue the journey of truly embracing the depth and beauty of the Catholic Church. For that, Italy never disappoints.

Each time I arrive in Italy, I breathe deeply and recall a particular verse — one of my favorites — in the Bible. In 1 Corinthians 2:9 we read, "No eye has seen, nor ear heard, nor the heart of man conceived, what God has prepared for those who love him."

For me, Italy is an exquisite example of the good Lord's handiwork — a place to admire and worship Him with all the senses. And so, each time I arrive, that verse echoes in my heart a little differently: "No eye has seen, nor ear heard, nor the heart of man conceived, what God has prepared for those who visit Italy!"

Everywhere you turn here, God's glory is revealed. From the natural beauty of the mountains and seasides and serene waterfronts, to the vibrance of the sunflowers and poppy fields, vineyards, and olive groves. All around, we see evidence of mankind worshiping his Creator: magnificent churches and cathedrals, famous sculptures, frescoes, fountains, painted ceilings, as well as ancient structures that are marvels of art and engineering. Each of these marvelous attractions testifies to the glory of God.

You could spend a lifetime traveling from one end of the country to the other, trying to see all the many treasures contained in the incredible villages and cities throughout Italy. It would be impossible to count all the gifts Italy has to offer, or to calculate the amount of time, talent, and treasure it took to create them all.

Consider, for example, how long it took to build St. Peter's Basilica in Rome, or the Duomo di Orvieto. How in the world were the people who walked the earth centuries ago, without the use of modern tools or technology, able to build such grandeur?

When leading tours and pilgrimages, as well as when serving clients through my travel coaching service, T's Italy, I often say God was just plain showing off when He made this country. Regardless of one's upbringing, whether they were raised in a devoutly religious household or rarely, if ever, stepped inside a church, it is hard to imagine that anyone visiting Italy could get back on a plane without giving at least some thought to the existence of God.

In Catholic circles, Dominick and I are called "reverts": cradle Catholics born and raised in the Faith who fell away and then returned to the Church later in life. Although we grew up surrounded by wonderful sacred images of Christ and the saints, like many Catholics we kept those images neatly packed away on the spiritual shelf, only to take them down during major holidays and holy days. We were married in the Church, of course. But it only took a few short years for us to get consumed by the pursuit of money and the success of the 80s "yuppie culture" and leave God in the rearview mirror.

And yet, soon after we said ciao to our Catholicism, our lives began to unravel. Through a series of trials, including a near divorce, things began to turn around when we were invited to a Bible study where we found ourselves falling back in love with each other, and most importantly with God and the Church—the Church Christ founded on St. Peter more than two thousand years ago, the Church based, of course, in the Eternal City of Rome.

Bishop Robert Barron says, "Begin with the beautiful and it will lead you to the good, and the good will lead you to the truth." St. Teresa Benedicta of the Cross (Edith Stein), a convert to Catholicism who died in Auschwitz, reminds us, "God is truth and anyone who seeks truth seeks God whether he is aware of it." In Italy we have experienced an abundance of all three transcendent godly attributes — the beautiful, the good, and the true. They have been central in the continued formation of our faith.

After spending two decades in the rough-and-tumble world of broadcast news, I found that Italy helped to settle my soul. It reminded me that the world is still a wonderful place. The hardship, sadness, violence, and stress that comes with covering major stories live each day had hardened me over the years. It took some time to shake off. Italy was and still is my form of long-term therapy.

The beauty of our marriage being healed and our lives being changed led us to discover the goodness and mercy of God. That goodness let us to a deeper interest in the fullness of truth in the Catholic Church, which then led us to Italy.

Although this book is not about our faith testimony, it is in many ways a testament to God as He is continually unveiled in this country through the beautiful, the good, and the true. It is also an effort of gratitude for all that God has done and for us how He has allowed us to enjoy this creation that is Italy and share it with others.

HOW TO USE THIS BOOK
SAVORING ITALY

— — — — — — —

After we had taken several trips "to the boot," family members and friends began asking me for advice in planning their dream trip to Italy. Before I knew it, I had spent hours and hours detailing the best places to "eat, stay, shop, play, and pray," as I say on my website, T's Italy (travelitalyexpert.com). Finally, with the encouragement of my friend John Hale, I started my Italy travel coaching service. Since 2019 I have advised a long list of satisfied customers on how to make the most of their time in Italy.

With so many people pouring into Rome for the Jubilee Year, I decided it was time to write this one-of-a-kind guidebook, *Italy's Shrines and Wonders*. I wanted to offer a faith-based resource that would offer more than getting you from one tourist attraction to the next. Italy is an encounter with greatness on so many levels. Even if you have only a week to spend there, this book will teach you to experience Italy as is meant to be: savored, not merely checked off the bucket list.

Slow down and enjoy. Gelato, anyone?

ITALY'S SHRINES AND WONDERS *IS . . .*

- *The ultimate guidebook for any type of trip to Italy, including pilgrimages or private tours.* Read it before you head across the pond — then be sure to stick it in your backpack or carry-on to use during your visit.
- *An enjoyable and informative read to help you better understand Italy's spiritual roots.* Whether you are a person of faith, nominally Christian, or have no faith affiliation at all, this book will enhance both your understanding and appreciation for the spirit of Italy.
- *A comprehensive collection of Italy's most important sights of religious significance.* Whether you're a first-time visitor, a veteran traveler, or you're only able to dream about visiting Italy, *Italy's Shrines and Wonders* is meant to help you dream and plan. Each chapter takes a different region of the country, and identifies . . .

  - *Beloved Saints of Italy, a lesser-known saint who is locally venerated, associated with each region.*
  - *Region Highlights, to help you plan your trip.*
  - *T's Must-Sees and Must-Dos points you to the "best of the best" from each region.*
  - *Sacred Spaces directs you to places where faith meets culture.*
  - *Fascinating Places includes not-to-be-missed gems for your itinerary.*
  - *Celebrations highlights a special event held in each region.*
  - *T's Travel Tips offers region-specific, friendly advice on how to have the best experience. You will find additional, more general assistance in the appendix.*

As you will soon discover, the "Sacred Spaces" segments in each chapter introduce you to Italy's most well-known and much-loved saints, including local shrines and powerful stories of how the love of and dedication to Italy's saints led the locals to sacrifice so much to build such architectural wonders in their honor and often off the beaten path.

The "Fascinating Places" sections will make you feel as though you are standing in the middle of the local piazza of each region. You will also learn in this book about popular attractions and not-to-be-missed celebrations and local cuisine and recipes, in order to help you plan and enjoy and savor your next trip!

The final chapter, "Going Home Again," will give you some additional food for thought (pun intended) for your next journey to Italy. Whether your next experience will be an "armchair pilgrimage" at home or another in-person visit, this chapter provides even more of what Italy has to offer in the remaining eleven of Italy's twenty fantastic regions.

So, whether you're a first-time visitor, an Italy veteran, or dreaming of Italy, grab a nice glass of vino, sit back, relax, and dive into *Bella Italia*. And as you turn the pages, my prayer is that *Italy's Shrines and Wonders* will enable you to answer, in your own special way, the question: What is it about this place?

Buon Viaggio!

PART ONE

Rome and the Lazio Region

MARVELS OF THE VATICAN AND BEYOND

DISCOVERING THE REGIONS OF ITALY

ROME AND
THE LAZIO REGION

Previous page: The Ponte Vittorio Emanuele II with St. Peter's Basilica in the background

WHAT YOU'LL EXPLORE...

ROME AND LAZIO REGION HIGHLIGHTS

- **Rome:** Ever the Eternal, Enigmatic City
- **Via del Corso:** Living the Sweet Life
- **Beloved Saint of Italy — St. Cecilia**
- T's Ultimate Must-Sees and Must-Dos in Rome
- T's Favorite Churches in Rome
- T's Ultimate Must-Sees and Dos in the Lazio Region

SACRED SPACES OF LAZIO

- **Ostia Antica:** Home of St. Augustine and St. Monica
- **Viterbo:** City of the Popes and St. Rose
- **The Greccio Sanctuary of St. Francis:** The First Christmas Crèche

FASCINATING PLACES IN THE LAZIO REGION

- **Civita di Bagnoregio:** The Lively "Dying City"
- **Vatican Views:** Castel Gandolfo, the Barberini, and Lake Albano
- **Tivoli:** Of Fountains and Flowers
- **Tarquinia:** An Ancient Etruscan Necropolis
- **Trastevere and Testaccio:** Roman Neighborhoods Worth Knowing

CELEBRATIONS AND SIGNATURE DISHES

- **Lungo Il Tevere:** June–August
- **Bucatini all'Amatriciana**

A PILGRIM'S PERSPECTIVE: MIKE RITCHIE

DON'T MISS THE JOY!
DISCOVERING THE REGIONS OF ITALY

— — — — — — —

So, you want to go to Italy? Let's plan the trip of your dreams!

To start, when you think of Italy, what is on your "bucket list" of the places you just *have* to go? Quite often, I find that travelers planning a tour of Italy think in terms of cities, not regions. When my clients fill out their "dream trip" questionnaire, their itinerary usually consists of Rome, Venice, Florence, and Assisi. The more adventurous might throw in the drop-dead gorgeous Amalfi Coast town of Positano.

Nothing wrong with that, of course, as those cities and areas contain some significant attractions. Unfortunately, this also means that, in their eagerness to reach the next big attraction, they might miss some truly breathtaking regions of Italy, such as Lazio, Umbria, and even Tuscany. Slowing down to enjoy the journey provides so much additional joy!

Italy has twenty regions that all have much for the traveler to embrace. Although there are certainly similarities when it comes to the Italians and their love of faith, family, food, and fellowship, each area of Italy is very different and quite stunning in its own way.

For example, if you hop on a train, hire a driver, or rent a car, in a little over thirty minutes you can leave the big, bustling Eternal City of Rome and find yourself in a quaint lakeside village, white wine country,

Opposite: The Colosseum at sunrise

or the former summer residence of the popes. In about an hour you could be walking through palace gardens, drinking cool water from fabulously carved fountains, or stepping back in time as you learn all about the ancient Etruscans in the seaside city of Tarquinia. All of this and so much more in the beautiful region of Lazio.

ROME: EVER THE ETERNAL, ENIGMATIC CITY

Roaming or strolling in Rome (as with everywhere else in Italy) happens to be the way of life. In such a crowded metropolis as Rome, walking is commonplace; minimal parking and excessive traffic make driving across town or even to the local market almost impossible. Roman drivers park anywhere and everywhere, so much so that is not unusual to be dining outdoors, alfresco, at one of Rome's quaint trattorias and have someone pull up and park their cute red Fiat right next to your table. That actually happened to us on our very first visit. And so it is no wonder that taking

View of St. Peter's Basilica over the Tiber River

"St. Francis' donkey" (our own two feet) is considered the best means of moving around.

Public transportation such as is offered by subways and buses is another option, of course, as long as the transportation workers aren't striking on the day you're trying to get to the Vatican for your tour. Cabs are abundant, yes, but they can be costly. Of course, if you're a native Roman or Italian, Vespas (a.k.a. "mosquitoes") also do the trick. But maneuvering a Vespa in and out of Roman traffic is not for the faint of heart or even for the most daring tourist, unless you are a glutton for punishment.

And don't forget, walking offers other benefits as well: the opportunity to take in what's laid out before you, at your own pace. It allows you to explore little alleys and side streets, where you may stumble on what might become your favorite wine bar, pizzeria, or section of Roma. Oh, and of course the more you walk the more calories you will burn (and the more gelato and pasta carbonara you can enjoy).

VIA DEL CORSO: LIVING THE SWEET LIFE

One of the most delightful memories I have of this city stems from our first visit more than twenty-five years ago. We were wrapping up our trip and were delighted our tour guide reminded us that we had another free night to enjoy a bit more of *la dolce vita* or "the sweet life."

So off we went, walking slowly through the colorful and busy streets. As my husband and I turned yet another delightful corner, tucked behind one of the main avenues, the Via del Corso, we discovered a small but quaint piazza that looked like it belonged in the countryside rather than smack in the middle of a hectic municipality. There were two or three restaurants, along with few shops and a Catholic church with its crisp white marble façade serving as the piazza's focal point. We noticed that the restaurants offered plenty of alfresco or outdoor dining.

We were able to grab a table outside at a charming trattoria, feeling like we were in the middle of a movie set. The meal was divine, and we

T's Italy

T'S TRAVEL TIP

Roamin' Rome

Although the pace of Rome is certainly comparable with other major cities in Europe and America, Romans still practice the popular pastime of the passeggiata. This term refers to a stroll after a meal and is often designed to end up in the town square or piazza, to gather with friends or to just catch up on the day. Once in Rome, it's easy to pick up the passeggiata vibe and walk from one Roman wonder to the next.

found ourselves lingering for hours, as we enjoyed yet another glass of *vino della casa* (house wine). Unfortunately, the restaurant went out of business long ago, but the memory is as fresh as if it happened last week. If we had decided to ignore our guide's advice to explore, we would have missed a magical evening that smacked of a true Roman experience. We would have also missed our first powerful encounter with pasta cooked perfectly.

That night we decided on a simple meal of *pasta pomodoro* and *insalata mista* (mixed salad). The pasta was served with tomato sauce so flavorful and robust that I had to pull the waiter aside and ask about it. As I mentioned in the introduction, we both grew up with very good Italian food, or so we thought. The pasta or macaroni of our childhood was always tasty and al dente. And yet, I don't remember it having the amount of flavor we enjoyed that night.

As someone who loves to cook Italian food, I was fascinated to discover the secret to flavorful pasta. Back in the States, we cook the pasta separately and then simply cover the noodles with sauce. In Italy they undercook the pasta and then finish cooking it in the sauce so that the flavors are wonderfully infused. If you're going to eat well in Rome, pasta has to be on the top of the list. Whether it's a good pomodoro sauce or perhaps a bowl of the perfect carbonara, please, avail yourself of the flavors of Italy. Don't worry, portions in Italy are not massive (gluten-free options are readily available), and because they are so perfectly prepared you won't feel the need to eat mounds of pasta. One course with some good *pane* or bread to soak up the sauce, and you're good to go.

HOW LONG SHOULD I PLAN TO STAY?

When planning your visit to Rome, keep in mind another cliché: the city truly was not built in a day. That means you're going to need several days to take in the major sights — more, if your travel schedule includes other cities in the area. Allowing four or five days for your Rome excursion will give you time to see ancient and Christian Rome as well as embrace not only a passeggiata here and there but also a bit of la dolce far niente — the sweetness of doing nothing. Embrace the Scripture from Psalm 46:10, "Be still, and know that I am God" by looking at the beauty around you. Sit and soak in the sweetness of doing nothing.

Most ancient and Christian Rome tours cover a lot of territory: St. Peter's, the Vatican Museums, the other major basilicas of St. John Lateran, St. Mary Major, and St. Paul Outside the Walls. Ancient Rome translates into several hours at the Forum and the Roman Colosseum or longer if you want to see other ruins. On paper, it may not seem like a busy schedule. But one must account for crowds, limited hours (many churches close in the middle of the day) and travel time (major attractions are not exactly conveniently located right next to each other). Even if you only stop in a handful of these amazing galleries, churches, and monuments, if you don't take time to stop and smell as well as drink the cappuccino, you'll end up exhausted and everything you've seen will seem like a blur.

Such was the case with a parish pilgrimage my husband and I helped plan years ago. Our limited itinerary included hotel stays at only two locations, Rome and Assisi. But because the group also wanted some other day trips, we suggested a stay of eight or nine nights. However, during a planning meeting with parishioners, the vast majority (who had never been to Italy) insisted that anything more than a seven-night stay was too much of a commitment. Some were even pushing for six nights. Our pastor, who had studied in Rome for several years and had traveled back and forth to Italy numerous times, agreed that more time, not less, was the best plan.

We understood the reasons some were pushing for a shorter trip. Many have limited vacation time, and we all have busy schedules. Those with family might have concerns about being away for more than a week or traveling so far with teens or younger children.

And yet, as an Italy travel coach, I try to get my clients to think about the time, money, and effort they're already putting into an overseas holiday. We explained that a longer trip would make the whole trip more enjoyable — and make it easier to face challenges at the beginning or end of the trip: jet lag, flight delays or cancellations, and the extra time we'd need at the airport to make an international flight home. Why not get the most out of their trip by staying even a few extra days?

However, despite our best efforts, nothing convinced the group to extend the trip, so we decided to meet the group in Rome after spending five days on our own in Siena. In addition to getting to know the medieval city that gave the world the great Doctor of the Church, St. Catherine, we also visited several other Tuscan towns, including the adorable San Gimignano, before heading down to the Fiumicino/Leonardo da Vinci airport in Rome to meet our group.

As we had anticipated, the more we moved through Rome and the Umbrian towns of Assisi and Orvieto, the more they regretted their insistence on a weeklong pilgrimage. That's a tough lesson to learn when you're flying overseas and investing your hard-earned cash. Keep these suggestions and scenarios in mind as you review our highlights of the Eternal City and begin to plan your own vacation to Italy.

BELOVED SAINT OF ITALY

St. Cecilia

- **Relics:** Basilica of St. Cecilia in Trastevere, Rome
- **Patron Saint:** Musicians, poets, singers
- **Canonized:** 1599 by Pope Clement VIII
- **Feast Day:** November 22

Born in Rome, St. Cecilia (third century) was a young Roman noblewoman who was martyred for refusing to sacrifice to the Roman gods. A virgin forced by her parents to marry, as the musicians played at her wedding, she sang in her heart to God to protect her virginity, and after the wedding she convinced her new groom and his brother to be baptized. After both men were martyred, she was sentenced to death: first by suffocation in the baths, then by three ax blows to the neck. She survived for three days before finally succumbing to her injuries.

ROME AND VATICAN CITY
HIGHLIGHTS

Italy offers the unique opportunity to be in one nation and step into another without ever hopping on a plane or in a car, leaving the boot in the rearview mirror. You can do this in the Lazio Region by visiting the Vatican, established as its own nation in 1929 by Lateran agreements approved by both the Church and the government of Italy. The name Vatican comes from the once marshy area along the Tiber River once known as the *Ager Vaticanus*. The Vatican is large in importance regarding faith, art, culture, and global affairs, but it is small in size, holding it all within a two-mile border.

The sovereign nation is home of the Catholic Church, the largest organized religion in the world. It is where the pope lives and carries out his ministry as the Vicar of Christ and the head of Vatican City

State. The Vatican is also where pilgrims can visit the tomb of the first pope, St. Peter, who as one of the first twelve apostles gave his life for Christ and the Church some two thousand years ago. Visitors wait for hours to see St. Peter's Basilica, the Sistine Chapel, the Vatican Museums, the Vatican Gardens, and the pope.

Step outside St. Peter's square and you are back in the Eternal City of Rome, established in 753 B.C. According to legend, Ancient Rome was founded by two brothers and demigods Romulus and Remus. Rome is the capital city of Italy, located in the Lazio region in the central part of the peninsula. With a population of more than four million, Rome is the most populated city in Italy. For over a thousand years, Rome controlled Western civilization in Europe and parts of Africa until the Empire slowly collapsed due to numerous challenges at home and abroad, until it was sacked by the Visigoths in A.D. 410. Fortunately, many of the original and famous structures survived.

Rebuilt over the centuries, Rome has given us historic churches, museums, monuments, architectural wonders, impressive piazzas, fountains, parks, and important archaeological sites. All of this attracts so many tours every year that it is one of the world's most popular destinations. Rome is called the "Eternal City" due to its enduring legacy, cultural impact, and historical significance.

Right: The Elephant and Obelisk at the Piazza della Minerva
Middle: The chair of St. Peter in St. Peter's Basilica
Left: Capitoline Wolf statue

ROME AND VATICAN CITY
T'S ULTIMATE MUST-SEES AND DOS

— — — — — — —

Although one can easily spend weeks — even months — in Rome exploring the endless churches, museums, monuments, and piazzas, we've put together a top ten list of the major sights you don't want to miss. If you only have a few days in the Eternal City, these "must-see" sights can be covered with the help of a guide. If you have at least a week in Rome, be sure to check out other "must-dos" in this chapter — including the list of my favorite churches — some of which can be visited on self-guided tours.

Ceiling of the Sistine chapel in the Vatican museum

VATICAN MUSEUMS AND SISTINE CHAPEL

The Public Museum of the Vatican City (including the Sistine Chapel) contains an immense collection of art, including the most renowned Roman sculptures and Renaissance art in the world.

FOUR MAJOR BASILICAS:

- St. Peter's Basilica — built over the shrine of St. Peter the apostle
- St. Mary Major (Santa Maria Maggiore)
- St. John Lateran
- St. Paul Outside the Walls

Basilica of St. John Lateran, Rome

Catherine of Siena statue, Castel Sant'Angelo

CASTEL SANT'ANGELO

Along the Tiber River near the Vatican, this beautiful castle once served as a papal fortress and is now a museum. It is a fun place to visit especially for the terrace. Don't miss the special statue of St. Catherine of Siena facing the Tiber.

PANTHEON

This former Roman temple was converted into a Catholic church dedicated to Mary and the martyrs in A.D. 609. Today it is one of the best-preserved monuments of Ancient Rome.

COLOSSEUM

This ancient Roman amphitheater is still the largest standing amphitheater in the world today.

ROMAN FORUM

A historic landmark of the old Roman public meetings, laws, courts, and ceremonies.

ROMAN CATACOMBS

Ancient underground burial places in and around Rome. Be sure to check out two along the Via Appia: St. Callistus (the largest) and the nearby St. Sebastian.

The Roman Forum

BORGHESE GALLERY AND GARDENS

A beautiful place to take a break to explore famous art and stroll the gorgeous gardens.

SPANISH STEPS

This beautiful gathering spot is named for its proximity to the Spanish embassy. To the right of the Spanish steps is the famous Column of the Immaculate Conception. Each year on the feast of the Immaculate Conception the pope places a bouquet of flowers at the feet of the Blessed Mother.

Column of the Immaculate Conception near Spanish Steps

TRINITA DEI MONTI

Walk up the Spanish Steps and visit the church where St. Thérèse, the Little Flower prayed before a painting of the Blessed Mother, asking for God to give her the grace to enter the convent at age fifteen.

Trevi Fountain

TREVI FOUNTAIN

Located in the Trevi district, this eighteenth-century fountain is the most famous of the three hundred monumental fountains in Rome.

T'S INSIDER TIP

Isola Tiberina

Treat yourself to some island time in the middle of Rome. Grab some wine, cheese, and don't forget the camera as you head to Isola Tiberina, between the Jewish Quarter and the Trastevere neighborhood. The lower part of the island is home to a local hospital but also includes a green space that welcomes visitors. Climb down the steps along the river, sit close to the rushing water, and watch the world go by in the Eternal City.

View of the hospital on Isola Tiberina

Map of Churches of Rome

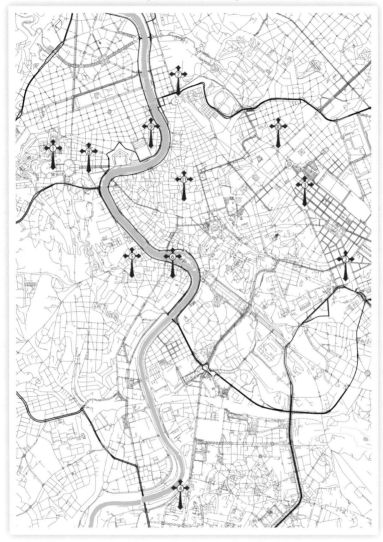

1. St. Peter's
2. Basilica of St. John Lateran
3. Basilica of Santa Maria Maggiore
4. Basilica of St. Paul Outside the Walls
5. Basilica of Santa Maria in Trastavere
6. Basilica of Santa Cecilia in Trastevere
7. Basilica of Santa Maria del Popolo
8. Santo Spirito in Sassia
9. Church of the Sacred Heart of Jesus/ Purgatory Museum
10. Church of Santa Maria della Vittoria
11. Santa Maria Sopra Minerva

ROME AND VATICAN CITY
T'S FAVORITE CHURCHES

Once you've seen St. Peter's and the major basilicas, there are several beautiful churches that I love to visit. These can provide such a profound spiritual experience just from their pure beauty.

SANTA MARIA TRASTEVERE

This beautiful basilica of Our Lady is one of the oldest churches in Rome. Located in the heart of our favorite Roman neighborhood, Trastevere, it is known for its mosaics.

Mosaics of Santa Maria Trastevere

SANTA CECILIA TRASTEVERE

Built on the home of St. Cecilia, this stunning church is tucked away in a quiet area of Trastevere with a museum and chapels connected to the martyr. This church was also visited by St. Thérèse, the Little Flower, during her trip to Rome.

Statue of St. Cecilia before the main altar of Santa Cecilia Trastevere

SANTA MARIA DEL POPOLO

Located in the Piazza del Popolo and home to amazing works by Raphael, Bernini, and Caravaggio, this church is run by the Augustinian Order.

CHURCH OF SANTO SPIRITO IN SASSIA

This beautiful church near St. Peter's Square is dedicated to the Divine Mercy and St. Faustina. Adorned with many paintings and frescoes spanning different time periods, this is a wonderful place to pray and meditate.

Church of Santo Spirito

CHURCH OF THE SACRED HEART

This parish houses the Museum of the Holy Souls, also known as the "Little Purgatory Museum" (*Piccolo Museo Del Purgatorio*). This is located in Prati near the Tiber River and is not far from Castel Sant'Angelo.

Church of the Sacred Heart

Ecstasy of St. Teresa (Maria Della Vittoria)

SANTA MARIA DELLA VITTORIA

In this beautiful church, dedicated to the Virgin, you will find Gian Lorenzo Bernini's masterpiece, *The Ecstasy of Saint Teresa*, located in the Cornaro Chapel.

SANTA MARIA SOPRA MINERVA

This Dominican church, located behind the Pantheon, houses the tomb of St. Catherine of Siena.

Tomb of St. Catherine of Siena in Santa Maria Sopra Minerva

T'S TRAVEL TIP

Before you visit, check the church's website for Mass (in Italian or English) and Confession times, and note if the church is undergoing renovations. An "English version" of their website may be found by adding "/en" at the end of the URL. Others have a British flag to click on for English.

LAZIO REGION
HIGHLIGHTS

Think of the Lazio Region of Italy as the "knee" of the boot shape of Italy. The word Lazio is from the Latin word *Latium*, which is the original name of the region around present-day Rome, where most spoke Latin. Lazio is the second most populous region of Italy and contains the largest and most famous city in all of Italy — Rome, which is home to more than five million people. Transportation to or from Rome is easy not only because of frequent flights to or from the city but also due to the region's high-speed rail lines: Rome's Termini Station is the largest train station in Italy and is one of the largest stations in Europe.

Outside of Rome, the region is mostly plains and hills, with some mountains near Rieti — Monte Terminillo measures over 2,200 meters. The northern section of this region contains an area of lower mountains with volcanic origins. These volcanic craters have made many beautiful lakes in this region, including Lake Albano to the south of Rome and Lake Bracciano in the northwest.

This region is also the center of the Catholic world, housing the Vatican City State, which has is its own country and governance. The Swiss Guards are the police for the Vatican and the pope. The Lazio Region is also known for producing Romaine lettuce, wine, and olives. It is also popular among the locals for its beaches along the Mediterranean coast. Thanks to not only Rome, but also to other locations with strong ties to early civilizations, including the Etruscans, the region is rich in archeology, history, and culture.

Right: View over Lake Albano
Middle: Anguillara Sabazia on Lake Bracciano
Left: Etruscan necropolis in Cerveteri

LAZIO REGION
T'S ULTIMATE MUST-SEES AND DOS

– – – – – – – –

- Take a day trip to one of the many lovely towns in this lovely region such as **Castel Gandolfo, Frascati**, or **Bracciano**.

- Visit Basilica di Santa Christina near Lake Bolsena, an ancient pilgrimage site dedicated to a young martyr where a famous eucharistic miracle occurred in 1263. (Bolsena is on the border between Lazio and Umbria — the story of the miracle is in the next chapter because the relic itself is venerated at a church there.)

- If you love flowers, head to the city of Viterbo for a visit to the beautiful botanical gardens. The Mountain Botanic Center, home to a unique and large collection of peonies in the Lazio region.

Basilica di Santa Christina, Bolsena, Lazio

Opposite: The Pontifical Gardens at Castel Gandolfo

LAZIO REGION
SACRED SPACES

If you have a few additional days after "roaming around Rome," consider heading beyond the city limits to the Lazio region. Even if learning about Church history or ancient civilizations isn't your thing, the areas we're highlighting outside of Rome are worth putting on your itinerary. They are sacred spaces on many levels. In addition to their religious and historic significance, they provide a peaceful and different perspective.

Don't get me wrong, Roma will always be Roma. It's an awe-inspiring city on so many levels. It is also a city that can zap your energy. St. Ambrose reminds us, "When in Rome, do as the Romans do." And since the Romans are wise enough to escape to the countryside or waterfront as often as possible on the weekends, perhaps we should be following close behind.

OSTIA ANTICA
Home of St. Augustine and St. Monica

The popular phrase, "When in Rome ..." referring to following the customs or traditions practiced by locals, is attributed to St. Ambrose, who served as bishop of Milan in the later part of the fourth century (A.D. 374 to 397). He played a major role in the conversion of another great

Opposite: Ruins at Ostia Antica

saint, St. Augustine of Hippo, originally from North Africa. When Augustine began experimenting with popular religions, his mother Monica — a devout Christian — begged him to change his ways and appealed to the bishop to intercede for her son. A long tug of war ensued: he was on one side, and God and his mother — and eventually St. Ambrose — were on the other. Finally, Augustine boarded a ship for Rome to get away from the pressure.

The ship landed in Ostia Antica, at the time the bustling harbor city of Rome at the mouth of the Tiber River. Eventually, after his conversion, Monica would follow him, and passed away there in 387. The influence and presence of two great saints, Monica and Augustine, are what make Ostia Antica a sacred space. It also carries a great deal of weight with travelers interested in discovering more about Italy's ancient civilizations.

Sixteen miles southwest of Rome, Ostia Antica is now an important and fascinating archeological site, known for its ruins and frescoes, which were well-preserved due to being buried under sand and silt after the city was abandoned following the fall of Rome. Given its vastness, it's not difficult to imagine what life was like there some sixteen hundred years ago, and why the adventure-seeking Augustine would call the city home. The site still contains remains of homes, inns, taverns, as well as public baths, and even a large, reconstructed amphitheater that is often still used during the summer months.

Archaeological Park of Ostia Antica

A visit to this gem in the Lazio region is a fun way to combine learning with leisure, although thanks to the landscaping being reworked over time Ostia Antica is no longer a coastal city. But the Mediterranean is close by. So, pack a beach bag. Tour the ruins in the morning and then hop back on the train to head to Rome's seaside.

VITERBO
City of the Popes and St. Rose

Palazzo dei Papi, home of the first papal enclave

When one thinks of European Christmas markets filled with rows and rows of crafts, mulled wine, and delectable holiday treats, Germany, Austria, and northern Italy come to mind. However, many regions of Italy — including lovely Lazio — come alive during this special time of year.

Spending Christmas in Rome had always been on my bucket list, so in 2019 we packed a small fake tree, some lights, and a few presents and crossed the ocean for our own *Buon Natale* (Merry Christmas). And though Rome was a fantastic scene, offering every kind of festive decoration and display, we also wanted to take in some of the celebratory scenes in areas outside the city. Many of my website clients had expressed an interest in seasonal activities outside of Rome.

I soon discovered that Viterbo is one area that is transformed into a delightful Christmas extravaganza from early December through early January, ending on the feast of the Epiphany, January 6.

The Christmas exhibits — including an ice rink and live nativity scene — stretched across the main piazza, where the palace and local cathedral are located, and through the village. The façade of the papal palace, Palazzo dei Papi, was adorned exquisitely in colorful lights, so much so that it was easy to forget the religious and historic significance of the building itself. Dating back to the thirteenth century, the palace was originally built as a fortress but later developed into the religious and political center of Viterbo.

Viterbo became known as the "City of the Popes" after the Curia moved its headquarters there in the year 1257. The first and longest papal conclave was convened in the palace in 1268, lasting almost three years. The people of the town became so frustrated by their inability to reach consensus that, at one point, they decided to remove the roof and restrict the participants' diet to bread and water in order to expedite the process.

While the Christmas market is spectacular, a visit should not be limited to the holidays as the city is a treasure trove. Medieval structures line the quaint cobblestone streets, and it is a place that has kept the Faith and an incredibly strong sense of its past in more ways than one. In addition to being known as the "City of the

Traditional Garb of Facchini of Santa Rosa

Popes," Viterbo is famous for one the most exhilarating events, the Macchina di Santa Rosa, held in honor of the patron, St. Rose.

Each year on September 3, a *macchina* (machine) lifts and carries a massive tower of lights and torches three quarters of a mile through the squares of the city. Standing ninety feet high and weighing about five tons, the tower is made of metal and fiberglass, and it is topped by a statue of the patron saint. It's moved slowly and very carefully by a group of 113 men known as the *Facchini*.

To say the *Facchini* are strong is a major understatement. The choosing of the *Facchini* is quite the process, as each man must go through a series of special tests or a *prova di portata* to determine if he's up to the task. And because of the physical strength needed and the risk involved in transporting the *macchina*, the *Facchini* are given a special blessing by the local bishop, known as the blessing in articulo mortis, meaning an indulgence at the moment of death.

I often wonder how St. Rose feels about the celebration each year, seeing people risking so much in her honor. Rose had a great love for the poor, and became a secular Franciscan when she was only ten years old after being rejected by the Poor Clares. She told the sisters, "You will not have me now but perhaps you will be more willing when I am dead."

Everything she did was for love of Christ. Rose preached courageously in the streets, calling the people to repent for their sins. Soon after, Rose and her family were sent into exile for siding with the pope against the emperor. Later, her efforts to start a religious community failed. Finally, she died when she was only eighteen years old.

St. Rose of Viterbo had only a short time on earth, and lived a life of great humility and holiness. And yet she is greatly loved and celebrated today by all the people, who credit her intercession for sparing the city from a seven-year plague (ending in 1664), and who have remained devoted to her ever since.

THE GRECCIO SANCTUARY
OF ST. FRANCIS
The First Christmas Crèche

The hermitage of the Greccio sanctuary, *Santuario Eremo di Greccio*, will have you singing Christmas carols no matter what time of year you visit. It is known all over the world as the "Franciscan Bethlehem," and this is exactly what St. Francis wanted. It was his hope and prayer that by creating the first live nativity scene, Christians would be better able to understand that although Christmas occurred long ago, Christ still comes to all of us in the present.

You'll find Greccio truly off the beaten path in the province of Rieti. It is immersed in peaceful natural surroundings that are part of the Sabine Mountains. Three years before his death in 1253, St. Francis chose Greccio as the site of the first representation of the nativity scene

Greccio Sanctuary

or Christmas crèche after he visited Bethlehem. Since he knew that very few faithful at that time would be able to make a pilgrimage all the way to the Holy Land, he wanted to bring the Holy Land to them.

With the townspeople gathered around, one of the Franciscan priests presided at a midnight Mass. Local residents dressed in costumes portraying Mary and Joseph. The scene also included a wax figure of Jesus along with a live donkey and an ox. One of the Franciscan priests presided at the Mass, along with Francis, who was a deacon, who preached and proclaimed the Gospel. St. Bonaventure, author of *The Life of St. Francis of Assisi* (TAN Classics), said that on the night of the first crèche, the forest resounded with many voices singing psalms of praise.

> The man of God [Francis] stood before the manger, full of devotion and piety, bathed in tears and radiant with joy; the Holy Gospel was chanted by Francis, the Levite of Christ. Then he preached to the people around the nativity of the poor King; and being unable to utter His name for the tenderness of His love, He called Him the Babe of Bethlehem.

The sanctuary is one of four erected by St. Francis in what is known as the Sacred Valley and is part of a pilgrimage route, the Way of St. Francis or *La Via di Francesco*, a trail connecting many of the places frequented during his life and ministry. Inside, visitors can see the original cave where that Mass with the first living crèche was celebrated and walk through the nearby hermitage used by Francis and his brother friars as a place of solitude, prayer, and meditation. The Nativity Grotto is adjacent to a precious Catholic church that houses a large collection of nativity scenes from around the world, including a magnificent life-size crèche.

Greccio, although remote, is not to be missed. As someone who has had the blessing of visiting the Holy Land many times, I can attest to the fact that St. Francis certainly captured the tranquility and sacredness of the little town of Bethlehem far away in the hills of central Italy.

LAZIO REGION
FASCINATING PLACES

— — — — — — — —

Often Rome travelers think that to discover exciting venues apart from the many museums and churches, they need to travel hours by train or car to another area of Italy. They don't realize just how rich the region of Lazio truly is. They would be surprised that some of Italy's most exquisite sites are much closer together than they think, less than an hour away from Rome. Inside the Eternal City, they will discover new worlds by simply going around the corner. Below are some of my favorite picks for "Fascinating Places" in the Lazio region.

CIVITA DI BAGNOREGIO
The Lively "Dying City"

About an hour northwest of Greccio, two hours north of Rome, is another Lazio gem, Civita di Bagnoregio. Thanks to its closeness to the Umbrian border, it's often part of a day trip for those visiting the more famous Etruscan city of Orvieto. The Civita is the kind of place that one needs to view from afar for a bit before making the short trek up the steep hill to enter its medieval gates. Founded 2,500 years ago, it is both serene and strikingly surreal — it is hard to believe that it is still standing. Hence the nickname "The Dying City."

Opposite: View of Lake Albano in Castel Gandolfo

This ancient hamlet is also connected to the Etruscans, and is perched on a plateau of volcanic rock in the middle of the Tiber River valley, a plateau that is continually eroding. The valley is often referred to as the "Badlands" because of the seismic activity and unstable geology. An earthquake in the late seventeenth century and the subsequent erosion led to the town being abandoned. Currently only about a dozen residents (and two dozen cats) live there full-time.

Although its location would qualify as "off-the-beaten path," this dying city is being reborn thanks to its remarkable landscaping, along with some creative tourism efforts. It doesn't take a large chunk out of your travel itinerary to experience. And if time is an issue, the nearby sister city of Civita di Bagnoregio offers the perfect viewing and picture-taking platform.

If you can make room in your itinerary, however, Civita di Bagnoregio is one of the country's most beautiful places, dreamy with its curious position, cobblestone streets, and buildings decorated with

Civita di Bagnoregio, the "Dying City"

vines and colorful flowers. It has several wonderful restaurants and shops featuring local products and wines. More importantly, it is the birthplace of St. Bonaventure, the biographer of St. Francis of Assisi.

Born here in the early thirteenth century, Bonaventure became very sick as a child and credited his healing to the intercession of St. Francis of Assisi.

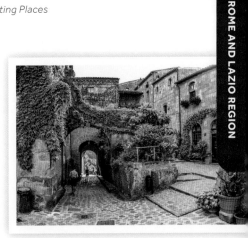

Civita di Bagnoregio

There is a cave open to travelers that contains an ancient olive press that is said to be the location of St. Bonaventure's miraculous recovery. The only remaining relic of the saint, who is known as the Seraphic or Angelic Doctor of the Church, is kept in the cathedral in Civita di Bagnoregio.

Civita di Bagnoregio does charge a five-euro entrance fee — the only city in Italy to do so — which goes toward the upkeep and preservation of the village. Once you pass through the arch or Porta San Maria, the village's only remaining entrance, the street will take you to Piazza San Donato, the charming main square. You've probably heard of the famous horse race, Il Palio; well, in Civita di Bagnoregio there is a similar race twice a year, Palio della Tonna, featuring donkeys.

The church in San Donato contains the relics of their ninth-century bishop, St. Hildebrand, or San Altibrando. Many miracles are attributed to him, most notably the miracle involving a stillborn child that came back to life after he was placed next to the body of Altibrando, which had been exposed in the church. San Donato also houses a wooden crucifix from the fifteenth century affiliated with the school of Donatello and carried in numerous processions.

Civita di Bagnoregio is small in size, abundant in character, and an unforgettable place that you must see to believe.

T'S TRAVEL TIP
Train of the Pontifical Villas

On Saturdays from mid-April through October, purchase a ticket on the "Train of the Pontifical Villas" (the "Pope's Arrow") that includes a tour of the Vatican Museums, the Vatican Gardens (behind St. Peter's and at Castel Gandolfo), and a round-trip train ride from the old Vatican City railway station to Castel Gandolfo.

VATICAN VIEWS
Castel Gandolfo, the Barberini, and Lovely Lake Albano

Only eighteen miles southeast of Rome is the scenic town of Castel Gandolfo, the former summer residence of the popes. It is a place that offers a true respite from the bustling metropolis and is easily accessible by train or car for a wonderful and leisurely day trip.

Many are familiar with the Vatican Gardens tucked behind St. Peter's Basilica, which are well worth visiting. However, the Barberini or papal gardens of Castel Gandolfo are just as beautiful, and provide breathtaking views of the Lazio countryside and of Lake Albano, a volcanic lake that also happens to be the deepest lake in the Lazio region. A ticket for a tour includes both a stroll through the gardens and an inside look at the apostolic palace.

The last pope to spend time here during the summer was Pope Benedict XVI. At the end of his papacy in 2013, he flew via helicopter over Rome to Castel Gandolfo and spent several weeks there. Pope Francis spends his summers in Rome, at the Santa Marta residence next to St. Peter's, and between 2014 and 2016 he opened both the Castel Gandolfo villa and gardens to the public. It's interesting to note that during the Second World War, Pope Pius XII allowed the palace to be used by refugees fleeing Rome.

Castel Gandolfo is owned by the Holy See and still has a great history associated with the Catholic Church. Also referred to as "the second Vatican," the palace was designed in the seventeenth century for Pope Urban VIII as a summer retreat. It currently operates as a wonderful museum containing many artifacts associated with the Vatican, including vestments of former popes. Tourists are also given access to the luxurious apartments and the papal portrait gallery.

In addition to the gardens and palace, the town and the area of the Alban hills are treasure troves of interesting attractions including:

- St. Thomas of Villanova, the local parish church designed by Bernini,
- the world's first postbox located in the main town square, Piazza della Liberta, and
- Lake Albano, a volcanic lake, which has a shoreline lined with restaurants and wine bars. Sip your vino or Aperol Spritz while taking in the views. Boat and kayak rentals are also available but swimming is not advised — given its depth of 560 feet, the water is simply too cold.

Regardless of how you get there, *do* get there. Castel Gandolfo is a short passage from the busy city to the Italian countryside, allowing tourists a much-needed slice of *la dolce vita* or "the sweet life."

Castel Gandolfo/Barbarini Gardens

TIVOLI
Of Fountains and Flowers

About an hour east of Rome is a UNESCO world heritage site, the historical villa of Tivoli or *Villa d'Este, Tivoli*. I don't know what is more plentiful in this beautiful setting, the fountains or the flowers and other plant life sprouting everywhere, but this palatial property is now an Italian museum, and another not-to-be-missed day trip.

There are more than two dozen trains daily traveling between the city and Tivoli, allowing you to leave the rental car and the traffic behind. Once you arrive you feel as if you are much more than twenty miles away from Rome, in another world entirely.

According to UNESCO, the Villa d'Este in Tivoli is a walk back in time for many reasons. At 771 feet above sea level, Tivoli has been a popular summer escape, going all the way back to the time of the Romans. The area itself has been inhabited for over three thousand years. It served as a country retreat for emperors such as Augustus, not to mention many poets, and has been a source of inspiration for artists and architects alike as it represents some of the best examples of not only Renaissance gardens but Renaissance architecture that the world has to offer.

Villa d'Este is also a hydraulic engineering marvel, given the intricate plans that had to be undertaken to keep the water flowing throughout this Roman oasis. The sixteenth-century estate has one of the first "gardens of wonder," or *giardini delle meraviglie*, containing thousands of varieties of trees, shrubs, perennials, and rare plants. With its countless cascades and grottoes, it also served as an early model for other magnificent gardens created around Europe.

Both the gardens and the villa were built on behalf of Cardinal Ippolito Il d'Este of Ferrara, a strong patron of the arts, after he was named governor of Tivoli. The sprawling property, covering about two and a half acres and including a monastery, was developed with the utmost care into a masterpiece, with gardens that stretch over two

Villa d'Este, Fountain of the Organ

slopes and with the central fountain, Fontana del Bicchierone, designed by the famous sculptor Gian Lorenzo Bernini. One of the highlights of any visit to Villa d'Este is the Fountain of the Organ, which took forty-three years to complete. Flowing water moves through a large organ, producing music that serenades visitors every two hours.

In addition to taking in the magnificent landscaping and feeling the refreshing spray from the luxurious fountains as they stroll the grounds, visitors will also experience the opulence of the Renaissance period as they walk through the actual estate, including the cardinal's living area. Although many of the extravagant trimmings are long gone, some rooms still contain frescoes and detailed decorations that provide photo opportunities every few feet.

You only need a few hours to visit the estate. But it will be an awe-inspiring experience that, as I'm sure you will agree, takes the idea of a garden party to an entirely different level.

TARQUINIA
An Ancient Etruscan Necropolis

How many times have you heard the phrase "If these walls could talk"? Perhaps you uttered those words aloud as you visited a place important to you such as a treasured family home or gathering space. No doubt those walls would probably have a lot to say about you and your experiences.

Well, in Tarquinia, the walls speak loudly and clearly, which is among the many reasons this ancient Etruscan city is worth discovering on your next trip to Italy. Tarquinia was not on my radar until just a few short years ago, when we were planning a pilgrimage focusing on the regions of Lazio and Umbria. Our wonderful guide, who had a doctorate in archeology, strongly suggested we included a tour of both the necropolis and the National Archeological Museum of Tarquinia in our itinerary, and I will be forever grateful that he did.

When planning a pilgrimage, it is important to give travelers the big picture of the country, including both religious and secular attractions with historic significance. We learn from previous generations and civilizations, and if we're open we often discover that ideas we often think are very modern or contemporary have roots that are hundreds, perhaps

Tarquinia Winged Horses,
(4th century BC)

even thousands of years old. Or as it says in the Old Testament Book of Ecclesiastes, *"What has been is what will be, and what has been done is what will be done; and there is nothing new under the sun" (Eccles. 1:9).*

The ingenuity and creativity of the people who built and lived in Pompeii, Herculaneum, and Paestum in the Campania region certainly exemplify this idea, and they also garner most of the attention when it comes to Italy's highly regarded archeological discoveries. Tarquinia, however, also deserves recognition.

Located not far from the coast, north of Rome, Tarquinia has an archeological heritage dating back to the seventh century B.C. It is home to a necropolis with thousands of tombs, two hundred of which "speak" to us through colorful paintings and important tools and artifacts left behind. Fifteen of those tombs are open to the public. The images, along with the vast collection of household items tell us of the everyday life of the Etruscans as well as their mythological beliefs and help us piece together Italy's incredible past.

When you visit the necropolis, be sure to visit the museum as well. It affirms the advancement of the pre-Roman Etruscan civilization with a massive artifact collection that is spread over three floors. It contains important sarcophagi from notable families, along with vast and ancient collections of bronze coins, gold coins, various types of jewelry, pottery, and tableware, and more. One of the most dramatic pieces exhibited at the museum is the terra-cotta high relief of the *Winged Horses of Tarquinia*, a sculpture that was once part of the largest Etruscan temple, dating back to the fourth century B.C.

The city of Tarquinia itself is lovely, especially the old town, as it is filled with several historic churches lining pleasant medieval streets. The Tyrrhenian Sea is so close by that visitors can catch a glimpse of the beautiful island of Corsica off in the distance. There are so many tales filled with art, history, and culture to be told from Tarquinia and its crypts; you won't regret taking this meaningful walk back in time.

Coronation of the Virgin, *Basilica of Santa Maria, Trastevere*

TRASTEVERE AND TESTACCIO
Roman Neighborhoods Worth Knowing

Get lost! Not exactly words you'd expect to hear from someone you've hired to help you navigate your way through Italy. However, getting lost is not only easy but so much fun to do in these marvelous Roman neighborhoods.

TRASTEVERE

It's easy to get lost in Trastevere, which stretches over a large area south of the Vatican along the west bank of the Tiber (its name means "beyond the Tiber"). This district has been featured in countless travel brochures, postcards, and movies; its charming cobblestoned streets are lined with colorful houses, historical churches, countless pubs, restaurants, pizzerias, wine bars, villas, boutiques, and other shops selling regional products and local art.

One of the most popular areas is Piazza di Santa Maria in front of the church where it gets its name, the Basilica of Our Lady of Trastevere. The fountain in the middle of the square is a popular gathering space. And while you could spend a whole day getting lost among Trastevere's cafes and cozy corners, you will want to step inside some of its most famous structures, including Our Lady of Trastevere, one of the oldest churches in the city. Inside, you'll find numerous detailed and dramatic twelfth- and thirteenth-century mosaics, including the *Coronation of the Virgin*. One of the chapels contains the medieval icon, the pearl-encrusted *Madonna della Clemenza*.

In addition to Our Lady of Trastevere, I highly recommend making your way to one of my favorite churches in this incredible neighborhood, the fifth-century church of the Basilica of Santa Cecelia. The church was built above the house of the saint. Her tomb is located at the main altar, and pilgrims can also tour the ruins below. You'll find this basilica in the quieter section of Trastevere populated by more locals than tourists. Although it's much less busy than Piazza Santa Maria, it still has its share of excellent Roman eateries and chic watering holes.

A great way to wrap up a day in this iconic area is a stop at Tiberina Island (Isola Tiberina). There is something special about sitting on the banks of the Tiber River, watching the sunset over Rome. *Bellissimo!*

TESTACCIO

Unlike picturesque Trastevere, Testaccio doesn't have fancy fountains and architecture. But similar to Trastevere, you'll soon come across good signs that you're about to discover more of the "real Rome": lots of locals and a long list of authentic restaurants serving classic Roman dishes.

Testaccio is an easy walk from Trastevere, which means that you could take in both neighborhoods in one day. The name comes from the Latin word *testaceus* or "broken clay vessels." Sounds odd, except when you realize that the neighborhood's most iconic landmark is something called Monte Testaccio — a small, manmade hill built up over time from "broken vessels" used in Roman times to store oil and wine.

Grave of English poet John Keats at the Protestant cemetery in Rome

This special region of Rome has some other distinctive attractions, including a Protestant cemetery where you can visit the grave of the famous poets Keats and Shelley, the twelfth-century B.C. Pyramid of Cestius, and a former slaughterhouse that is now a modern art museum. Go figure.

For the foodies out there, check out the amazing Testaccio Market. It's a wonderful collection of sandwich shops, bakeries, fruit and vegetable stands, and even fish markets. I would say that it's a great place to grab a "quick bite." However, deciding what to have for that "quick bite," based on the variety and quality of the items offered, could take a while.

So, when it comes to these neighborhoods worth knowing, getting lost is good advice, as you'll soon discover the benefit of not having a particular destination in mind. It leads to so much more being found.

T's Italy

T'S INSIDER TIP

Relics of one of the early virgin martyrs, St. Appolonia, can be venerated in Our Lady of Trastevere; several popes are buried here as well. The patroness of dentists, she is often pictured holding a tooth with pincers or wearing a golden tooth around her neck

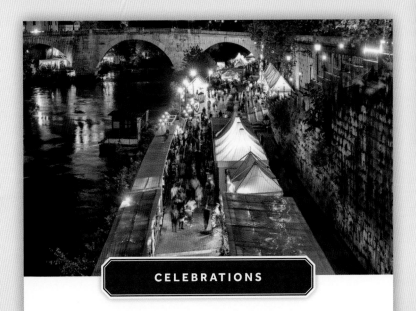

CELEBRATIONS

Lungo Il Tevere
JUNE — AUGUST

Lungo Il Tevere, or "along the Tiber," is a popular summer festival transforming the banks of the river into a three-month cultural celebration. It has been taking place since 2003 and offers a variety of local and international food, free concerts, art exhibits, and nightlife galore. It begins in June and ends in late August or early September. This festival takes some of the summer heat off (literally), as some of the temporary riverfront establishments offer the opportunity of sipping a cocktail or vino not only along the river, but right next to the small but powerful rapids. *Salute!*

LAZIO REGION
SIGNATURE DISHES

- - - - - - -

Bucatini all'Amatriciana
A RECIPE FROM TERESA'S KITCHEN

The region of Lazio (including Rome) is known for its pasta dishes. Expect to find carbonara, made with eggs, cheese, and pancetta, along with *cacio e pepe*, or cheese and pepper pasta, readily available. This is another wonderful pasta dish you will see on the menus of any Roman eatery worth its weight in sauce.

The name is taken from Amatrice, a town in Lazio east of Rome. It's one of my favorites because it is simple but has so much flavor thanks to the San Marzano tomatoes (from the Campagna region known for its quality *pomodoro*) and the *guanciale* (cheek of a pig or boar).

When I make it at home, I love to kick it up a notch by adding a healthy dash of red pepper to this dish. Most recipes call for bucatini noodles, but it also works well with rigatoni or linguine. I also use canned diced tomatoes from San Marzano — it saves time and they are just as good as fresh, as long as you use a good brand. *Godere!*

INGREDIENTS

- 1 lb. San Marzano tomatoes (or diced plum tomatoes)
- 12 oz. bucatini pasta
- 4 oz. guanciale (bacon-like cured cheek meat)
- ¾ cup grated Pecorino di Amatrice (about 3 oz.), or alternatively, ½ cup (about 2 oz.) Pecorino Romano
- 1 fresh red chili pepper (or ¼ to ½ teaspoon of crushed red pepper flakes)
- extra-virgin olive oil
- salt and pepper

DIRECTIONS

1. Bring a pot of water to a boil, adding a good amount of salt.

2. Cut the guanciale into ¼" strips.

3. Heat a drizzle of oil in a pan, sauté the guanciale until cooked (around 3–5 minutes), and then remove and set aside.

4. Cook the pepper and tomatoes for 30–40 minutes in the same pan as the guanciale, then return the guanciale to the pan. Add some of the pasta water if more liquid is needed.

5. Cook the bucatini for about 2 minutes less than called for.

6. Add the pasta to the tomato sauce to finish the cooking process, making sure not to overcook the pasta.

7. Top with grated Pecorino.

8. Godere! Enjoy!

A PILGRIM'S PERSPECTIVE

MIKE RITCHIE
AS TOLD BY JOHN HALE

A highly respected and successful Detroit-area businessman, Mike Ritchie has been a friend and mentor for many years. In July 2018, one of the world's oldest and finest choirs, the Cappella Musicale Pontifica Sistina (the Sistine Chapel Choir, sometimes called the "Pope's Choir") was about to make their first U.S. national tour. And so, when a colleague began to organize a special trip in December 2017 for the benefactors and organizers of the tour to come to Italy to hear the choir perform in the Sistine Chapel, I invited Mike to come and bring his family. Although I was unable to go, I wanted Mike to witness this once-in-a-lifetime experience for lay people to hear the choir in the Sistine Chapel, and there would be other highlights including the possibility of greeting Pope Francis at a papal audience.

To my surprise, he initially declined due to his schedule — and the fact that he was taking his family to Italy the following May. But when I persisted, saying that the Holy Father would like to thank him for all Mike did to facilitate the choir's historic tour, Mike agreed after his supervisor encouraged him to go. And so he relented; it seemed that the Holy Spirit was leading him to go.

As it turned out, the group was unable to greet the pope on that trip — which had been the primary reason Mike decided to go, or so he thought. When this opportunity did not materialize, Mike was forced

Mike Ritchie on his first trip to Rome

to reflect on why the Holy Spirit had inspired him to accept the invitation. Was this just another trophy, one more cool experience to tell people about? The more he thought about it, the more Mike realized that the audience could have become just one more extraordinary experience. Mike said that he felt on reflection that his heart wasn't in the right place. In fact, he was *very* grateful that he didn't receive that gift.

What he received instead was much more valuable, Mike said, than the greeting that had drawn him to accept the invitation. He experienced in a new way a deeper sense of God, the universality of the Church, and the deep consolation found from meeting people all over the world: the young and old, the happy and sad, the struggling and seemingly self-assured. All of these people were together in Rome, brought together by a hunger for something, *Someone* more.

In Rome, Mike became overwhelmed by how many people are hungry for God, who come from all corners of the earth to find fulfillment of the same universal desires. Mike himself was consoled and satiated in Rome in a way he had not been before. He also experienced a deep connection and friendship that prepared him for his family's trip just a few months later, making their pilgrimage even more meaningful. Meeting these brothers and sisters in Christ, Mike realized that his openness to the Holy Spirit had produced rich fruit in his life, and that God had blessed him on this trip beyond his greatest expectations.

This experience continued to bear fruit after Mike returned home. Over the years of reflecting on this and other invitations, Mike came to understand the complicated nature of such divine invitations. For Mike, and for all of us, an invitation must be pondered and even deconstructed (after the fact) to be fully understood and appreciated.

First, we must acknowledge the *risk*, our aversion to something new and out of our routine — and foreign to our concerns about safety and security. Next, we must be willing to surrender to the *mystery*, knowing that we must accept the fact that we cannot foresee all the contingencies and circumstances ahead.

An invitation to pilgrimage is a bit like walking through an open door. We might think we know what is on the other side — and we might be right. Or we might be surprised. Walking through a door usually leads to other doors, which must each be considered in turn: Should it be opened and walked through, or does it mean taking another path?

Adventure, then, is inextricably linked to invitation. Whether it is an invitation to a pilgrimage or a party, it can lead to an unexpected adventure. Even the unplanned moments — unpleasant and pleasant, from traffic delays to casual conversations — can be catalysts for the thrill of adventure as we surrender our experience to the Holy Spirit.

Finally, there is a matter of *time*. The gift and giving-up of our time are often greater than the financial sacrifice. We must be good custodians of our time, for we cannot reclaim it. And yet on pilgrimage we are releasing control of our time, our prerogatives, and even our preferences to someone who knows more about the place we are going. It requires an act of faith.

And yet, the smallest step, taken in faith, is blessed by God. He anoints it and uses it for our growth and good. God acts through our foibles and follies to bring good through our faith. In that way, a pilgrimage is a metaphor for our entire lives.

One of the hardest lessons we must learn is that we are not ultimately in control of our own lives. We are not in control on the pilgrimage, and we are not control when we return home. We all encounter trials and tribulations beyond our control. And so, on pilgrimage, we are given an opportunity to practice this lesson by saying yes to the mysteries, adventures, and risks by accepting God's invitation. In this very act, God blesses us both spiritually and physically by causing to grow within us very real and unexpected fruit.

This fruit does not grow effortlessly. There is an element of *sacrifice* that God asks of those who invite and of those who accept an invitation. Sacrifice is not an option; it is required in Scripture. In Matthew 6:16, Jesus says, "When you fast…" Jesus does not say, "If you would *like* to fast" or "If you *choose* to fast." He says *when*, not *if*. Nothing in the spiritual life is without cost. We must give up something to get something bigger.

When we begin to recognize and accept the Holy Spirit's invitations, it emboldens us to extend invitations to others. The following spring, Mike brought his family to Italy, having already experienced what God could and would do. The family enjoyed Rome and then moved to the beautiful region of Umbria and Assisi for an extended period of time.

Instead of a typical day trip to Assisi, they spent multiple days going off the beaten path. They experienced God in varied and surprising ways through the serenity of empty streets, the vast and colorful never-ending landscapes, and through the profound witness of the saints of this region, Rita, Clare, and Francis!

By graciously accepting these two invitations to pilgrimage in Italy, Mike and his family have been profoundly changed. Sitting with his family in an audience with the Holy Father several months after his first pilgrimage, Mike had a deep sense of God's Providence that permitted him to experience God in ways that were surprising and consoling. His

The Ritchie family, Easter in Rome

faith took on a tangible quality, as the reality of the Church came alive to him and as the Bible stories and saint stories he had read in books came alive. Ours is a bodily faith, where the physical and spiritual unite and renew us to all that is most real.

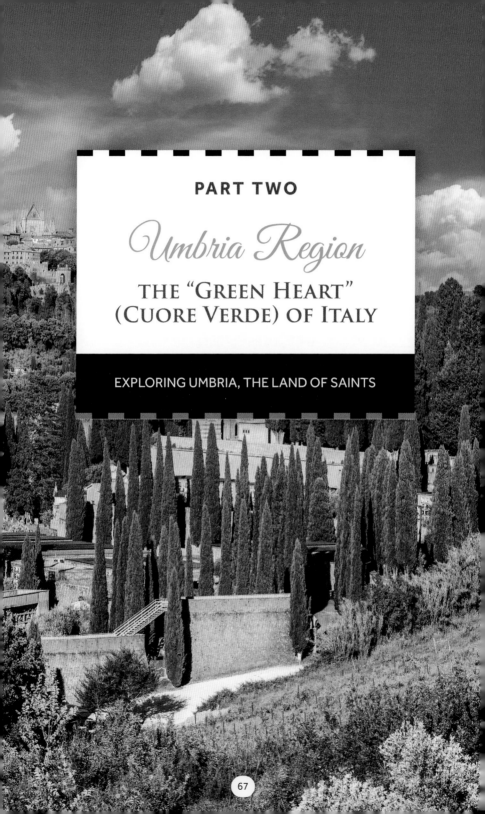

PART TWO

Umbria Region

THE "GREEN HEART" (CUORE VERDE) OF ITALY

EXPLORING UMBRIA, THE LAND OF SAINTS

Umbria Region

Previous page: Orvieto, Italy

WHAT YOU'LL EXPLORE...

UMBRIA REGION HIGHLIGHTS

- **Get to Know Umbria's Saints**
- **Beloved Saint of Italy — St. Angela of Foligno**
- T's Ultimate Must-Sees and Dos in Umbria

SACRED SPACES OF UMBRIA

- **Casa Dolce Casa:** Home Sweet Home in Umbria
- **Orvieto:** A Medieval Miracle, A Majestic Cathedral
- **Assisi and Montefalco:** St. Francis, St. Carlo, and the Two Clares
- **San Francesco della Pace:** The Taming of the Wolf of Gubbio
- **Santo Anello of Perugia:** Mary's Ring and a Prayer
- **Sanctuary della Madonna dei Bagni:** A Grateful Sign of Love

FASCINATING PLACES IN UMBRIA

- **The Via Flaminia and Nera River Park:** Discover the World's Tallest Manmade Waterfalls
- **Spectacular Spello:** The City of Flowers and the Infiorate
- **Orvieto Underground:** A Hidden Gem
- **St. Patrick's Well:** What Goes Down, Must Come Up

CELEBRATIONS AND SIGNATURE DISHES

- **Calendimaggio of Assisi:** A Celebration of Spring
- **Tagliere:** Not Your Typical Antipasto Platter

A PILGRIM'S PERSPECTIVE: SR. RITA CLARE (ANNIE YOCHES)

THE HEART OF THE MATTER:
EXPLORING UMBRIA,
THE LAND OF SAINTS

- - - - - - - -

Umbria is "the other Tuscany," a land of quaint medieval villages, lush landscapes, and fascinating saints. This small region in central Italy has all the beauty boasted by its stunning neighbor to the north, Tuscany, but garners much less attention. That's fortunate in one sense for those

Sunset in Umbria
Opposite: Picturesque alley near Santa Maria Assunta in Orvieto

71

of us who spend a lot of time here as much of the area remains unspoiled. But it is unfortunate for visitors who merely pass through with a quick stop in Orvieto or Assisi and move much too quickly on to what they think are greener, pun intended, pastures. But those who slow down and discover a different pace of life will enjoy all that this beautiful region has to offer.

I remember when I told one of my colleagues, Matteo, who works in the Rome bureau of EWTN, someone who was born and raised in Umbria, that my husband and I were finally, after years of discernment and prayer, making the move to live in Italy part-time. When I explained that we would be settling in Umbria, he was beyond thrilled. "Teresa," he said to me, "you have chosen to live not only in the green heart of Italy but in the land of the saints."

So true on both accounts. Umbria is a small landlocked region filled with forests, vineyards, and olive groves. If you enjoy good food, great wine, rolling hills, art, history, and important religious sites, Umbria has everything you need for a wonderful Italian holiday.

While Assisi and Orvieto get the lion's share of tourists and pilgrims, Umbria doesn't have the crowds and the high prices associated with Italy's more sought-after places. It also has the most medieval villages in all of Italy and a long list of Catholic saints who were either born in Umbria or connected to it through their lives and ministries. These brave men and women, many of whom are martyrs, made their mark on the Church and the world from here.

GET TO KNOW UMBRIA'S SAINTS

In addition to the most well-known saints of the region such as St. Francis and St. Clare of Assisi and the twins St. Benedict and St. Scholastica of Norcia, Umbria is associated with nearly two dozen saints, including ten connected to the medieval town of Todi in the central part of the region.

Medieval Todi, a city of saints

ST. FRANCIS OF ASSISI (1181–1226), for whom the Franciscan Order is named, is a patron of Italy along with St. Catherine of Siena (see p. 94).

ST. CLARE OF ASSISI (1194–1253), one of St. Francis's first followers, founded the Order of Poor Ladies, also known as the Poor Clares (see p. 98).

St. Clare and St. Francis, Santa Chiara, Assisi

ST. AGNES OF ASSISI (1197–1253), Clare's younger sister who died just three months after her, was one of the first abbesses. She is also buried in the Basilica of Saint Clare.

ST. AMATA OF ASSISI (1200–1250), Clare's niece, was miraculously healed by her aunt and then joined her in the convent.

ST. CLARE OF MONTEFALCO (1268–1308), who after her death was found to have the Cross of Christ emblazoned on her heart, is one of my favorite intercessors (see p. 100).

ST. ANGELA OF FOLIGNO (1248–1309) was a Franciscan laywoman and mystic who founded a religious community to care for the poor. (See p. 78).

St. Amata of Assisi

ST. RITA OF CASCIA (1381–1457), widow and Augustinian nun. She is the patron of marital problems and abused spouses. Buried in the Basilica of Santa Rita da Cascia in Perugia.

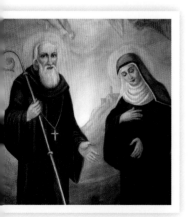

ST. BENEDICT OF NURSIA (480–547), founder of Western monasticism, established the first Benedictine monastery at Monte Cassino, where he is buried.

ST. SCHOLASTICA OF NURSIA (480–543), foundress of the Benedictine nuns and twin sister of Benedict. Her story is recorded in the *Dialogues* of Gregory the Great. She is buried with her brother inside the reconstructed cathedral of Monte Cassino.

Sts. Benedict and Scholastica

ST. VERONICA GIULIANI OF CASTELLO (1660–1727) was a Capuchin Poor Clare, mystic, and abbess. Her shrine is located in Città di Castello.

ST. MARGARET OF CASTELLO (1287–1320) was an educator and Dominican tertiary. Born blind and with spinal curvature, she was repeatedly abandoned by both parents and those entrusted with her care. When the townspeople welcomed her, she opened a school for poor children of working parents. She was later admitted to the Third Order of St. Dominic, and she was buried inside the Church of San Domenico in Castello. She was canonized by Pope Francis in 2021.

ST. UBALDO OF GUBBIO (1084–1160) was orphaned at a young age, then raised by his uncle, the bishop of Gubbio. Known for his gentleness and healing powers, his practice of heroic virtue enabled him to protect Gubbio from attack by the emperor Frederick Barbarossa in 1155 — an event that is celebrated to this day (see p. 103).

St. Ubaldo of Gubbio

ST. TERENTIAN OF TODI (d.118), first bishop of Todi, was martyred under Hadrian. His remains were stolen in thirteenth century, but his sarcophagus is located in the church of San Terenziano, outside Todi.

ST. FORTUNATUS OF TODI (d.537), sixth-century bishop, is one of five patron saints of Todi, along with martyr-convert **St. Cassian** (d.435), hermit and miracle-worker **St. Romana**, anchoress **St. Digna** (fourth century), and defender against Arianism and martyr **St. Callistus** (sixth century). They are buried in a sarcophagus in the crypt of the Basilica of San Fortunato (where Fortunatus's arm is displayed as a relic).

BL. JACOPONE OF TODI

(1230–1306), Franciscan friar, mystic, and poet, wrote the famous hymn "Stabat Mater." He is buried in the Basilica of San Fortunato.

Bl. Jacopone of Todi

BL. LUCY BROCADELLI OF NARNI

(1476–1544) was pulled between her desire to be a Dominican and her duties as a wife. (Her husband, Pietro, later had a strong conversion and became a Franciscan preacher, and Lucy joined a group of Dominican tertiaries in Viterbo.) Appointed prioress to the Convent of St. Catherine of Siena in Narni, Bl. Lucy was soon replaced and spent nearly forty years in silent seclusion. She is interred, incorrupt, in Ferrara Cathedral in northern Italy.

St. Valentine

ST. VALENTINE OF TERNI

(third-century bishop). After Emperor Claudius II outlawed marriages, St. Valentine continued to celebrate the sacrament, leading to his martyrdom in Rome. Couples come to Terni on his feast day (February 14) for a blessing of their love.

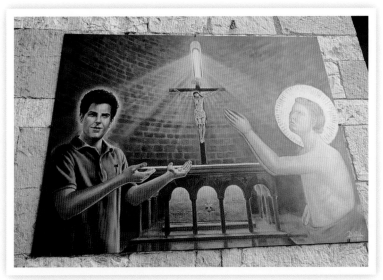

Outside St. Mary Major in Assisi

The canonization of another modern-day saint, Carlo Acutis, was announced by Pope Francis in 2024. Carlo was not born in Assisi, but he is buried there. He admired the life of St. Francis of Assisi so much that he wanted to be buried at St. Mary Major in Assisi. The church is located on the spot where St. Francis renounced his wealthy lifestyle.

This is the land of the saints indeed. Trust me when I say that your visit to Umbria and Italy's *cuore verde* (green heart) will be sure to capture *your* heart, too!

BELOVED SAINT OF ITALY

St. Angela of Foligno

- **Relics:** *Oratorio del Gonfalone, Foligno, Italy*
- **Patron Saint:** *Those seeking conversion, spiritual growth, and profound repentance*
- **Canonized:** *October 9, 2013, by Pope Francis*
- **Feast Day:** *January 4 (January 7 in the United States)*

Born in Foligno, Italy in 1248, Angela married young to a prominent wealthy man, had several children, and lived a worldly life. After experiencing war, storms, and an earthquake she felt the need for repentance.

When at nearly forty she received a vision of St. Francis of Assisi, Angela saw the emptiness of her own life and had a major conversion. After her mother, husband, and children died in quick succession, Angela rid herself of her possessions, realizing that she was being called to a higher purpose, and joined the Third Order Franciscans.

Angela continued to have many ecstasies and mystical experiences, and she wrote many instructional books about prayer. Vatican News explains, "Angela drew around her person a cenacle of spiritual children, who saw in her a guide and a true teacher of faith: for this reason her figure embodies one of the models of the feminine genius in the Church."[1]

After her death on January 3, 1309, her remains were placed in the Church of San Francesco in Foligno, but this church was closed in 2016 after an earthquake and her relics were moved to Oratorio del Gonfalone in Foligno for veneration.

---

[1] "St. Angela of Foligno, Franciscan," Vatican News, accessed August 29, 2024, https://www.vaticannews.va/en/saints/01/04/st--angela-of-foligno--franciscan.html.

UMBRIA REGION
HIGHLIGHTS

The Umbria Region is in northern central Italy just southeast of Tuscany. The most famous towns in this region are Perugia, where the famous chocolates are made; Assisi, where St. Francis is from; and Orvieto, home of a spectacular Eucharistic miracle. This miracle took place in 1263 at Bolsena, a town just southwest of Orvieto, where a priest witnessed the miraculous appearance of drops of blood on a Host that he was consecrating at Mass.

The Tiber River crosses this region, making rich soil perfect for cultivating corn, potatoes, sugar beets, grapes, and olives. The white wine of Orvieto, Orvieto Classico, is one of the most well known throughout Italy. Much of the cuisine of Umbria originates from its Etruscan roots and incorporates locally grown ingredients. Umbria is Italy's largest producer of black truffles, so many dishes in this region are made with this expensive delicacy.

Panoramic view from Ristorante Umbria in Todi

Right: Decorative cask in Gubbio, Umbria
Middle: Piazza IV Novembre in Perugia
Left: Rooftop view of Santa Maria Assunta in Orvieto

UMBRIA REGION
T'S ULTIMATE MUST-SEES AND DOS

— — — — — — —

Although there is a lot to see and do in Umbria, try to allow extra time just to stroll the quaint cobblestone streets and spend some quality prayer time in the beautiful basilicas.

ST. MARY OF THE ANGELS

Located in lower Assisi housing the tiny church where St. Francis first heard the call to rebuild for Christ. (Cross Ref pg #)

BASILICA OF ST. FRANCIS

The tomb of St. Francis is housed in Assisi in this magnificent church that tells his life story on the walls of the upper sanctuary.

BASILICA OF ST. CLARE

Housing the tomb of St. Clare and the San Damiano Cross that spoke to Francis.

ST. MARY MAJOR CHURCH

The tomb of St. Carlo Acutis is in this beautiful church.

EREMO DELLE CARCERI "HERMITAGE"

Caves/hermitage above Assisi, a four-kilometer drive or a several hour hike. But the views are so worth it! Your hotel can arrange for a driver. (We took a minibus.)

Opposite: Assisi, birthplace of St. Francis

TEMPLE MINERVA

In the Piazza di Commune. This former pagan temple is now a church. The piazza is a lovely place to take in the sights and sounds of the town with several good restaurants and lovely shops with beautiful religious items. (CRP#)

ROCCA MAGGIORE

This incredible fort at the top of Mt. Subasio is more than eight hundred years old. (CRP#)

ORVIETO

Located about an hour north of Rome, this stunning Etruscan town is set high upon a hill; the main cathedral contains the miraculous Host from the eucharistic miracle of Bolsena. The town has wonderful ceramic shops, restaurants, and wine stores well stocked with its famous local white wines. If you have time, take a tour of "Orvieto Underground," an ancient city still used by locals today. (CRP#)

LAKE TRASIMENO

Tucked away in the rolling northern hills of Umbria on the border of Tuscany lies this lovely lake that offers beaches, boat rides, and ample opportunities to get away from the crowds for a day or more. Consider taking the ferry over to Maggiore Island, where St. Francis spent an entire Lenten season. Once you step off the boat, enjoy its peaceful atmosphere with wonderful views of Tuscany and Umbria.

VISIT A WINE SPA

Umbria offers unique spa treatments at four- and five-star resorts across the region that are often half of what you would pay in neighboring Tuscany. (Check with your hotel concierge for recommendations.) Red wine contains antioxidants that are good for the skin. Be sure to enjoy a glass or two while getting that facial or massage.

VISIT A CERAMICS FACTORY IN DERUTA

If you love ceramics and pottery, be sure to visit Deruta, between Todi and Assisi. This quaint village has produced beautiful pottery and ceramics for centuries. Additional shops and factories line the streets of the lower part of the city just off the freeway. Most of the pottery producers offer great deals and will ship the amazing products home. Deruta — get your ceramics here!

Deruta, Ceramics Capital of Umbria

UMBRIA REGION
SACRED SPACES

— — — — — — —

When one thinks of visiting Umbria, for many Catholics the town of Assisi immediately comes to mind, the hometown of the great and much-loved saint, Francis of Assisi. Of course, there are many sacred spaces associated with this patron along with other saints who are buried in this medieval gem.

Umbria, however, has much more to offer in terms of sacred and special spaces to visit. These spaces in the central part of Italy provide venues filled with opportunities for reflection and contemplation regardless of one's faith affiliation. Whether it's a shrine of gratitude built by a married couple, a small church in the middle of a hilltop town tied to a beautiful Catholic tradition, or a remote mountain hermitage, it will take no time at all for Italy's "green heart" to tug at your own heart as you slow down and take in all the artistic and natural beauty.

CASA DOLCE CASA
A sweet home in Umbria

My husband and I now call this incredible region home six months out of the year — a fact that often puzzles locals, given that our heritage is a mixture of four different regions, none of which is Umbria.

Opposite: Sunset over the Basilica of St. Francis in Assisi

Both my father's parents were born in the region of Reggio, Calabria, along Italy's southwestern coast, not far from the island of Sicily and an eight-hour drive from central Umbria. My maternal grandfather was born in a tiny, remote village in the region of Campania, about two hours south of Naples. My maternal grandmother traces her roots back to the region of Basilicata and the lovely town of Anzi, about an hour from the famous ancient village of Matera, where *The Passion of the Christ* was filmed.

My mother-in-law's parents both came from Campania, and Dominick's paternal grandparents have their roots along the Adriatic in the Abruzzo region, which is known for its massive and magnificent mountain regions that attract hikers and adventure seekers from around the world.

If you were to look at a map of Italy, all these areas would be hundreds of miles southwest and southeast of Umbria. The regions of Italy are in many ways like different countries. Each area has its own dialect and, depending on the size of the region, some have more than one dialect. And each region has its own customs, foods, and festivals that celebrate what the area has to offer.

Most of the residents in our quaint medieval village are locals, and roots run deep. There is only one other American couple residing here part-time, and two other families that moved here from different parts of Europe. Although this peaceful farming community seems to have sprung up in the middle of nowhere, our hamlet is easily accessible, with Rome and Florence only a two-hour drive away. Perugia, Assisi, and Orvieto can all be reached in forty minutes or less. We are close to amazing restaurants, wineries, spas, and more; it is the perfect slice of real Italian life.

On our first few trips to the Motherland, we thought that if we ever made the plunge to purchase a place of our own, that it would be along the coast or in a larger, more well-known area. (It's very easy to quickly get enamored with locations in Italy that frequently appear on postcards and travel brochures.) But when we discovered we'd have to put most of our hard-earned savings into a place the size of a large broom closet and deal with tourists all day long, we decided to look elsewhere. And so, after many years of visiting the precious and breathtaking hill towns of Umbria and getting to know the many saints of this region, we decided to plant our Italian American selves in Italy's *cuore verde*, or green heart.

The residents have welcomed us warmly, graciously inviting us to various local events, most of which are connected to their strong Catholic roots. In Italy the feast days of saints are not just important days on the liturgical calendar; they're usually national holidays. In the small towns these feast days have become remarkable celebrations, as with Lazio's Viterbo and St. Rose.

Before moving on to highlight some of Umbria's gems, let me close with a favorite story of our life in *Bella Italia*. It is one of those moments that stays in my mind and always makes me smile. The sweet exchange with one of our new neighbors happened shortly after we moved in, as we were taking friends through our little village, a journey that takes ten minutes or less. One of the villagers was outside watering her plants. She happens to speak English and was very interested in why Americans from a big city moved to a place that is barely on Italy's map.

"Why here?" she asked. "There is really nothing."

"That's it, exactly," we replied. "Niente." Nothing but the kind of peace and quiet that can be hard to find in the United States. Most of us don't take the

View from our balcony

time even to sit down for a meal; if we dine at a restaurant, we're done in an hour or less and on to our next task. We tend to feel guilty if we're not packing every waking minute of the day with activity.

Not so in *Bella Italia*. Don't get me wrong. Italians are not lazy. But when it's quitting time, it's quitting time. They don't live to work. They work to live, and what *la dolce vita*, "sweet life," it is. Fr. John Riccardo, my friend who wrote the foreword for this book, led a small pilgrimage years ago with the theme "how to live like an Italian," savoring all that life has to offer. And as we continue to discover, and you will too, in Umbria there are many such lessons to be learned.

ORVIETO
A Medieval Miracle, a Majestic Cathedral

One warm September afternoon we walked up the Via del Duomo, the main street that takes visitors to the Orvieto cathedral, having a grand time admiring the colorful ceramics, the lively wine bars, and shops filled with truffles and other local gourmet goodies. The sky was, as I always refer to it, that deep Italian blue. We were making a stop in Orvieto on our way down to Rome, where we were to meet up with our group arriving that day. Orvieto was not on our original pilgrimage itinerary, but we thought that since we were driving right by, we might as well check it out.

Duomo in Orvieto

I had not expected to be so overwhelmed by the church's majesty and bright brilliance. When you are walking up the Via del Duomo, the façade of the grand gothic structure slowly begins to emerge. Then, suddenly, you observe it in all its glistening and graceful glory. Colorful mosaics depicting scenes from the life of the Blessed Mother sparkle in the sunlight, and bas-reliefs detailing scenes from the Old and New Testaments adorn the front of the church.

The duomo in Orvieto, known as the Santa Maria Assunta (Assumption of the Blessed Virgin Mary), took three hundred years to build — its construction began in 1290 to establish a worthy place to hold the miraculous Corporal of Bolsena. The towering structure commands your full attention, and you imagine what wonder and awe pilgrims over the centuries must have felt approaching the magnificent structure to adore the miraculous bleeding Host from the 1263 eucharistic miracle of Bolsena.

The town of Bolsena is the lakeside village where the eucharistic miracle actually occurred, and it is located on the border of Lazio and Umbria. In 1263 a priest, Peter of Prague, was making a pilgrimage to Rome and was celebrating Mass at the Church of Santa Christina. The priest was struggling in his faith and having doubts about the Real Presence of Jesus in the Eucharist and the transubstantiation when the host and wine become the actual Body and Blood of Christ. Shortly after the consecration of the Eucharist, the Host began to bleed on the altar cloth.

The priest took the Host and cloth to nearby Orvieto, where the pope was residing at the time. After a detailed investigation, the pope ordered the miracle to be available for veneration. It is exhibited several times a year in the cathedral's Chapel of the Corporal. The chapel is adorned with amazing frescoes painted between 1357 and 1363 focusing on the Eucharist. On the left side are frescoes of other eucharistic miracles and on the right are the paintings depicting the miracle of Bolsena.

In addition to the Chapel of the Corporal, not to be missed is the San Brizio Chapel, famous for its frescoes depicting the Last Judgment begun by Beato Angelico in 1447 and completed by Luca Signorelli between 1499 and 1504. These frescoes are said to have greatly influenced Michelangelo and his most famous work, the Sistine Chapel. The San Brizio Chapel is also famous for a portion of the frescoes known as *The Preaching of the Antichrist*. It is a chilling image and a timeless reminder of how evil portrays itself as good, with the devil shown whispering into the ear of a man on a pedestal who is speaking to a crowd. The man looks like Jesus, but the darker color and shades of paint used on the figure hint that he represents just the opposite, the antichrist.

Everywhere you look — the bas-reliefs, the mosaics and frescoes, as well as the various sculptures — visitors then and now are being catechized in the Catholic Faith. The message is clear: follow Jesus and

Preaching of the Anti-Christ *by Luca Signorelli (1499–1502)*

go to Heaven. Reject Christ and end up like the tortured creatures on the façade or on the walls of the church.

Such religious history lessons are so important. While some criticize the Catholic Church for building such expensive and elaborate houses of worship, it's important to remember that until recently most of the faithful could not read (illiteracy was commonplace), nor did they have the means to purchase a Bible. The façades, stained glass windows, and paintings taught the faithful what they most needed to know.

Today, Bibles are easily accessible in many different formats, yet few take the time to read it. And so, every time I see a line to enter the duomo in Orvieto or St. Peter's in Rome, I say a little prayer for the visitors. I pray they not only "look up" at the images before them but take their deeper meaning to heart.

ASSISI AND MONTEFALCO
St. Francis, St. Carlo, and the Two Clares

Assisi … it is hard not to fall in love with this medieval jewel perched in the center of the mammoth Mt. Subasio (part of the Apennine Mountain range). It stands nearly thirteen hundred feet above sea level and is filled with caves, forests, green meadows, and beautiful scenery that are part of a phenomenal regional park. It is always such a joy to watch the looks on pilgrims' faces and hear them gasp in delight as we exit the highway and start the approach to the town on a hill (a very big hill) that is home to two of the Catholic Church's most well-known and beloved saints, St. Francis of Assisi and his close friend and fellow religious, St. Clare.

The two Clares were born and raised in Umbria. Carlo Acutis, although not from the Umbrian region, chose this area as his resting place thanks to his love of St. Francis and all things Franciscan.

Assisi, a religious pilgrimage site for more than seven hundred years, is a popular day trip from Rome or Florence. And although a half-day tour can cover the major basilicas and other important sites related to Francis, to fully experience life in one of the best-preserved medieval villages in Italy treat yourself to at least a one- or two-night stay.

With its quaint cobblestone streets and views over the Umbrian countryside, Assisi is an entirely different place to experience after the crowds of tourists head back south to the Eternal City or north to Tuscany. Spend more time in Assisi and you will find yourself easily embracing and repeating to passersby the well-known greeting of St. Francis, *pax et bonum*, St. Francis's encouragement of peace and good things or peace and goodness.

ST. FRANCIS OF ASSISI

Francis of Assisi, the founder of the Franciscan Order and a patron of Italy, was a great mystic and poet, and is one of most beloved saints in the Catholic Church. Born in the late twelfth century to a wealthy Italian

Return of St. Francis Statue, Assisi, Umbria

fabric merchant and a French noblewoman, Francis lived a life of indulgence and grew up occupied with worldly matters. He began to change his life after he was imprisoned following a difficult battle with Perugia, a rival city of Assisi. He put his earlier attractions behind him and dedicated himself to a life of prayer and solitude.

Francis was said to have been directed by his many dreams, in which he experienced powerful exchanges with Christ. In one of those dreams, he believed he was being called to join the papal army as a knight. Soon after, he suited himself up with armor, bought a horse, and headed off to Rome. He is said to have been small in stature. But what he lacked in size he made up for in his larger-than-life outgoing personality.

On his journey, he made a stop in the Umbrian city of Spoleto, where he had yet another dream. The Lord encouraged him to fight for God in a very different way by serving the Church. One of my favorite images of St. Francis that exemplifies his willingness to follow God's will instead of his own is embodied in a beautiful equestrian statue in front of the basilica named after him. *Il Ritorno di Francesco* or *The Return of St. Francis* was created by artist Norberto Proietti. The statue portrays Francis returning to his birthplace on horseback but not in a triumphant manner. Instead, he is seen head down, in a definite position of humility, with even his horse in a similar pose, seemingly understanding what was in his master's heart. He was placing his life in God's hands to serve as a soldier of Christ.

It was at the church of San Damiano, just outside Assisi, where St. Francis's ministry would truly begin. As he prayed in front of a large crucifix, Francis heard the Lord asking him to rebuild His Church.

Francis, go repair My Church which is in ruin.

At first, Francis interpreted this literally, that he was to rebuild that crumbling chapel. Gradually, after continued prayer and contemplation, he realized he was being asked to undertake a much more significant assignment, that of renewing the Catholic Faith.

Canonized in 1228, St. Francis is buried in the crypt of the basilica, which is considered the mother church of the Order of Friars Minor (Franciscans). Built into the side of Mt. Subasio not long after Francis's death in 1226, the basilica is actually made up of two overlapping churches.

Step inside and you feel like you are getting a glimpse of Heaven as you are greeted by innumerable frescoes of the life of St. Francis, painted in bold colors and intricate detail between 1297 and 1300. In the upper basilica, you will also find frescoes depicting the history of salvation; the lower basilica contains depictions of the three religious vows of poverty, chastity, and obedience.

Tomb of Bl. Carlo Acutis

ST. CARLO ACUTIS: GOD'S INFLUENCER

Although they are separated by some eight centuries, St. Francis and St. Carlo share much in common, connected through their deep love of Jesus in the Eucharist, their dedication to the poor and downtrodden, and their dynamic personalities. Both were outgoing and loved Christ with a deep joy that was contagious, so much so that the informal title given to Carlo Acutis, "God's Influencer," could certainly apply to St. Francis.

St. Carlo Acutis is buried in Assisi not far from the saint he loved. In July 2024 the College of Cardinals in the Catholic Church approved a vote for his canonization. He was only fifteen when he died of leukemia in 2006, born to Italian parents in London, England and raised in Milan.

Although his parents weren't active in their faith when Carlo was a child, they say that their son was drawn, at a very early age, to all things Catholic. He loved to pray the Rosary and after making his First Holy Communion tried to get to Mass as often as possible. The youngster was naturally gifted with computers and in computer technology.

Carlo is such an example for teens and for all of us who find ourselves spending way too much time in front of a screen. According to 2024 statistics from the Pew Research Center, 85 percent of teens say they play video games, with four in ten saying they do so daily.[2] Also, in 2024 the surgeon general of the United States, Dr. Vivek H. Murthy, called for putting warning labels on social media platforms stating that they are associated with mental health harm in adolescents.[3] Young people now spend nearly five hours a day using social media.

---

[2]   Jeffrey Gottfried and Olivia Sidoti, "Teens and Video Games Today," Pew Research Center, May 9, 2024, https://www.pewresearch.org/internet/2024/05/09/teens-and-video-games-today/.

[3]   Ellen Barry and Cecilia Kang, "Surgeon General Calls for Warning Labels on Social Media Platforms," *New York Times*, June 18, 2024, https://nytimes.com/2024/06/17/health/surgeon-general-social-media-warning-label.html.

Much of the time Carlo spent online was dedicated to researching and collecting information concerning eucharistic miracles. His spiritual director confirmed that the Italian teen believed his efforts would help Catholics have a deeper appreciation for the Real Presence of Christ. Eventually Carlo, with the help of his family, would put together an exhibit that has been displayed at thousands of parishes around the world on five continents.

During his short lifetime Carlo loved to visit Assisi and had a strong devotion to St. Francis. The young man was known to emulate the great saint's concern for those in need, spending time serving the poor in a Milan soup kitchen run by Mother Teresa's Missionaries of Charity. His parents said he often used his allowance to buy items for the homeless sleeping on the streets.

He had a desire to be buried in Assisi. In 2007 his body was moved from its original resting place to St. Mary Major in Assisi and placed a glass tomb. The basilica is built on a location that would have suited Carlo — it is said to be the spot where St. Francis renounced his wealth by tearing off his expensive clothes in front of his father.

ST. CLARE OF ASSISI: *ALTER FRANCISCUS*

St. Clare of Assisi was an early follower of St. Francis. Born in the same Umbrian town into a prominent family, she was described as beautiful and extremely faithful, dedicating herself to prayer at an early age. She was eighteen when she heard Francis preach for the very first time during a Lenten service.

Not long after, on Palm Sunday 1212, she headed to the chapel of the "little portion" or Portiuncula. The name relates to the small portion of land on which it was built. At the time, this was where Francis's followers lived and where Francis received a deeper understanding of his calling, grappled with temptations. It is also where Francis experienced several visions, and is the place where Francis asked to be taken as he was dying. His death occurred in a small hut next to the church now known as the "place of transit." The Portiuncula and the "place of transit" are now located inside St. Mary of the Angels Church in lower Assisi.

St. Mary of the Angels, Portiuncula Chapel

It was here at the "little portion" church where St. Clare committed herself to the religious life. She allowed Francis to cut off her hair and joined the Franciscan community, exchanging her luxurious garments for a plain robe and veil. Her family, distraught over her decision, tried to force her to return home. She refused, claiming that Christ would forever be her only spouse.

She is the founder of the religious order known as the Poor Clares. She became the superior of the convent based at San Damiano, the same location that housed the cross that spoke to St. Francis. The Poor Clares lived an austere life as cloistered nuns, their days filled with prayer and manual labor. Her prayer life and her simple existence was so like that of St. Francis that she was referred to as *alter Franciscus*, "another Francis." She was known for her devotion to the Eucharist, so much so that it enabled her to perform two miracles. On one occasion, when Muslim invaders attempted to overrun her monastery outside the city walls, Clare determinedly went to a window and held aloft the Blessed Sacrament, the sight of which drove the mercenaries into the Umbrian hills.

Today Clare is also known as the patron of television, the title granted to her by Pope Pius XII in 1957 after the invention of the device. As her declining physical condition made it difficult for her to attend Mass, she was able to watch the Mass from her bed — an image of the liturgy miraculously appeared on the wall of her cell: "It is reported that in Assisi, on Christmas Eve, Clare, who had been brought to her convent by illness, heard the fervent songs that accompanied the sacred ceremonies and saw the nativity scene of the Divine Child, as if she were present in person in the Franciscan church."[4]

Clare is buried in upper Assisi in a basilica named after her; the construction began in 1257, just three years after her death. The San Damiano cross hangs inside the Chapel of the Crucifix (Cappella del Crocifisso). St. Clare's remains can be venerated in the lower part of the church where pilgrims are also able to view several important relics of both Francis and Clare.

ST. CLARE OF MONTEFALCO: THE SAINT WHO CARRIED THE CROSS IN HER HEART

Because we live close to their tombs, I sometimes like to visit these saints in person to ask for their intercession. I recently had an opportunity to experience this in a special way with St. Clare of Montefalco.

St. Clare of Montefalco, *artist unknown (14th century)*

4   Pius XII, apostolic letter proclaiming St. Clare Patroness of Television (February 14, 1957).

Dominick and I were in Montefalco for yet another wine tasting, wrapping up a weeklong vacation celebrating our fortieth anniversary. We had traveled north, from the Calabrian coastal town of Tropea to Eastern Umbria. Since we had visited "the other Clare's" tomb once before and enjoyed learning about her, we decided to go back before the wine tasting to pray before her relics, which include her heart imprinted with an image of the Cross.

I asked St. Clare to intercede for this latest and important writing assignment, seeking her intercession not just for my contribution but for all the team members working on the book project. Little did I know until I later spoke with my friend and co-author, Kelly Wahlquist, that our editor's husband was struggling with a rare heart condition. He had been awaiting major surgery at the same time that I was praying in front of the reliquary containing her heart. Coincidence? I don't think so.

The picturesque town of Montefalco sits about twenty-two miles south of Assisi. The small walled city is a popular Umbrian attraction, known for its wines, including the rich red Montefalco Sagrantino. St. Clare of Montefalco (also known as St. Clare of the Cross) is not as well-known as her saintly Umbrian neighbors, even though she lived around the same period, in the thirteenth century.

Before becoming an Augustinian nun, Clare joined a convent of secular Franciscans, sharing similar faith practices. In 1290 that same group founded the Holy Cross Convent and chose to live under the rule of St. Augustine, which was very similar to that of the Franciscans. Followers were expected to live detached from the world, practicing their faith through fasting, prayer, caring for the sick, and in silence.

Though Clare of Assisi is recognized for her love of the Eucharist, Clare of Montefalco experienced God through her dedication for Christ's Passion and particularly the Cross. Four years after the founding of the Holy Cross Convent, Clare fell into a state of spiritual ecstasy that lasted several weeks. During this experience, she had a vision in which she was being judged by God. The vision included a profound encounter with Christ, Who appeared to her as a poor beggar weary from carrying His Cross. When she approached Him and asked to help carry it, the Cross was planted in her heart. Following the vision Clare is said to have experienced pain in her heart for many years. Upon her death her heart was opened, and within the fibrous tissue the Cross and other instruments of Christ's Passion could be seen.

Clare is the beloved saint of Montefalco and is buried in the church outside the city walls. Pilgrims can venerate a statue of her body inside a glass sarcophagus. Her heart is also displayed there for veneration.

SAN FRANCESCO DELLA PACE
The Taming of the Wolf of Gubbio

Each year on May 15, since 1160, the northwestern Umbrian town of Gubbio has been celebrating the Festa dei Ceri. This spectacular event involves men (known as the *ceraioli)* carrying or racing three *ceri* or giant

Gubbio, Giant Ceri "candles"

wooden candles, each measuring just over thirteen feet tall, up and down the crowded city streets.

Topping the three *ceri* are statues of St. Ubaldo (Gubbio's patron), along with St. George and St. Anthony. After a nearly two-and-a-half-mile journey they reach their destination: the basilica of St. Ubaldo, located at the very top of Mt. Ingino.

This festival carries a great deal of spiritual and historical meaning for Gubbio residents, each year attracting thousands of locals and tourists alike. It is a way to show gratitude to St. Ubaldo, who saved the town from several sieges, and who since 1973 has been so culturally important that the *ceri* have come to symbolize the Umbrian region.

Given the celebration's importance to Gubbio and the surrounding area, it would be quite appropriate that most of the city's attention be given to the saints at the center of the competition. However, a quick stroll through this captivating commune reveals another saint who receives just as much recognition: St. Francis.

Of course, the image of St. Francis of Assisi in Gubbio is very different from those in his hometown or on holy cards, in religious catalogs, and in Catholic churches. In Gubbio St. Francis shares the stage with his animal friend, known as the Wolf of Gubbio.

This sweet story of St. Francis and the taming of the wolf inspired the building of a small church in the center of Gubbio, San Francesco della Pace, or St. Francis of Peace. The words "dedicated to God and Francis, the peace bestower" are inscribed above the door of the church as you walk in.

In the crypt, visitors will find a sarcophagus with remains of a large wolf that were found in the late nineteenth century. Tradition holds that the site of the church is where Francis met the wolf early in the thirteenth century. The wolf had been attacking livestock and other animals in the nearby woods, causing local residents to be afraid of going outside the city walls.

Francis heard about the attacks and decided to head west to Gubbio to meet the infamous wolf. When the two met in the woods, the wolf was ready to attack Francis, but the gentle friar made the Sign of

the Cross and the wolf became like putty in Francis's hands. In lower Gubbio, as a matter of fact, there is a large statue of Francis, outside another church, with the wolf sitting calmly in the lap of the saint, looking like a tamed pet longing to be petted by his master.

It is said that Francis rebuked the wolf and told him that if he promised to change his ways, the townspeople would keep him well fed. According to tradition, "Brother Wolf," as Francis named him, lived for a few more years and was embraced by the townspeople so much so that they mourned him when he died.

Of course, the tale of the wolf could be seen as an allegory or fable, reminding us to be more like Francis and to encourage peace, harmony, and a love for all God's creatures. However, the story is well known in Umbria and is found in several books including *Deeds of Blessed Francis and His Companions*, written by the fourteenth-century Franciscan friar Ugolino Boniscambi, and *The Flowers of St. Francis* (author unknown).

Should the story be taken as fact? That's up to you to decide. But in Gubbio you won't get very far before you bump into yet another plaque, painting, sculpture, or figurine of Francis and his furry friend.

T'S TRAVEL TIP

Get a Madman Certificate. Get certifiably crazy in Gubbio! The beautiful city of Gubbio is also affectionately known as the "City of Fools." Some say the label comes from the fun-loving nature of the residents. Others suspect locals could have been impacted by toxins coming from rock formations in the area. To earn your own "Madman's Certificate," just pay a small fee and go three times around the Fontana dei Matti (fountain). You can grab that certificate from a shop near the fountain. They make a unique souvenir with a great story!

Opposite: Francis and the Wolf of Gubbio

SANTO ANELLO OF PERUGIA
Mary's Ring and a Prayer

The Gospel of St. Matthew tells us of the betrothal of Joseph and Mary. An angel appears to Joseph in a dream, saying:

> Joseph, son of David, do not fear to take Mary your wife,
> for that which is conceived in her is of the Holy Spirit.
> (Matt. 1:20)

In some parts of the Church, a special feast day is celebrated on January 23 called the Espousal of the Blessed Virgin Mary. Dating back to the fifteenth century, this little-known feast is a reminder of the importance of the Sacrament of Matrimony in the life of the Church.

It was around this same time that a remarkable discovery came to light in the Church of San Lorenzo in Umbria's capital city of Perugia. A special ring — believed to be the Blessed Virgin's wedding ring — was discovered. According to tradition, an Italian goldsmith in the Tuscan town of Chiusi originally received the ring from a Jew-

Mary's Ring at Santo Anello

ish merchant at the beginning of the tenth century. The merchant claimed that the ring had been passed down over hundreds of years after the Blessed Mother appeared to him in a dream.

The ring was eventually given to a local convent in Chiusi and then to the church in Perugia, where it is kept in a side chapel in an ornate reliquary. The ring is stored high above an altar, behind several metal doors with some fourteen special keys needed to reach it.

It was the writings of Bl. Anne Catherine Emmerich that led to the ring becoming more well known outside of central Italy. Emmerich is said to have had a vision in 1821 in which she saw the unusual wedding ring.

> I saw the Blessed Virgin's wedding-ring; it is neither of silver nor of gold, nor of any other metal; it is dark in color and iridescent; it is not a thin narrow ring, but rather thick and at least a finger broad. I saw it smooth and yet as if covered with little regular triangles in which were letters. On the inside was a flat surface. The ring is engraved with something. I saw it kept behind many locks in a beautiful church. Devout people about to be married take their wedding-rings to touch it.[5]

Although the keepers of the ring at the cathedral of Perugia remind pilgrims that there is no confirmation that the object belonged to Mary, thousands of pilgrims flock each year to San Lorenzo's for veneration. Many engaged and married couples are allowed to touch their wedding rings to the holy ring and can also receive a special prayer for their marriage.

Did the ring truly belong to the Blessed Mother? The Catholic Church does not affirm this; however, in a world where marriage and commitment are often seen as a burden rather than a blessing, the ring symbolizes something important. So, if you know of someone about to be married or celebrating a milestone anniversary, or if your own marriage could use some encouragement, head to the cathedral in Perugia and see the Santo Anello. We don't know if the ring is real, but the graces God sends to those who ask for them certainly are.

---

[5]   Bl. Anne Catherine Emmerich, *The Life of the Blessed Virgin Mary*, trans. Sir Michael Palairet, ed. Donald R. Dickerson, Jr., online ed., chap. 7, https://www.ccel.org/ccel/emmerich/lifemary.xi.html.

SANCTUARY DELLA MADONNA DEI BAGNI,
A Grateful Sign of Love

The *Sanctuary della Madonna dei Bagni* ("Madonna of the Bath") is a little shrine truly off the beaten path that has this grateful kind of love written and painted all over it. The origin of the shrine's name is unknown, but if you put Madonna of the Bath on your Italy pilgrimage itinerary you will discover a beautiful sanctuary built around a love story. And it is a love story not only between a husband and wife, but between the Blessed Mother and her many grateful children.

We would often see small signs mentioning Madonna dei Bagni on the side of the *autostrada*, or highway, on the way to or from Assisi or Perugia. At first we didn't give the sight much thought — until we were encouraged to visit by one of our pilgrimage guides. It is quite small compared to other well-known pilgrimage attractions, so we didn't know what to expect. But we soon learned it is indeed worth the visit.

Madonna dei Bagni is tucked away in the hills south of the lovely village of Deruta, famous for its ceramic creations. The sanctuary was built in the seventeenth century. According to tradition, in the mid-1600s a Franciscan priest found a broken fragment of pottery in the woods. The fragment was decorated with an image of the Blessed Mother and the Infant Jesus. To protect the image, the priest decided to place the fragment in the branches of an oak tree.

Eventually, it fell to the ground where it stayed until a local merchant, Cristoforo di Filippo, discovered the shard on his way to work and decided to nail it to the tree for safe keeping.

A few years later, his wife became extremely ill and he thought of the pottery shard. Returning to that tree, he found the shard and asked for the intercession of the Blessed Mother. When he arrived home that same day, he found that she had fully recovered. To express their gratitude, the couple then commissioned an artist in Deruta to create a ceramic plaque in honor of the healing.

And thus began the devotion to Madonna dei Bagni. The same tile that adorned the oak tree, was placed behind the altar of the church and can still be seen today. But what makes this church so special is not just the story of the di Filippo's and their tile, but the literally hundreds of other tiles covering the walls. Over the centuries, some seven hundred tiles have been made by the loving

Sanctuary of Madonna dei Bagni

hands of Deruta-based ceramicists, commissioned by the faithful who believe serious injuries were prevented or their very lives saved after asking for the intercession of the Madonna of the Bath.

The plaques depict dramatic images of near-fatal calamities, such as coming dangerously close to being mauled or trampled by wild animals or being saved from a car accident, an earthquake, or a fire. An interesting part of the votive tiles centers around the letters *PGR* inscribed in each one of them; *per grazia ricevuta* or "for grace received."

It's powerful to reflect on not only the grace received by the hundreds of people over time whose prayers have been answered, but also on the grace received by all the artists who painstakingly created the scenes on those tiles and inscribed those three letters. Just imagine all the visitors graced by those willing to put that attitude of gratitude in writing and in living color to be seen long after they've moved on. Madonna dei Bagni is a deeply moving place, built and decorated by some smart cookies indeed.

UMBRIA REGION
FASCINATING PLACES

— — — — — — —

Fascinating places come in all shapes, sizes, and structures. In Italy, they are also found in the most unusual locations. Whether it's a huge waterfall where Roman soldiers rerouted a river to improve their water supply, or the cobblestone streets turned into a colorful floral canvas, or a sixteenth-century underground well that is an engineering masterpiece, the green heart of Italy provides adventurous travelers with an assortment of noteworthy excursions.

THE VIA FLAMINIA AND NERA RIVER PARK
Discover the World's Tallest Manmade Waterfalls

The Romans not only went over the river and through the woods to carve out the Via Flaminia, but they moved stagnant marsh water as well! The ancient road begins in Rome and winds through the Apennines all the way northeast to the Adriatic and to the coastal city now known as Rimini. A significant portion of this road runs through Umbria and through Carsulae, one of the most important archeological sites in Italy.

The municipality dates back to 300 B.C. and is a metropolis that began as a popular rest stop for travelers, tradesmen, and Roman

Opposite: Cascata delle Marmore, the tallest man-made waterfalls in the world

soldiers. The area was eventually abandoned, until the seventeenth century when the first excavations began under Pope Pius VI. Among the ruins, visitors will find the remains of a theater, amphitheater, a public square or forum, thermal baths, remnants of a church, a public meeting place, and two Roman temples. All this ancient history just ninety minutes from Rome!

Do you like waterfalls? Head twenty-five minutes southeast to Nera River Park and Cascata delle Marmore or the Marmore Falls, the tallest manmade waterfalls in the world. The falls get their name from the Italian word for marble, *marmo*. They powerfully cascade down from a height of nearly 550 feet.

Ancient Roman settlement of Carsulae
(2nd century BC)

The falls date back to 271 B.C. and were constructed by the Romans to drain the local marshes from their highest point into the Nera River. Although the flooding problems continued, the falls provide endless and awe-inspiring views and photo ops, including the romantic Lovers Balcony located at the end of a tunnel, where you can stand behind the falls and touch the Velino River.

T'S TRAVEL TIP

Make sure you time your visit just right, as the falls flow at different levels during different times of the day. Check online for more information.

SPECTACULAR SPELLO
The City of Flowers and the Infiorate

Spello is all about flowers. Just stroll through the streets on a warm spring or summer day, and you will be hard pressed to find a staircase, terrace, balcony, or front door that doesn't belong on the cover of a gardening magazine. Although many Umbrian towns celebrate the feast of Corpus Christi in June with a flower festival, no place says it with flowers like the Infiorate of Spello, more formally known as the Infiorata del Corpus Domini. (*infiorate* means "to cover with flowers.")

Infiorate Flower Festival

Every year, Spello's elaborate, colorful, and extremely detailed floral decorations are made with only natural plant elements and the images, mostly religious, line their streets in celebration of the eucharistic miracle of Bolsena (the holy relic is preserved at Orvieto Cathedral).

The event attracts hundreds of thousands of people each year. Though the main celebration occurs on the actual feast day (the Thursday after Pentecost Sunday), the festivities begin days before with music, photo exhibits, a children's flower show, and a floral cooking class. On the eve of the feast day, visitors can watch the city transform on the Night of Flowers.

T's Italy

T'S TRAVEL TIP

If you plan to attend the Infiorate, pack your patience and arrive early. The event is one of the most popular spring gatherings in Italy, and parking is limited.

ORVIETO UNDERGROUND
A Hidden Gem

The city of Orvieto sits on a giant volcanic rock, *la rupe* (the cliff), providing a dramatic position in the valley and allowing for the development of an entirely separate city underneath. So if you have more than a few hours in Orvieto, head over to Piazza del Duomo 23 (the tourist office in front of the main cathedral) and book yourself a tour of the Orvieto Underground.

The tour covers a lot of interesting ground, including some twelve hundred caves dug between the Etruscan era (eighth through third century B.C.) to the Renaissance. The underground city has cisterns, old olive mills, dovecotes, tunnels, and traces of the ancient Etruscans. The main tour is just under an hour and gives you just enough flavor of ancient and medieval life in this part of Italy without information overload.

ST. PATRICK'S WELL
What Goes Down, Must Come Up

On the other side of town, close to the funicular station, you'll find another underground structure that will have you scratching your head and asking yourself "How did they do that"?

Commissioned by Pope Clement VII when he took refuge here during the "Sack of Rome" in 1527, it was renamed St. Patrick's Well (Pozzo di San Patrizio) in the 1800s when local monks said it reminded them of the cave where St. Patrick prayed.

When the pope commissioned the well to build up the city's emergency water supply, one of Italy's most respected and sought-after engineers, Antonio da Sangallo the Younger, created a unique design to access underground water efficiently. It consists of a two-hundred-foot circular shaft with two spiral staircases that wrap around each other like

St. Patrick's Well

a DNA Helix (as my engineer husband describes it), so that mule-drawn carts could go in one way and ascend on the other to collect water without bumping into each other.

Although the well is no longer used, it now serves as an important local attraction. You will feel as if you are time-traveling back to the sixteenth century as you climb 248 steps (each way) by the light of seventy-two windows to marvel at this architectural wonder.

CELEBRATIONS

CALENDIMAGGIO OF ASSISI
A CELEBRATION OF SPRING

In all our travels to Italy we have experienced some incredible festivals up and down the Italian peninsula, but nothing quite prepared us for Assisi's Calendimaggio, a historic celebration in the merry month of May (Calendario di Maggio) that welcomes in spring in quite dramatic fashion. Calendimaggio lasts several days; thanks to our friends Don and Monica, expats from California who now live in Assisi full-time, we had front row seats to this medieval extravaganza.

This gathering, located in Assisi's main square, the Piazza del Comune, is complete with music, colorful parades, authentic costumes, dramatic presentations, and various competitions (much of it done on horseback). The festival features a friendly rivalry between residents in the upper and lower parts of the city that is taken very seriously by locals. A "jury" panel made up of experts from various backgrounds is even brought in to examine how closely each side adheres to the authenticity of Assisi's history.

Each group has its "headquarters" — San Rufino for the upper Assisi group, and the Basilica of St. Francis for the lower group. As the festivities begin, the groups parade through the streets, dressed to the nines in their medieval costumes. The city itself takes a step back in time, with streetlights replaced by torches and restaurants turned into old world taverns.

Seating is set up in the main piazza in front of the Temple of Minerva (no ticket, no seat). Tickets can be purchased through the Assisi ticket office in the main square and online.

While the region of Umbria has some of the most celebrated festivals in Italy and Europe, Calendimaggio is by far one of the most impressive.

UMBRIA REGION
SIGNATURE DISHES

- - - - - - -

Tagliere Not Your Typical Antipasto Platter
RECIPE FROM TERESA TOMEO'S KITCHEN

You will find *tagliere* in the appetizer section of the menu. The word means "cutting board" in English and refers to a serving board or platter piled high with Umbrian savories such as high-quality pork products and cheeses.

When ordering *tagliere* in central Italy, remember to "size down." For example, when we were dining out with friends at one of our favorite eateries near our Umbrian residence, we ordered the *tagliere* for two even though there were four of us. We barely got through half of it and had to take the rest home.

Tagliere's impressive presentation makes it ideal for company; it looks like you've worked all day in the kitchen, but the only prep required is shopping at a decent Italian market and putting the board together.

So, how can you take your guests on a culinary tour of Umbria without ever leaving your home? Below are some suggestions with some or all of these delectable items are found on the typical *tagilere* in Umbria.

Just imagine the impression you'll make on your guests when you bring this plate of Umbrian goodness to your table. All those bravas or bravos without cooking a thing.

INGREDIENTS

- **Prosciutto di Norcia PGI** — Italian ham that has received the coveted seal meaning (protected geographical indication). You can wrap it around some melon if in season or also try wrapping it around some good crunchy breadsticks.

- **Capocollo** — Another popular Umbrian cured pork product. Capocollo is well seasoned and served thinly sliced, cut from the neck or the shoulder of the pig.

- **Salame Corallina** — This cured meat product is among the most popular of the cured meats in Umbria along with the Prosciutto di Norcia.

- **Pecorino di Norcia** — A sheep's milk cheese aged for at least two months, often on a bed of herbs to add even more flavor. You will also find the cheeses in Umbria flavored with the famous truffles.

- **Caciotta Cheese** — Umbria's most well-known cheese. It is cured for only about twenty days to maintain its soft and lighter texture.

- **Torta al testo** — No tagliere would be complete without chunks of this famous Umbrian flatbread.

- **Suppli** — Delicious Italian finger food snack made of fried rice croquettes, often filled with cheese or chopped meats.

- **Crostini al Tartufo** — Grated Umbrian truffles are combined with olive oil and anchovies and are spread on small crunchy pieces of Italian bread or crostini. And don't worry about having to make the truffle spread as it can easily be found at a good Italian market or online.
- **Olives**
- **Marinated Artichokes**
- **Grilled Vegetables**

DIRECTIONS:

Arrange your favorite antipasti items on a large tray or cutting board with a knife.

Godere! Enjoy!

A PILGRIM'S PERSPECTIVE
SR. RITA CLARE (ANNIE YOCHES)
AS TOLD TO JOHN HALE

- - - - - - - -

In the carefree days following college, Annie Yoches was living what she thought was her best life. Until it wasn't. Annie had a dream job training athletes at a gym she helped start and was playing women's professional football for the Detroit Demolition. She partied every chance she could and had no real understanding of Who God was or what plans He had for her.

Annie Yoches and her mother on their first trip to Assisi

Out of habit, she continued to go to Mass, rolling out bed each Sunday just in time to meet a group of friends at a "last chance" 7:00 p.m. Mass at the St. John Center for Youth and Family. These weekly Masses were celebrated by a young, dynamic, and holy priest, Fr. John Riccardo, who drew many young adults to this ministry.

Like many lifelong Catholics who come into a closer relationship with Christ in adulthood, Annie's conversion was a process. In July 2003, Annie went to Mass feeling sick and empty, hungover from the night before. For the first time, she realized that her lifestyle was not sustainable. That weekend Fr. John preached on 1 Corinthians 11:27–30: "Whoever, therefore, eats the bread or drinks the cup of the Lord in an unworthy manner will be guilty of profaning the body and blood of the Lord. Let a man examine himself, and so eat of the bread and drink of the cup. For any one who eats and drinks without discerning the body eats and drinks judgment on himself. That is why many of you are weak and ill, and some have died."

That homily hit her *hard*. Annie knew that she was sick and dying on the inside from her lifestyle. She decided to go back to Confession for the first time in more than a decade. Yet she continued to lead a double life, going to Mass and Confession and then partying the rest of the time.

Shortly after this initial moment of conversion at Mass, Annie's friend Diana invited her on a Fall 2004 pilgrimage to Assisi and Rome with Fr. John Riccardo. Annie had been to Europe several years before, but right away she sensed that this was different. She thought and prayed about the trip and talked with her mom — who said she would like to go, too! Her mother's encouragement and support made Annie decide to accept Diana's invitation.

The first couple of days in Italy, Annie wondered if she'd made a mistake. Why spend her limited vacation time and financial resources to travel with a group of older "church people"? She could have gone on a fun party trip to Cancun instead! Annie felt somewhat out of place and quickly realized how little she knew about her Faith.

On the day of the papal audience, Annie couldn't understand why everyone was waiting so long to see Pope John Paul II, this "old and clearly infirm guy" being driven around St. Peter's Square. But as the pope was driven by Annie and the pilgrimage group, something happened inside of her. She was deeply moved, inspired by the goodness of this "old man." His mere presence passing by so closely was her next invitation to conversion. In that moment she became convinced that she was supposed to be there, and she experienced a deep peace that she hadn't felt previously.

Looking back, Annie believes that this silent invitation — sent by God through the very presence of this future Saint — prepared her to receive her calling. But that night she was strongly tempted to return to her old ways; the wine was flowing, and Annie was the life of the party. She left the group and continued the party at the Hard Rock Café, returning to the hotel at two o'clock in the morning and feeling sick. The group had an early departure for Assisi at 6:00 a.m.

Annie was physically sick all the way to Assisi and could not even look up at the frescoes in the Basilica of St. Francis, nor did she receive the Eucharist there because of the state of her soul. She barely made it across town to the Basilica of St. Clare in Assisi, and was half-listening to the tour guide showing them the San Damiano Cross when she heard how Jesus spoke to St. Francis from that cross, saying, "Francis, rebuild My Church which is falling into ruin."

That's extraordinary, Annie thought, wondering if such a thing was possible. She said to God, "If You really spoke to St. Francis from this cross why don't You say something to me when I pray in front of it?"

The cross was silent. Annie began pleading and begging, but she didn't hear anything. So she walked out of the Church and stood against the railing in the courtyard, overlooking the beautiful valley of Assisi, where she noticed some sisters standing outside of the basilica. It was *there*, in her heart, that she felt the Lord's invitation to religious life. "You could do this; you *should* do this," He said to her as she gazed at the nuns.

Annie knew the Lord was speaking to her, and she knew what He meant. But she was sure He must have the wrong person. "You want me to do *what*?! Become a nun? Are You crazy? Do You know who I am and what I have done? Do You know what I did just last night? There is *no* way I could become a nun!"

Sr. Rita

There was no response. And yet she couldn't dismiss what had happened. It was all so real. She went to Confession with Fr. John, who encouraged her to pray in front of St. Peter's bones the next day on the Scavi tour; the apostle was someone who had also messed up and turned his back on the Lord.

Through the quiet acceptance of each of these three invitations — one from a dear friend to go on pilgrimage, another at the sight of Pope St. John Paul II to continue her journey, and third from the Lord in Assisi to follow Him radically as a consecrated religious sister — that Annie is no longer Annie, but Sr. Rita Clare, a member of the Franciscan Sisters T.O.R. of Penance of the Sorrowful Mother in Steubenville, Ohio.

Last year, Sr. Rita Clare took a group of her students to Rome and Assisi. Sober and alert and completely changed into the person Jesus had called her to be, she was filled with gratitude to return to the place where she first received her invitation to religious life. This time she could look up and explain every fresco of St. Francis's life to the students. She felt at home on the cobblestone streets of Assisi, leading the students off the beaten path into a deeper relationship with Christ.

PART THREE

Campania and Puglia Regions
Italy Coast to Coast

THE AMALFI COAST "BITES DEEP"

Campania and Puglia Regions

Puglia Region

Campania Region

Previous page: Panorama of Amalfi, Italy, overlooking the Gulf of Salerno

WHAT YOU'LL EXPLORE...

CAMPANIA AND PUGLIA REGION HIGHLIGHTS

- **The Amalfi Coast "Bites Deep"**: Why John Steinbeck Was Right
- **Beloved Saint of Italy — St. Joseph of Cupertino**
- T's Ultimate Must-Sees and Dos in Campania
- T's Ultimate Must-Sees and Dos in Puglia

SACRED SPACES OF CAMPANIA AND PUGLIA

- Coastal Saints and Sanctuaries
- **Church of Santa Maria Assunta:** "Posa, Posa! Put Me Down in Positano"
- **St. Andrew Cathedral:** Amalfi, the Apostle Andrew, and the City by the Sea
- **Monte Sant'Angelo:** The Miraculous Apparitions of St. Michael
- **San Giovanni Rotondo:** St. Padre Pio and Companions
- **Basilica San Nicola, Bari:** The Story behind the Christmas Legend

FASCINATING PLACES

- Exploring Coastal Italy
- **Remarkable Ruins:** Pompeii, Herculaneum, and Paestum
- **Path of the Gods:** A Heavenly Landscape on the Amalfi Coast
- **Pearls of the Tyrrhenian:** Basilicata and Maratea
- **Sassi di Matera:** City of Timeless Wonder
- **Trulli Worth a Visit:** Quirky and Unique Alberobello
- **Island Time:** Capri, Ischia, and Procida

CELEBRATIONS AND SIGNATURE DISHES

- **Praiano's Luminaria di Domenico:** A Celebration of St. Dominic
- **Limoncello:** Sweet Memories

A PILGRIM'S PERSPECTIVE:
THE SWORD OF GALGANO: JOHN HALE

THE AMALFI COAST "BITES DEEP"

WHY JOHN STEINBECK WAS RIGHT

— — — — — — —

"Positano bites deep. It is a dream place that isn't quite real when you are there and becomes beckoningly real when you are gone."

John Steinbeck

"You haven't heard a word I said, have you?"

I looked away from the glistening Amalfi Coast for a second, and I turned to my husband and smiled. "You're right. I have not." We both laughed as we pulled our chairs a little closer to the railing for an even better view of what was before us as we enjoyed another cappuccino.

It was our very first time to the coast and we were enjoying our breakfast on the hotel terrace, which had an incredible view of Positano, known as the Jewel of the Amalfi Coast. The combination of the pink, blue, and yellow houses built into the side of the mountains and all the vibrant colors combining as everything cascaded down to the turquoise blue waters of Mediterranean created a "frozen moment," as my godmother Jenny Aielli used to say, etched permanently in our memories.

In the 1950s, the renowned American novelist and playwright John Steinbeck visited Positano, and was also captivated by its surreal beauty, as was quoted in the May 1953 issue of *Harper's Bazaar*:

Opposite: Church of Santa Maria Assunta in Positano by Gail Coniglio

Its houses climb a hill so steep it would be a cliff except that stairs are cut in it. I believe that whereas most house foundations are vertical, in Positano they are horizontal. The small curving bay of unbelievably blue and green water laps gently on a beach of small pebbles. There is only one narrow street, and it does not come down to the water. Everything else is stairs, some of them as steep as ladders. You do not walk to visit a friend. You either climb or slide.

Of course, to us Positano and the coast looked very different than in the 1950s, when there was barely a tour group to be found. The city itself is much larger now, with several streets leading down to the beach lined with art galleries, restaurants, jewelry stores, boutiques, and even shops making sandals on the spot. It is often too crowded for my taste, but it is still a magical place.

I would add that it's not only Positano that "bites deep." The entire Amalfi Coast quickly captivates visitors from all over the world. Positano, Praiano, Ravello, Amalfi, Atrani, and Sorrento (the gateway to the Amalfi Coast) all provide picture-perfect settings for an incredible holiday along the water.

The Mediterranean coast, including the nearby islands of Capri, Ischia, and Procida have much to offer in terms of jaw-dropping scenery as well as hiking and boating. If you love history and archaeology, be sure to take a tour of Pompeii and Herculaneum to the north and the remarkably well-preserved temples of Paestum to the south.

But if the only activity that strikes your fancy is relaxing by the ocean, watching the yachts and the cruise ships pass by, the Amalfi Coast is made for this. Don't just do something, sit there!

Praiano Coastline, Campania by Gail Coniglio

BELOVED SAINT OF ITALY

St. Joseph of Cupertino

- **Relics:** *Basilica of San Giuseppe da Copertino, Osimo (Province of Ancona, Marche Region)*
- **Patron Saint:** *aviation, astronauts, pilots, the learning disabled, and exam-takers, students*
- **Canonized:** *1767 by Pope Clement XIII*
- **Feast Day:** *September 18*

St. Joseph of Cupertino was born in a barn on June 17, 1603. His family lived in great poverty in Cupertino, in the Province of Lecce. Learning-disabled but very devout, he began receiving visions and ecstasies at eight years old.

Joseph's ecstasies caused him to be misunderstood, rejected, and poorly treated. He would stop speaking mid-sentence or drop whatever he was carrying or doing, and would stand motionless, his mouth agape. Recognizing that his challenges stemmed from a deep love for God, the Conventual Franciscan Order allowed him to enter as a servant to take care of the donkey. Through a series of providential happenings, Joseph became a priest, even without an education, and he became well known for miracles of healing, multiplication of food, bilocation, and of his friendship with animals and birds. Continuing to have ecstasies while in prayer, he frequently levitated and even flew up into trees or hovered in the sky.

Popular with the laity, he was kept in strict seclusion for years until his death on September 18, 1663, in Osimo, Italy (Province of Ancona, Marche Region).

Opposite: Path of the Gods, a beautiful hiking trail on the coast of Amalfi

T's Italy

CAMPANIA REGION
HIGHLIGHTS

The Campania Region is home to one of the most popular tourist destinations in the world, the Amalfi Coast. It is in Southeast Italy along the Tyrrhenian Sea and includes Naples, the Phlegraean Islands, and the stunning Isle of Capri. It is the third-most populous region of Italy with over five million people. This region is the proud mother of Italy's three most recognized foods: macaroni, pizza, and tomato sauce, and boasts of its amazing water buffalo mozzarella cheese.

Though all of Italy has its beauty and charm, nothing compares to the Amalfi coast. The mix of the water, the mountains, the cliffside views, and the scent of lemons, along with the fresh local cuisine makes for the most perfect spot to visit in beautiful Italia. I promise a visit to this iconic area in Italy will not disappoint.

Right: The Campania region is the mother of some of Italy's most recognizable foods, including tomato sauce
Middle: The Fountain of the Giant on the Naples seaside
Left: View of the small island Scoglio del Monacone off the coast of Capri

CAMPANIA REGION
T'S ULTIMATE MUST-SEES AND DOS

— — — — — — —

TAKE IN THE VIEW FROM SORRENTO'S PIAZZA DELLA VITTORIA

This wonderful piazza sits high on a cliff overlooking the Mediterranean and Sorrento's Marina Piccola. On a clear day Mt. Vesuvius is visible. The piazza has a popular wine bar with great cocktails, as does the nearby five-star Bellevue Hotel.

ENJOY A MEAL AT ONE OF SORRENTO'S WONDERFUL FISH RESTAURANTS ON THE MARINA GRANDE

It's a ten-minute walk from the heart of town but a lovely stroll through the older streets of this seaside city. My favorite is Ristorante Delfino (Dolphin Restaurant).

VISIT THE FAMOUS ISLE OF CAPRI

Ferries to the island are available from Naples, Sorrento, Positano, and Amalfi. Skip the main piazza on Capri with its expensive shops and over-crowded streets, and head up to Anacapri. Then go even higher on the Monte Solaro chair lift for the most incredible views overlooking the Bay of Naples on one side and the iconic Faraglioni rocks, three towering formations that jut out of the ocean.

The Faraglioni rocks, which tower above the water off the coast of Capri

IF THE SHOES OR SANDALS FIT, BUY THEM

The Amalfi Coast is known for many fine products including colorful clothes, ceramics, and of course all things lemon. But in Positano there are shops that make gorgeous sandals on the spot. You pick out the style and the bling, go have *pranzo* or a gelato, and when you return you will have a unique gift from this glitzy town on the coast.

Colorful vases with lemon ornamentation on display in Positano

VISIT GORGEOUS ST. ANDREW'S IN AMALFI

The cathedral with an incredible grand staircase in the center of town is worth a lot more than just a backdrop for another selfie. It is also an important pilgrimage site as it houses the relics of the apostle Andrew, the patron and protector of the maritime city.

STAY IN A SMALLER TOWN ALONG THE COAST

Praiano is my pick when I want to plant myself in this stunning area of Italy, with lovely hotels and great restaurants located between two amazing beaches.

T's Italy

T'S TRAVEL TIP

Be sure to pack sturdy walking shoes — it may take many steps (or a few steep ones) to get to a particular church, beach, hotel, or restaurant you want to visit on the Amalfi Coast. Not all have steep steps, but it is best to be prepared.

FIND OUT WHY EVERYONE RAVES ABOUT RAVELLO

This mountaintop town has breathtaking views, exquisite gardens (including Villa Rufolo), great restaurants overlooking the ocean, and an amazing summer concert series. Ravello is known as *la città della musica* ("the music city") thanks to composer Richard Wagner, who spent time here in the late 1880s. It is said its beauty inspired him to finish the second act of *Parsifal*, an opera he had been working on for more than a decade.

Villa Rufolo, Ravello

PUGLIA REGION
HIGHLIGHTS

For many Americans visiting the "heel of the boot," the region of Puglia ("Apulia") rarely seems to make it on their "bucket list." And that's a shame. A good number of travelers from the States are interested in the life of the popular saint, Padre Pio, and will visit San Giovanni Rotondo and the nearby Cave of St. Michael on Puglia's dramatic Gargano peninsula. However, that's where their Puglia experience ends.

And yet, Puglia is one of the least crowded areas of the boot with so much to offer in terms of beautiful beaches, fascinating religious history, archeological gems, along with breathtaking hilltop towns

Right: Olive grove in Salento
Middle: The town of Locorotondo, like neighboring Alberobello, is known for its whitewashed facades
Left: View of Vieste from Lido di Portonuovo on the Gargano peninsula

filled with crisp, whitewashed buildings. And it has great food and drink as well — Puglia produces some of the best wines in the country as well as the best olive oil.

Located on the easternmost region in Italy, Puglia is a narrow peninsula, bordered by two seas, the Ionian and the Adriatic, and has the longest coastline in Italy. It is the least mountainous region but is occupied by many gorgeous plains and hills. Supported by the local aqueduct, this region is among the biggest Italian producers of tomatoes, salad, carrots, olives, eggplants, artichokes, almonds, and citrus fruit.

Gravina in Puglia

PUGLIA REGION
T'S ULTIMATE MUST-SEES AND DOS

— — — — — — —

If you are staying overnight in Puglia, I recommend you stay on the coast in Monopoli or my favorite, Polignano a Mare, and then take in a few nearby towns such as Lecce, Alberobello, and Matera. There are plenty of other great towns to visit in the heel of Italy but remember, given the beauty of this area and the great sandy beaches, much different from the rocky beaches along the Mediterranean, do give yourself lots of time for *la dolce vita*. When you are ready to go exploring, here are some of my favorite places:

ALBEROBELLO
Known for its hilltop whitewashed stone huts with conical roofs, called "Trulli homes."

SASSI DI MATERA
The city of Sassi (meaning "rocks"), in the region of Basilicata, is where many famous movies have been filmed, including *The Passion of the Christ*.

SAN GIOVANNI ROTONDO
Home of the incorruptible saint, Padre Pio. He is buried in the crypt of the new sanctuary.

Alberobello, known for its whitewashed Trulli homes

Polignano a Mare

ST. MICHAEL'S CAVE

About an hour's drive from San Giovanni Rotondo, this cave on the Gargano Peninsula contains a church said to be consecrated by the archangel himself and has been visited by countless popes and saints (See p. 149).

VOLARE

Domenico Modugno, the artist behind the famous song "Volare," was born in stunning Polignano a Mare, about twenty miles south of Bari. *Volare* means "fly," and in his city by the sea you can take an iconic photo in front of his statue, imitating him with your arms spread out wide and with the deep blue Adriatic behind you. Another iconic photo op.

COASTAL SAINTS AND SANCTUARIES

SACRED SPACES

- - - - - - -

Italy is a large peninsula with nearly five thousand miles of coastline along the Ligurian and Tyrrhenian Seas (which are part of the Mediterranean) on Italy's west coast, the Ionian Sea to the south, and the Adriatic Sea bordering the east coast.

Given the popularity of the country's wonderful waterfront areas for vacationers, most don't associate the coast with sacred spaces. However, those who want their Italian holiday to combine faith and fun in the sun will be able find plenty of both.

Along the Amalfi Coast, for example, you can start your day with Mass and prayer at the tomb of St. Andrew the apostle and then hop the ferry over to the famed Isle of Capri.

On the Adriatic Coast, you'll learn about St. Michael the archangel in the whitewashed town of Gargano. St. Padre Pio will amaze you in San Giovanni Rotondo. Further south, you will learn how St. Nicholas ended up in Bari. In between, enjoy the beach, perhaps at Pugliano a Mare, not far from the ancient and fascinating city of Matera. Coast to coast Italy is filled with the scenic and the sacred.

Opposite: Cathedral of St. Andrew, Amalfi

CHURCH OF SANTA MARIA ASSUNTA
"Posa, Posa! Put Me Down in Positano"

Even if you have yet to visit Positano, you're probably familiar with photos featuring the golden *cupula* (dome) of its main church with its bright majolica tiles. That church, Santa Maria Assunta (Assumption of Our Lady Parish), shows up in practically every brochure, postcard, website, and magazine featuring the town. If Positano is on your itinerary, don't just take a few photos from the outside. Step inside and learn more about the church's history and strong ties to the local community. Begin with the famous icon of the Black Madonna, La Madonna Nera.

According to the parish website, the church is closely connected to a Benedictine monastery built after a Byzantine icon of the Virgin Mary arrived. Parishioners and residents along the coast, to this day, treat that arrival, through processions festivals, and feast days, as miraculous. The festivities are always held close to the Catholic holy day of obligation, the feast of the Assumption of the Virgin Mary, on August 15.

Parish archives, tradition, as well as stories passed on through many generations, say the icon was brought to the abbey in the twelfth century. One tradition says it came by way of monks who were sailing along the coast of southern Italy. Another claims the icon had been stolen, and that pirates had been transporting the icon along with other stolen goods.

The ship was about to pass Positano when it came to a complete stop in suddenly calm waters, unable to move. After several attempts to set sail again failed, the sailors heard a voice saying, *Posa, posa!* or "Put me down!" That's where the name of the village came from. The captain believed that it was the icon of the Virgin expressing a desire to stay put. When they decided to do just that, the ship began to sail again. The icon was then given to the inhabitants who chose the Virgin as their patron and built the church near the abbey in her honor. Since that time, the village has been called Positano in honor of the Blessed Virgin's command.

The church underwent a major five-year restoration beginning in 1717. In 1783 the archbishop consecrated the church and topped the icon with a golden crown. Once you visit this striking place, you'll agree with the Blessed Mother. After all, who wouldn't want *posa, posa* — to be put down in Positano?

ST. ANDREW CATHEDRAL
Amalfi, the Apostle Andrew, and the City by the Sea

*As he walked by the Sea of Galilee, he saw two brothers,
Simon who is called Peter and Andrew his brother, casting
a net into the sea; for they were fishermen. And he said to
them, "Follow me, and I will make you fishers of men."*

— Matthew 4:18–19

How apropos that St. Andrew, a fisherman from Galilee who became a fisher of men, is buried in a city so strongly associated with the sea. Amalfi, the city where the famed coast takes its name, was at one time the capital of a crucial seaport connecting the East and West; its importance as a coastal powerhouse once rivaled Genoa and Pisa. Along with the other dreamy seaside towns of the Amalfi Coast, Amafi lies in the region of Campania and is now a major tourist attraction, serving as one of Italy's most important resort areas.

Reliquary of St. Andrew in the Cathedral of St. Andrew, Amalfi

Amalfi sits at the mouth of a deep ravine. This UNESCO heritage site is surrounded by dramatic cliffs. Cruise ships arrive daily, which means you want to visit after throngs of cruisers grab their limoncello, the famous local liquor, and head back on board. Late afternoon is a great time to visit.

This star along the sea is dominated by the Cathedral of St. Andrew, a cathedral with a major "wow" factor. As you enter Amalfi through a beautiful archway and walk down a busy street lined with bustling gift shops, bakeries, and restaurants, suddenly the crowds clear. There in front of you is this monumental church and complex dedicated to the brother of the first pope, St. Peter. It is believed that St. Andrew's remains were brought here from Constantinople in 1206 and placed in a crypt below the main altar.

One of the most dramatic elements of the cathedral's exterior is the grand staircase leading up to the church's main entrance. Once you climb the sixty-two steps, you'll find a portico with intricate mosaics and original bronze doors from the eleventh century with scenes from the life of Christ and St. Andrew. The majesty of the cathedral continues with more mosaics on its façade with a dramatically detailed mosaic by Domenic Morelli, the *Triumph of Christ*.

The cathedral's construction can be traced to the ninth century, although the staircase and façade were rebuilt in the late nineteenth century after the collapse of the originals. Combining different architectural styles such as baroque, Gothic, Moorish, and Romanesque, St. Andrew's is an impressive place to be savored for hours, slowly walking through its chapels, cloisters, and caverns and reflecting on the time and effort it took to bring it to life. It is considered one of region's greatest treasures, with myriad mosaics, frescoes, sculptures, and most importantly the tomb of Sant'Andrea, the patron and protector of Amalfi.

MONTE SANT'ANGELO
The Miraculous Apparitions of St. Michael

Cave of St. Michael

The Gargano Peninsula, jutting out into the Adriatic in southeastern Italy, is home to Monte Sant'Angelo, a whitewashed village named after St. Michael. It is also home to one the oldest shrines in Western Europe, the site of four apparitions that occurred between late fifth and seventeenth centuries.

Monte Sant'Angelo is about twenty miles from where Padre Pio spent most of his life, San Giovanni Rotondo. Padre Pio had a strong devotion to St. Michael and encouraged many of his followers to ask for his intercession, instructing them to walk all the way up Monte Gargano on their way to the shrine as a form of penance. This was no easy task, considering the shrine atop Monte Gargano sits some 2,600 feet above sea level.

The apparitions of St. Michael, approved by the Catholic Church, are commemorated on May 8 as well as on the feast of the archangels,

September 29. (The feast of the archangels also includes St. Raphael and St. Gabriel.)

The first apparition occurred in 490, when a wealthy resident ordered a servant to fire an arrow at his bull who had wandered near a cave. Instead of striking the bull, the arrow boomeranged and hit the archer instead. The man shared the story with the bishop, St. Lorenzo Maiorano, who believed that supernatural forces might be involved and called for three days of prayer and penance. After the prayer period ended, the bishop encountered Michael in a vision.

> I am the Archangel Michael, and I am always in the presence of God. This cave is sacred to me. And because I have decided to protect this place on earth and its inhabitants, I have decided to attest in this way that I am the patron and guardian of this place and of everything that happens here. At the opening in the rocks, people's sins can be forgiven. Whatever is requested here in prayer will be heard.

Archangels are not mythical creatures. Their presence and involvement in the lives of believers is prominently mentioned in Scripture and the Catechism (see *Catechism of the Catholic Church*, 325–354). St. Michael is known as a guardian of Israel, the guardian of the Catholic Church, as well as a warrior against evil. In the book of Revelation (chap. 12), we read about Michael the archangel engaging in celestial battles with Satan. There is much more to say about the significance of St. Michael for Catholic Christians. Even this short explanation hopefully helps one understand the popularity of the shrine in Puglia.

Getting to the Sanctuary of St. Michael requires quite a journey, even if you're attempting to reach it on wheels — it really is "off the beaten path." First you will take a nail-biting ride up the side of Monte Gargano with continuous twists and turns along the way. Then you will have a half-mile walk through winding cobblestone streets of bright white houses and buildings. As you walk through the gates, you'll find yourself in a little courtyard in front of a small church with a lovely bell tower built in the thirteenth century. But you're not there yet! There are many more steps — eighty-six of them — before you reach the destination.

After you descend the five flights of stairs to the cave, which is now a Catholic Church, be sure to look for St. Michael's footprint at the bottom of the steps. Upon entering you will also see some of the words spoken by St. Michael to Bishop Maiorano, to whom he appeared. "Here are where the stones open the sins of men are blotted out, this is the special house where any evil deed is washed away."

T'S TIP

Pray to St. Michael the Archangel for peace and protection each morning as you set out for your day. Here is a simple yet powerful prayer for protection:

*St. Michael the archangel,
defend us in battle.
Be our defense against the wickedness
and snares of the devil.
May God rebuke him, we humbly pray,
and do thou,
O prince of the heavenly hosts,
by the power of God,
thrust into Hell Satan,
and all the evil spirits
who prowl about the world
seeking the ruin of souls.
Amen.*

SAN GIOVANNI ROTONDO
St. Padre Pio and Companions

San Giovanni Rotondo is best known as the home and final resting place of one of the most popular Catholic saints, St. Padre Pio of Pietrelcina, a twentieth-century priest, mystic, and stigmatist. Pietrelcina was his birthplace in the region of Campania, about two hours away.

Thanks to the proximity of St. Michael's Shrine and San Giovanni Rotondo, both pilgrimage sites can be visited easily in a day. Combining the two makes for a very moving experience, especially since Padre Pio had such a strong devotion to St. Michael. Often when we take groups here, we stay one night in San Giovanni Rotondo, touring the church and monastery of Santa Maria delle Grazie, Padre Pio's home for more than fifty years and where he received the stigmata, the wounds of Christ, and then we move on to visit St. Michael.

Padre Pio Pilgrimage Church, San Giovanni Rotondo

The Capuchin monastery where Padre Pio arrived in 1916 as a young priest was built in the sixteenth century. To walk through the monastery connected to the church is to encounter this great and humble man in a very personal way. This was his spiritual ground zero, where he heard countless Confessions, celebrated Mass, and received the throngs of followers needing hope, healing, and guidance. This is also where he built a world-renowned hospital to serve the poor.

As you glimpse inside his small and simple cell, you can imagine the conversations he had with God, the Blessed Mother, and his guardian angel while he was there. Visitors will also see other belongings including books, vestments, bandages, and bloodstained gloves and stockings, evidence of the stigmata.

Next to his tomb, the most touching place in all of San Giovanni Rotondo for me was the room with the collection of letters. The thousands of envelopes that line the shelves no doubt represent only a small portion of the correspondence he had with devotees from around the world during his eighty-one years of life.

In 2004, to accommodate the millions of pilgrims that visit San Giovanni Rotondo, a new church was built. Modern and ornate, it is large enough to seat 6,500 inside the nave. And while it is wonderful that such a large church allows for more of the faithful to receive the sacraments and visit the saint's tomb, I prefer the simpler, smaller, and much more traditional church of Santa Maria delle Grazie. Try to pay a little visit if you can.

BASILICA SAN NICOLA, BARI
The Story behind the Christmas Legend

Therefore, since we are surrounded by so great a cloud of witnesses,
let us also lay aside every weight, and sin which clings so closely,
and let us run with perseverance the race that is set before us,
looking to Jesus the pioneer and perfecter of our faith.

— Hebrews 12:1–2

Next, Puglia's great cloud of witnesses will take you about one hundred miles south along the Adriatic coast, from San Giovanni Rotondo to our next stop in Bari. Let's get to know another of Padre Pio's heavenly companions, St. Nicholas of Myra, who is buried in Bari.

Church of St. Nicholas in Bari

St. Nicholas was a fourth-century Christian bishop serving in the Greek city of Myra, now in modern-day Turkey. Mostly associated with the Christmas season, St. Nicholas is remembered as a generous soul with a soft spot for the poor. His feast day is December 6.

St. Nicholas, who is said to have come from a wealthy family, became aware of a local family in need. The recently widowed father was distraught over the fact that he did not have enough money to provide dowries for his three daughters — and without dowries his daughters would be forced into prostitution. Hearing of the family's plight, Nicholas dropped bags of gold coins through the window while the family was sleeping. Over time, the story was passed down through the generations until it became the legend of Santa Claus. (I'm not sure at what point he started climbing down the chimney.)

Like St. Michael the archangel, St. Nicholas has two feast days: December 6 is the day St. Nicholas died in 343. The second feast day, May 9, is the anniversary of his relics being moved to Bari. Those relics can still be venerated in the gated crypt beneath the main altar. This twelfth-century Romanesque basilica that carries his name has served as a template or blueprint for the design of many other churches across Italy and Europe.

The Basilica of St. Nicolas sits in Bari's historical center, just steps from the waterfront — a fitting tribute, as this saint is also the patron of sailors.

EXPLORING COASTAL ITALY
FASCINATING PLACES

- - - - - - - -

The variety of experiences available when traveling along and between Italy's Amalfi and Adriatic Coast will delight all kinds of travelers. The Campania and Puglia regions will draw the faithful pilgrim closer to Christ and His saints; the thrill seeker can see the world from high above the ocean, and the history buff can get lost in a maze of ancient Greek or Roman ruins. There is even plenty of room for the beach bums who love to search for the perfect spot to plant that lounge chair, Aperol Spritz in hand. And even if you and your fellow sojourners have different tastes and priorities, no worries. You've just given yourselves more reason to return again and again.

REMARKABLE RUINS
Pompeii, Herculaneum, and Paestum

Roaming around ancient ruins is not only educational, but it can also be exciting as it connects you to the people of early civilizations in a very personal way. These ruins take you inside homes, villas, shops, and political centers, giving you a taste of their inhabitants' everyday lives. As you explore these fascinating ruins in the shadow of Mt. Vesuvius, one of Italy's several active volcanoes, you can't help but wonder what it must have been like to live right next to such a powerful force of nature.

Opposite: Casa della Fontana Grande, Pompeii

POMPEII

This UNESCO world heritage site covers an area of over 4.6 miles, so put on your walking shoes! Each time I've toured the ancient city of Pompeii, I've been fascinated by the creativity and ingenuity of the people who built the city thousands of years ago. I was even impressed with the ingenious ways stones were used in and along the city streets to assist travelers.

For example, did you know that the ancient city roads had crosswalks? As you're walking along, notice the larger stones lined up, connecting the roads. It allowed residents to use them as steppingstones to avoid water and mud; they were just wide enough for carriages and cars to pass through. The roads in Pompeii also included strategically placed small white stones that acted as natural reflectors in the moonlight to guide nighttime travels of horse-drawn chariots. Wow!

Pompeii, about fourteen miles southeast of Naples, was destroyed in A.D. 79 by the volcano, Mt. Vesuvius, buried in almost twenty feet of ash and debris. Historians believe close to twenty thousand people lived there at the time of the eruption. Although it took a devastating toll on the city's population, much of the city was preserved for centuries under that layer of volcanic ash. The excavations, which began in the eighteenth century, give us a detailed look at life in the ancient world. As you walk, you'll quickly realize that this town was a bustling place with many fine buildings, fine homes decorated with colorful mosaics, luxurious baths, and large courtyards. You will even see a market street where vendors would sell their goods.

Archeological experts observe that Pompeii is "the only archaeological site in the world that provides a complete picture of an ancient Roman city."[1] The excavations recovered not only the city but human remains with more than 1,100 victims, both human and animal. Some

---

[1] "Archaeological Areas of Pompei, Herculaneum and Torre Annunziata," UNESCO World Heritage Convention, UNESCO World Heritage Centre, accessed August 31, 2024, https://whc.unesco.org/en/list/829/.

one hundred of these have been studied and are on display, their bones encased in plaster casts.[2]

Although I've been to Pompeii many times, I would not want to live there! Mt. Vesuvius is an active volcano, and geologists say it is not a matter of if Vesuvius is going to erupt again but when.

HERCULANEUM

Eleven miles north of Pompeii, closer to Naples, is another Roman city, Herculaneum (named after the pagan god, Hercules), that was also destroyed by Mt. Vesuvius in A.D. 79. Like Pompeii, this ancient city was preserved nearly intact. However, Herculaneum was not buried under volcanic ash, but covered with what geologists call "pyroclastic material," a fluidized mixture of gases and volcanic rock moving at high speeds.

Villa of Papyri (Herculaneum)

2 Natasha Sheldon, "Human Remains in Pompeii: The Unique Case of the Body Casts," History and Archaeology Online, November 5, 2017, https://historyandarchaeologyonline.com/human-remains-in-pompeii-the-unique-case-of-the-body-casts/.

Geologists say that this type of destruction for Herculaneum makes the most sense as it was much closer to Mt. Vesuvius than Pompeii.

Herculaneum was a popular resort town, as evidenced by the large, more sophisticated waterfront homes and boats and the expensive materials used to build them. While the wealthy resided in both Pompeii and Herculaneum, Herculaneum would have been where the upper crust or elites of Roman society would go. (Think of Pompeii as a functioning city, like a smaller version of Miami or New York. Herculaneum would have been more like the Hamptons or Boca Raton.)

Proof of the opulent living conditions can be found in one of the most popular Herculaneum ruins, Villa of the Papyri, named after ancient Roman scrolls, discovered there in the mid-1700s. This was the mother of all the local waterfront villas, spreading out over 220,000 square feet with a library, gardens, a pool, a covered walkway, boathouses, and more. Many living at Herculaneum at the time tried to escape the eruption by hiding in those boathouses.[3]

Visiting Herculaneum and Pompeii is a fascinating way to learn firsthand how ancient people lived, worked, and celebrated life. They are also a stark reminder of how it can all quickly be taken away.

PAESTUM

Head south of the Amalfi Coast, well past the seaside city of Salerno, and you will think you have crossed over the Italian peninsula and landed in Greece. That's because sixty miles south lies the ancient Greek city of Paestum. Ancient Roman cities in Italy — that makes sense. But Paestum is a surprise because of its Greek roots. It was founded by the Greeks in 600 B.C. and then conquered by the Romans several hundred years later.

While Pompeii and Herculaneum are known for their beautiful villas and other buildings, Paestum is known for its Greek temples. The

---

[3]   Daisy Dunn, "The beautiful ancient house discovered in ashes," bbc.com, July 8, 2019, https://www.bbc.com/culture/article/20190705-the-beautiful-ancient-house-discovered-in-the-ashes

ruins are made up of three major temples. Probably the most impressive of the temples is the Temple of Neptune. Even compared to Greek temples in Agrigento (Sicily) or Athens (Greece), this one is said to be one of the best preserved in the world. It's 195 feet high and eighty feet wide, a great spot to stand if you need a little dose of humility — it certainly makes you feel and look small. Paestum also boasts Roman ruins and an amphitheater along with ancient tombs.

Paestum, it needs to be noted, is not exactly just around the corner. It's a bit of a challenging drive from the Amalfi Coast. We drove there from Praiano, about fifty miles north, and it took almost two hours. The good news is that the journey takes you right through buffalo mozzarella country. Paestum specializes in this delicacy, so don't pass through without making a stop. Visit one of the factories, watch them make the cheese (or take part in the cheese making), then take some delicious fresh mozzarella back with you.

This is one time we did not follow our own advice; we were in too much of hurry to get to Paestum and back. And although we enjoyed the temples, every time my husband and see fresh buffalo mozzarella in the stores we kick ourselves. We're still working on getting back to those factories to try our hand at mozzarella making.

PATH OF THE GODS
A Heavenly Landscape on the Amalfi Coast

For a completely different view of the Amalfi coast, take the Path of the Gods for an unforgettable hike. The three-and-a-half-mile mountain trail, 2,065 feet above sea level, stretches between Positano and Praiano and is one of the most popular hiking trails in the world.

In Italy it's known as Il Sentiero degli Dei. Local legend has it that the path was carved out by the gods as they came down from the sky to save Ulysses from the song of the mermaids coming from the Le Sirenuse Islands below.

There are three different starting points, including Praiano, just south of Positano where we were staying. So we thought that it made the most sense to begin there. We hired a guide, which I highly recommend, but little did we realize that we would have to climb one thousand steps from our Praiano base before even getting to the actual path itself. Mamma mia!

Despite that challenging start, it was one of the most memorable experiences we have had along this gorgeous coastline. I think it was even more amazing than hiking Cinque Terre next to the Ligurian Coast, a more difficult hike due to some of the rocky terrain, but even more beautiful as there is hardly a time when you don't see the blue waters of the Mediterranean below. It also takes you through old vineyards hanging on the side of the mountains, olive groves, and lush fields, and you might even bump into a donkey or two as we did. They're still used today to transport food and other items to the tiny towns dotting the path through the mountains.

It should be noted that the Path of the Gods is not for the faint of heart. It takes almost four hours, has twists, turns, ups, downs, and some difficult terrain at several points (which is why having a guide helps as they have done the path before and give you plenty of warning of what's ahead). That said, if you are in good health and can climb steps and walk without difficulty it's worth it.

PEARLS OF THE TYRRHENIAN
Basilicata and Maratea

After having been to the Amalfi Coast half a dozen times, I decided to find a different seaside location to wrap up one of our vacations. Inspiration struck when I came across an article in one of my Italian tourism magazines highlighting an obscure area referred to by Italians as the "pearl of the Tyrrhenian" or "the other Amalfi Coast." You can bet those titles grabbed my attention! I was even more thrilled to learn that Maratea was in Basilicata, the region where my maternal grandmother was born.

Basilicata is another undiscovered region of Italy. It is filled with farmland, mountains, rugged terrain, and a fair number of villages listed in the Borghi Più Belli (most beautiful villages of Italy association). The association's website explains that the group was founded "with the aim of enhancing and promoting the greatest heritage of history, art, culture and landscapes present in small Italian towns."[4] Their list includes more than 350 *borgos* that have been selected and certified.

What struck me about Maratea was its location. Maratea happens to be a clifftop town along the Tyrrhenian Sea and is the only town along the Basilicata's twenty miles of coastline. The region, which is mostly landlocked, is nestled below Puglia, east of Campania, with Calabria hugging its southernmost border.

Winding road to Maratea

[4]   I Borghi più belli d'Italia, accessed August 31, 2024, https://borghipiu-belliditalia.it/en/.

Christ the Redeemer (Maratea)

Maratea is a peaceful paradise, giving you all the Amalfi Coast has to offer including beach life, boating, hiking, four- and five-star hotel properties, Michelin star restaurants, and all of this without massive tourism. It's a go to place for Italians who want to avoid the busyness of the Amalfi Coast. Although reachable by car, it is quite a distance from major attractions. The city of Amalfi, for example, is almost three hours away.

Maratea also holds a wonderful gift for Catholics looking to explore unique shrines. At the summit of Monte San Biagio (the Mountain of St. Blaise) sits a sanctuary high up in the Lucanian Dolomites. It is so high up, in fact, that your car will only get you so far. At a certain point, you must park your vehicle and hop in a small shuttle bus to reach your destination. When you arrive, you're greeted by a seventy-foot statue of Jesus with His arms open wide, known as Christ the Redeemer of Maratea.

On a clear day the statue's platform allows 360-degree views of the coast and Lucanian Mountains. What's so moving to me is that Maratea's Jesus has His arms outstretched but He is facing inward or toward the people and the land, looking directly at the Basilica of St. Biagio (St. Blaise), which is dedicated to Maratea's patron.

Locals told us that the statue, erected in 1963, looks inward to bless the residents, especially the farmers in the area as poverty has been widespread since World War II. This remote shrine provides an opportunity to venerate the relics of the martyr and fourth-century bishop; St. Blaise is the patron of those suffering with throat illnesses. His relics have been preserved in the basilica since the eighth century.

SASSI DI MATERA
City of Timeless Wonder

"Where are they going?"

My husband and I were eating lunch in a restaurant in the city center of modern Matera. We were sitting in a booth with a partially restricted view and could not figure out what was going on as more and more people kept passing our table and heading up a small staircase.

Sassi di Matera, "Capitol of Culture"

Prior to our *pranzo* break, we had spent some time looking for the Sassi di Matera (Stones of Matera), but we couldn't find it. We couldn't find the tourist office either. So, we did what most Italians do when the going gets tough: we got something to eat and drink (*mangiare e bere*). But as we were waiting for our pizza, all these people passed our table until the reporter in me couldn't stand it any longer: I got up and climbed the staircase.

At the top was a very large picture window with a breathtaking view of a large section of the Sassi, the rock formations and ancient cave dwellings. It reminded me of the landscape of the Holy Land, and it was easy to understand why many religious movies including the blockbusters *The Passion of the Christ* (2004) and *Ben Hur* (2016) were filmed there.

After lunch we found the tourist office, grabbed a self-guided tour sheet, and spent several hours walking back in time over hills, along polished stone pathways, and down haphazard staircases. It was easy to see why Fodor's described Sassi di Matera as "one of the most unique landscapes of Europe."

The Sassi area, a designated UNESCO world heritage site, is made up of 1,500 of the longest-occupied cave dwellings on the globe, dating back seven thousand years.

The story of its people, at least for me, is equally compelling. As recently as the mid-twentieth century, the Sassi and its sixteen thousand residents were considered the shame of Italy, living in extremely poor and unhealthy conditions without running water. Most of the people worked the local farms and were too poor afford to buy or build their own homes, so they moved into the cave dwellings and made the best of a very bad situation, even allowing farm animals to share the space to help keep them warm.

A major turnaround would occur after the release of the book *Christ Stopped at Eboli* in 1945. The book was written by Carlo Levi, an artist and doctor. He was punished by Mussolini for his anti-fascist views and activism and banished to the remote towns of southern Italy.

His book detailed the day-to-day difficulties of the people in the area. It exposed a national scandal of an entire population forced to live in grim conditions, and as a result the population was relocated to new housing facilities in the nearby city of Matera. The Sassi was left vacant for decades, but then experienced a major rebirth, becoming a popular tourist attraction, complete with many cave hotels and restaurants, but with a major focus on passing on the good, the bad, and the ugly of the Sassi history.

We keep returning to the Sassi and have even stayed overnight in one of the remodeled cave dwellings. I feel close to my roots here; my maternal grandmother was born in a town only an hour away. I want to embrace those roots and never forget the struggles of the people known as the Lucani, from the harsh yet hauntingly beautiful region of the Sassi di Matera in Basilicata.

TRULLI WORTH A VISIT
Quirky and Unique Alberobello

This part of Italy will take you on a rollercoaster of emotions: one minute you're reflecting on thousands of years of history and the dramatic dilemmas faced by struggling inhabitants in the Sassi. Then just an hour away in Puglia, you feel like you're in the middle of a fairy tale or Pixar animation as you walk through the adorable streets lined with the famous Trulli homes of Alberobello. Welcome to southeastern Italy. Never a dull moment.

Trulli homes

Once in Alberobello, you are half-expecting hobbits or Snow White and her seven dwarfs to be peeking through the curtains of these structures, the conical or cone-shaped houses very specific to the Itria Valley in central Puglia. There are several different theories about how *trulli* came to be so prominent here. The area was originally settled in the eleventh century, and some of the conical homes may have been built at that time; in the sixteenth and seventeenth centuries these homes were heavily populated by the peasants who worked on the farms.

On our last visit, our guide explained that the distinctive construction had a practical benefit: those trying to avoid paying taxes to the king or landowner could dismantle the trulli and get out of dodge quickly, and then reconstruct it elsewhere.

The houses are made of local stones, built without mortar and treasured by their owners, as many have been in families for generations. You'll find that many of the cone-shaped roofs are adorned with painted symbols having to do with religion or astrology.

Thanks to the distinctive construction of its houses, Alberobello was named a world heritage site by UNESCO in 1996. The trulli can be found in other nearby towns but the heaviest concentration is in Alberobello, a name that means "beautiful tree." Alberobello sits is surrounded by olive and almond trees. Today the city is filled with wonderful shops selling regional products, not to mention restaurants and plenty of boutique hotels — you guessed it — all located inside the treasured trulli.

ISLAND TIME
Capri, Ischia, and Procida

ROMANTIC ISLE OF CAPRI

No chapter about the coastal areas of southern Italy would be complete without talking about living life island style. Among the most well-known islands is the romantic Isle of Capri. While Capri certainly stands out thanks to being so close to the famous towns of the Amalfi Coast, two other islands are also not to be missed, Ischia and Procida.

Beginning with Capri, I would advise if your schedule allows to treat yourself to at least a one-night stay as it is a completely different experience after the last ferries head back to Positano, Sorrento, or Naples. Here too, like on the Amalfi Coast, be prepared for the crowds. That said, the unbelievable natural beauty of the island does make battling those crowds a bit easier to take.

There are plenty of ferries available from the main Amalfi Coast towns including Amalfi, Positano, Sorrento, and Naples. The boat ride from the coast to the island is also a treat. Once you set foot on Capri, you'll notice quite a few local tour operators encouraging you to spend a small fortune on the famous Grotta Azzurra (Blue Grotto). Skip it. If grottos are your thing, consider the grottos around Praiano, just as brilliantly blue but much less crowded and much easier on the wallet. Not to mention that the Blue Grotto often has very limited access due to the ever-changing water levels.

My favorite activity on Capri, which my husband and I discovered by accident on our first visit there, is the lift to the top of Mt. Solaro located in the town of Anacapri on the upper part of the island. Once you get to the top you won't want to leave. This is the perfect place to view the famous symbol of Capri, the Faraglioni rock formations, and there is of course no better place for your Kodak or selfie moments.

Once you make it back down the mountain to Anacapri you might want to visit the Villa San Michele, one of the most popular sights on the island. It's the former home of physician Axel Munthe and now serves as a museum. Munthe was also a popular author. His book about this magical place, *The Story of San Michele*, was published in 1929 and quickly became a bestseller. The views from the villa are out of this world, and you feel like you could reach out and touch the clouds, if there are any, as Capri is known for its crystal-clear skies.

Before you step off the island, have a cocktail in Piazza Umberto (Piazzetta), the main piazza. It's a lovely square and the perfect spot to rest before or after shopping, whether you window shop to get an early scoop on the latest fashion trends or a scout out a tasty scoop of gelato. (If you've been waiting to grab the latest designer bag, head to Via Camerelle to choose from some of the most popular fashion names on the planet.)

ISCHIA: *THE OTHER CAPRI*

Maratea is described by Italians as the "other Amalfi coast" and Ischia as "the other Capri." We were encouraged to visit Ischia by a friend of ours whose in-laws call the island home. I'm so glad we took his advice.

More than four times larger than Capri, Ischia covers an area of forty-six miles; that means you have many more options regarding hotels and restaurants. This idyllic isle in the northern area of the Gulf of Naples is known for its beautiful beaches and thermal springs and is frequented more by locals than international travelers (who tend to converge on Capri).

Ischia feels very authentically Italian. Residents are proud of their heritage and still express it through well celebrating with festivals and great food. There are six cities of varying size to explore, with bright pastel-colored houses and buildings that cover the island. Ischia even has its own "island on the island," Castello Aragonese d'Ischia, which sits on a rock formation in the gulf that can only be reached by a

Castello Aragonese d'Ischia in Ischia, the "Other Capri"

footbridge. I could not stop staring at the castle as we dined on freshly caught fish at a wonderful waterfront *ristorante* located at the beginning of that footbridge.

Thermal baths are a must-try as the springs are known for their healing qualities. Ischia has built several parks around them along the waterfront — and the sunsets, oh the Ischia sunsets. There are several boat operators that offer sunset tours. However, having an Aperol Spritz at a seaside wine bar will more than suffice.

In 2022, Ischia was honored as Italy's Capital of Culture. The title has been handed out by the government since 2015 as another way to promote regional history and cultural values. I also love staying here because it is just a ferry ride away from one of my favorite little islands: precious Procida!

PROCIDA: A PRECIOUS LITTLE SLICE OF PARADISE

It might seem corny to call it that, but the island of Procida really is precious. The smallest of the three islands with plenty of ferry access, little Procida is slightly north of Ischia.

The best way to describe Procida is to think of the brightest, most vivid watercolor painting you've ever seen hanging in a museum or an art gallery. Then get ready to walk right into the middle of that explosion of color. It's known for the yellow, pink, orange, and turquoise buildings that dot the waters of tiny fishing villages.

Procida also has been the backdrop for many a film including *The Talented Mr. Ripley* (1999) and *Il Postino* (*The Postman*, 1994). It's popular with artists and writers and those looking for a truly laid-back holiday, offering a variety of rentals, bed-and-breakfasts, and high-end hotel properties.

We spent a wonderful leisurely afternoon there during our time on Ischia, walking to the top of one of its hills that provided an incredible view of the gulf. We then rewarded ourselves by eating *spaghetti alle vongole* (spaghetti with clams) as we watched the little sail boats rock back and forth in the little bay in front of us. *Bellissimo!*

CELEBRATIONS

Praiano's Luminaria di San Domenico
A CELEBRATION OF ST. DOMINIC

Praiano is my absolute favorite town on the Amalfi Coast, with some of the best restaurants and hotels located up and down the sides of the Lattari Mountains. It has some spectacular rooftop views, two incredible beaches, and a very friendly family and faith-based community that we have come to know over the years. My husband Dominick and I especially love the five-day celebration leading up to the feast day of St. Dominic (August 8). It's known as Luminaria di San Domenico.

Although St. Dominic was born in Spain, he is revered in Italy. He is buried in the northern Italian city of Bologna, yet he also has a special connection to Praiano: Dominican monks came to a local monastery there in 1606, the Monastery of Santa Maria a Castro, built above a hill in the town.

The festival in Praiano is based on a vision of St. Dominic's mother. While pregnant with Dominic, she dreamed of a dog with a torch in its mouth. The torch was a symbol for how her son would spend his life, setting the world on fire with the love of God.

In honor of that vision, for five days each year leading up to the saint's feast day the town sets the world ablaze with of thousands of luminaries and candles on windowsills and on streets, and particularly in front of San Gennaro Church. The main event is not to be missed: in honor of St. Dominic, dance troupes put on dramatic performances with fire!

CAMPANIA AND PUGLIA REGIONS
SIGNATURE DISHES

– – – – – – –

Limoncello: *Sweet Memories*
FROM JOAN LEWIS' KITCHEN IN ROMA

Limoncello is a lemony Italian liquor that has its home along the southwestern coast in the Campania region (Sorrento, Positano, and Amalfi). No surprise there, given that the endless summer sunshine lends itself to producing the citrus fruit that is central to the limoncello recipe.

Limoncello is very strong and must be served ice cold. Its high alcohol content means you can store it in the freezer and not worry about it turning into a block of solid lemon ice. It's served year-round as an after-dinner drink but is especially popular in the warmer weather.

Limoncello from the kitchen of EWTN's Joan Lewis

Most Italian families have their own recipes, but the main ingredients are lemons, sugar, and lots of grain alcohol. My dear friend, Joan Lewis of EWTN and *Joan's Rome* fame, has lived and worked in Rome for decades. She shared her own special limoncello recipe with me and agrees that ice cream or gelato can be made even more delicious by a few drops of this special Italian liquor.

INGREDIENTS:
- **1 liter (about 34 ounces) of grain alcohol (do NOT use vodka or anything else)**
- **1 liter of water**
- **1 kilo (2.2 pounds, about 5 cups) of sugar**
- **Zest of 8 lemons**

DIRECTIONS:

1. Trim the zest from the lemons and set inside a large glass jar.

2. Pour 34 ounces of alcohol over the zest. Place the container in a dark, cool place. Stir once daily.

   When the alcohol turns bright yellow and there is no yellow left on the zest (this can be 4 or 5 days or perhaps even 8 or 10 — it all depends on the lemons!), strain and throw zest away.

3. Put the liter of water and kilo of sugar in a large pot. Heat and cook over medium temperature until the sugar is entirely absorbed, stirring constantly. Cool and after one final stir add the alcohol mixture. Stir well. Pour into liter-sized bottles (should have about 2.5 liters total).

4. With all the right ingredients you should have a great limoncello!

5. Place the bottle in your freezer several hours before serving guests. I also place my glasses (prosecco flutes are nice) in the freezer about a half hour before serving. The chilled limoncello and chilled glasses really please the palate.

6. Salute!

A PILGRIM'S PERSPECTIVE
THE SWORD OF GALGANO
BY JOHN HALE

— — — — — — —

An encounter with God may happen anywhere. In my experience, precious moments of God often occur in little-known monasteries or quiet churches, away from the hype and roar of crowds. I find I often hear God's voice in the lesser-known places conquered and won over for Christ by brave and courageous brothers and sisters whose names have

Sword of Galgano

all but been forgotten to many of us. They were no less brave than the saints who we all know and love, and I can hear God more clearly without the long queues, security checks, and the crowds swarming around me.

Near the ruins of the Abbey of San Galgano, in the rolling hills of one of my favorite parts of Italy, the Val d'Orcia region of Tuscany, is a small church that houses the relic of the sword of St. Galgano. Galgano Guidotti lived in the twelfth century and, like many saints, led a worldly life of violence and hedonistic pleasure before his conversion. After the death of his father, Galgano had a dream in which St. Michael the Archangel appeared to him to tell him to change his way of life. As a result of this dream, he vowed to give up worldly pleasures and his waging of war.

As a decisive pledge of this commitment, Galgano miraculously plunged his sword into a *stone* near what are now the ruins of a magnificent Abbey. That sword, still in the stone, now is ensconced in the Rotondo Church, which St. Galgano had dreamt would be built. Contemporary scientists have confirmed that the materials of the sword are from the time of St. Galgano.

I was visiting this Abbey several years ago with my young son Andrew, zipping over on a Vespa from a nearby hotel. As we passed through the incredibly colorful fields of sunflower and wheat, I felt a welcome lift in my heart, and I settled in to enjoy the wild ride.

The pandemic had a devastating impact on our travel business, our team, and our clients and family. Nearly eighteen grueling months later, by God's Providence, our business was still standing. I was now experiencing profound gratitude at the beauty that surrounded me as I contemplated how God had brought us through a very difficult time. It was exhilarating to be riding with my son to visit an incredible Gothic thirteenth-century monastery that is over eight hundred years old.

Marveling at God's created beauty, I let the ride enable me to shed the pain of the previous months and focus on something more profound than my own pain and self-pity. Galgano's courage and visible, tangible act of courage became a metaphor for how I must daily plunge all that is not of God into that stone. I must take my all my foibles, folly, and sin and leave it daily in that rock. Doing so renews me and frees me from those things that unnecessarily weigh me down.

God invites each of us to divest ourselves of the things in our lives that hold us back from Him. I will always be grateful to have had a chance to hear St. Galgano's story, which likely inspired the legend of King Arthur, who had a profound conversion at this spot and whose miracle from that conversion can still be seen today.

John and Andrew Hale, Val d' Orcia, Tuscany

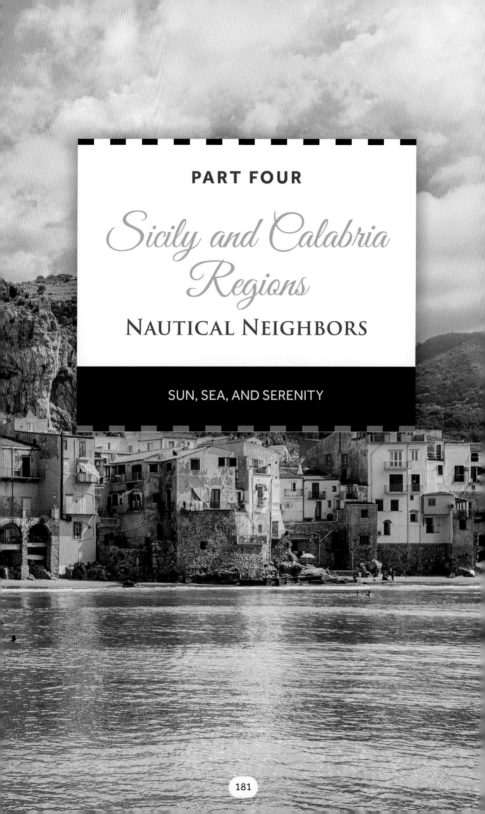

PART FOUR

Sicily and Calabria Regions

NAUTICAL NEIGHBORS

SUN, SEA, AND SERENITY

SICILY AND CALABRIA REGIONS

Calabria
Region

Sicily Region

Previous page: Cefalù in northern Sicily

WHAT YOU'LL EXPLORE...

SICILY AND CALABRIA REGION HIGHLIGHTS

- **Sun, Sea, and Serenity:** The Good Life in Sicily and Calabria
- **Beloved Saint of Italy — St. Francesco di Paola**
- T's Ultimate Must-Sees and Dos in Sicily
- T's Ultimate Must-Sees and Dos in Calabria

SACRED SPACES OF SICILY AND CALABRIA

- **St. Rosalia of Monte Pellegrino:** A Little Saint and a Big Cure
- **Palermo:** Capella Palatina
- **Church of Piedigrotta di Pizzo :** Faith on the Rocks

FASCINATING PLACES OF SICILY AND CALABRIA

- **Tropea:** The Pearl of Calabria
- **Ancient and New:** Agrigento, Mt. Etna, and Taormina

CELEBRATIONS AND SIGNATURE DISHES

- **Sagra della Ricotta e del Formaggio:** Vizzini, Sicily
- **T's Holy Cannoli Recipe:** From Grandma Squillace

A PILGRIM'S PERSPECTIVE:
A SORRENTO STORY OF BREE SOLSTAD

SUN, SEA, AND SERENITY
THE GOOD LIFE IN SICILY AND CALABRIA

We were heading for Reggio Calabria as our car ferry pulled out of the dock in Messina, Sicily. As we drove, my feisty Calabrese grandmother, Paolina Mazza Squillace, was on my mind. Being born and raised in Calabria, my father's mother would often reminisce about her homeland,

Lungomare of Reggio
Opposite: Fishing boats off the coast of Levanzo

sharing stories of the Calabrian coast and how she loved to swim near Reggio in the Strait of Messina.

The "toe of Italy," as Calabria is often described, practically touches the big island of Sicily. Reggio has a lovely *lungomare* or water-front that stretches for just over a mile directly across from Messina, with plenty of beach access and amazing seaside restaurants.

In addition to its beaches, Calabria is also known for its the famous iconic sweet red onions, Cipolle di Tropea, and the not-so-sweet but wonderfully spicy chili peppers, which pack a powerful punch in their famous Nduja sausage spread.

Not to be outdone in the food category, Sicily has been referred to as "God's Kitchen" thanks to such delectable dishes such as *pasta alla norma*, Sicilian pizza, and the famous cannoli which were originally created on the island.

Sicily is also a great example of Italy's marvelous melting pot. The island's location, north of Africa, brought in visitors and settlers from many corners of the earth: Greeks, Spanish, Normans, and Arabs. Such diversity has resulted in different dialects as well as dishes and recipes reflecting the wonderful mixture of cultures over the centuries.

Both southern regions are filled with ancient ruins, stunning churches, and some of the best resorts in all of Europe. And since they are so close to each other, it is easy to include a few sites from the island and the toe in your next Italy getaway.

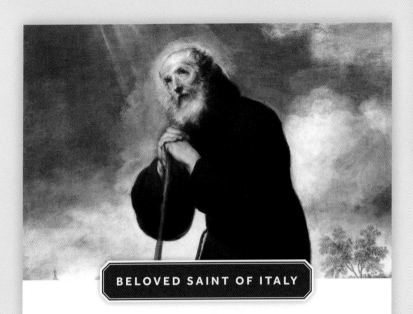

BELOVED SAINT OF ITALY

St. Francesco di Paola

- **Relics:** *The Sanctuary of Saint Francis of Paola, in Paola (Province of Cosenza, Calabria Region)*
- **Patron Saint:** *boatmen, mariners, naval officers, and Calabria*
- **Canonized:** *1519 by Pope Leo X*
- **Feast Day:** *April 2*

Born on March 27, 1416, Francesco grew up in a devout family in Paola. At fifteen, he moved to a cave to live as a hermit. By 1436, enough men had also come to live in solitude to found a religious order, which later became the Minims. They vowed poverty, chastity, obedience, and year-round abstinence from meat and other animal products to encourage fasting among the laity during Lent. Francesco cured the sick, raised people and even animals from the dead, ended plagues, and even could carry burning coals in his hands, giving him the nickname "Francis the Firehandler."

Blessed with a prophetic gift, Francesco gave advice and comfort to thousands of people — including King Louis of France, who as he lay dying summoned Francesco, who later became tutor to the king's heir, Charles VIII, as well as advisor to his successor, Louis XII. Francesco spent the rest of his life in France, dying in Touraine on April 2, 1507.

In 1562, vandals raided his tomb in France, burned his incorrupt body, and scattered the remains. People gathered the relics, which were given to several churches, including one in Paola.

The famous sanctuary where he lived as a hermit is among the most popular tourist destinations in Calabria.

Opposite: Temple of Dioscuri in the Valley of the Temples

SICILY REGION
HIGHLIGHTS

The Island of Sicily is located just off the mainland of Italy, separated by the Strait of Messina which is only two miles wide. Sicily is the largest and most populous island in the Mediterranean Sea and one of the twenty regions of Italy. The capital of Sicily is Palermo, and its most prominent landmark is Mt. Etna, the tallest active volcano in Europe and one of the most active in the world, currently 3,357 meters high. The island has a typical Mediterranean climate.

The earliest archaeological evidence of human activity on the island dates from as early as 14,000 B.C. By around 750 B.C., Sicily had three Phoenician and a dozen Greek colonies, and it was later the site of the Sicilian Wars and the Punic Wars. Since it is an island, Sicily became a crossroads of sorts throughout history and a melting pot for a dozen or more ethnic groups.

The hilly island of Sicily is a beautiful tourist destination due to its beautiful beaches and picturesque hilltop views. It contains two natural parks (Madonie and Nebrodi), where from each summit covered with century-old olive and chestnut trees visitors can enjoy panoramic views of the island as far as the sea. Sicily is surrounded by many smaller islands, such as Ustica and the Eolie or Lipari group (known as the "Seven Sisters" islands), and it is comprised of two active volcanoes, Stromboli and Vulcano.

Sicily is a great producer of wine and oil, citrus fruit, almonds, and vegetables, and it is one of the top fishing regions in Italy. Minerals such as sulfur, salt, natural gas, and petroleum are prominent as well.

The Italian dialect spoken in Sicily is known as Sicilian, which is also spoken in its satellite islands. A variant, Calabro-Sicilian, is spoken in nearby southern Calabria, where it is called Southern Calabro. This is spoken especially in the metropolitan city of Reggio Calabria.

Right: Praetorian Fountain with the Church of Santa Caterina d'Alessandria in the background, Palermo
Middle: Suspended umbrellas for outdoor dining in Catania
Left: View of Mt. Etna from Taormina

SICILY REGION
T'S ULTIMATE MUST-SEES AND DOS

— — — — — — —

The Capital City of Palermo in northwestern Sicily has much to offer in the way of museums and bustling street markets. It also has beautiful mountaintop sanctuaries including the shrine of Monte Pellegrino, dedicated to its patron, St. Rosalia. If you only have a short time, concentrate on Cappella Palatina and Cattedrale di Monreale. These two mosaic masterpieces will leave you awestruck.

VALLEY OF THE TEMPLES IN AGRIGENTO

This ancient marvel is Sicily's most important archeological site that hugs the island's southern coast and boasts eight of the world's best preserved Greek temples, sanctuaries, and cemeteries, dating back to the fourth and fifth centuries.

TAORMINA

Across from the Strait of Messina on the northeastern coast, stunning Taormina offers the old and the new. Visit its ancient theater boasting among the best views of Sicily. Stroll its famous Corso Umberto, lined with shops, beautiful buildings, and quaint wine bars.

CATANIA

South of Taormina and close to Mt. Etna, this city offers many sites of historical, archeological, and religious significance.

MT. ETNA

This massive volcano is still active, and there are ways to see it up close and personal, including a tour that includes a combination cable car ride and a drive making the trek to the top up bit more doable.

AEOLIAN ISLANDS

Off Italy's northeastern coast is a group of seven protected islands. They're famous for beautiful beaches, island-hopping, and another active volcano, Stromboli, after which one of the islands is named. Take the ferry ride from Calabria or Sicily to the Aeolian Islands for a perfect day at the beach, then take a later ferry back from the Aeolian Island of Stromboli so you can see this active volcano light up the sky at dusk with its dramatic eruptions.

Isle of Stromboli

CALABRIA REGION
HIGHLIGHTS

The region of Calabria is often referred to as Italy's "toe." It sits between two seas, boasting five hundred miles of coastline, with the Tyrrhenian on the west and the Ionian on the east. That explains why Italians and Europeans flock to the area's beautiful beaches, especially the popular town known as the "Pearl of Calabria," Tropea.

Calabria offers tourists a variety of different landscapes and historic and religious attractions, including an ancient grotto carved into a cavern along the ocean, in addition to its beaches. The capital city of Reggio boasts the lungomare, one of the region's most beautiful boardwalks along the Strait of Messina where you can stop for lunch, a swim, or just a stroll, slowly taking in the views. Reggio is also home to the National Archaeological Museum, which holds many ancient treasures including its famous Riace bronzes, dating back to the fifth century B.C.

And let's not forget the food. Many of the menu items are built around the famous pepper pepperoncini and the sweet red onions Cipolle of Tropea. Being surrounded by so much water, look for fabulous fresh fish as a mainstay of many dishes. Make sure you try the spicy Nduja sausage, a spreadable delicacy that is also used on pizza and in many pasta dishes.

Peppers at a market in Tropea, a common site in the region

Right: Tropea, known as the "Pearl of Calabria"
Middle: Vespa in Tropea
Left: Riace bronzes, Reggio

Calabria Region
T'S ULTIMATE MUST-SEES AND DOS

— — — — — — — —

REGGIO

Reggio is the third-largest city in Calabria, filled with beauty and history. Among the many attractions:

- *Castello Aragonese* — Located in the center of the city, this well-preserved castle is in great condition and is considered an icon.

- *Lungomare Falcomatà* — This beautiful boardwalk stretches along the coastline and includes beautiful beaches, parks, and outdoor restaurants.

- *Reggio Calabria Museo Nazionale* — Not far from the beach promenade sits a treasure filled with history about the city and the Calabrian region. Its main stars are the Riace bronze statues and two full-size Greek bronze statues discovered by a diver in the 1970s and most likely cast between 460 and 450 B.C.

THE PEARL OF CALABRIA: TROPEA

North of Reggio along the Tyrrhenian coast, this lively, colorful city is a popular tourist attraction and boasts some of southern Italy's best beaches and resorts, not to mention cafes, wine bars, and a collection of fine restaurants nestled its quaint streets.

THE SANCTUARY OF SANTA MARIA DELL'ISOLA

Located along the beaches of Tropea, this clifftop monastery, built originally in the fourth century, offers incredible views of the coastline and is well connected to Tropea's history and faith community as it houses a twelfth-century portrait of the Blessed Mother, considered the protector of the town.

Chianalea di Scilla

LITTLE VENICE OF THE SOUTH, CHIANALEA DI SCILLA

(Pronounced "Sheila") a magical seaside town unknown to international tourists but popular with locals. It is known for its ancient tradition of swordfishing.

EASTERN CALABRIAN BEACHES

Don't ignore the eastern coast of Calabria, which also has some of the best beaches the region has to offer, in addition to the west coast, known as the Coast of the Gods.

T's Italy

T'S TRAVEL TIP

Watch the sunset over the Tyrrhenian Sea while sipping a cocktail from one of Tropea's famous hilltop terraces.

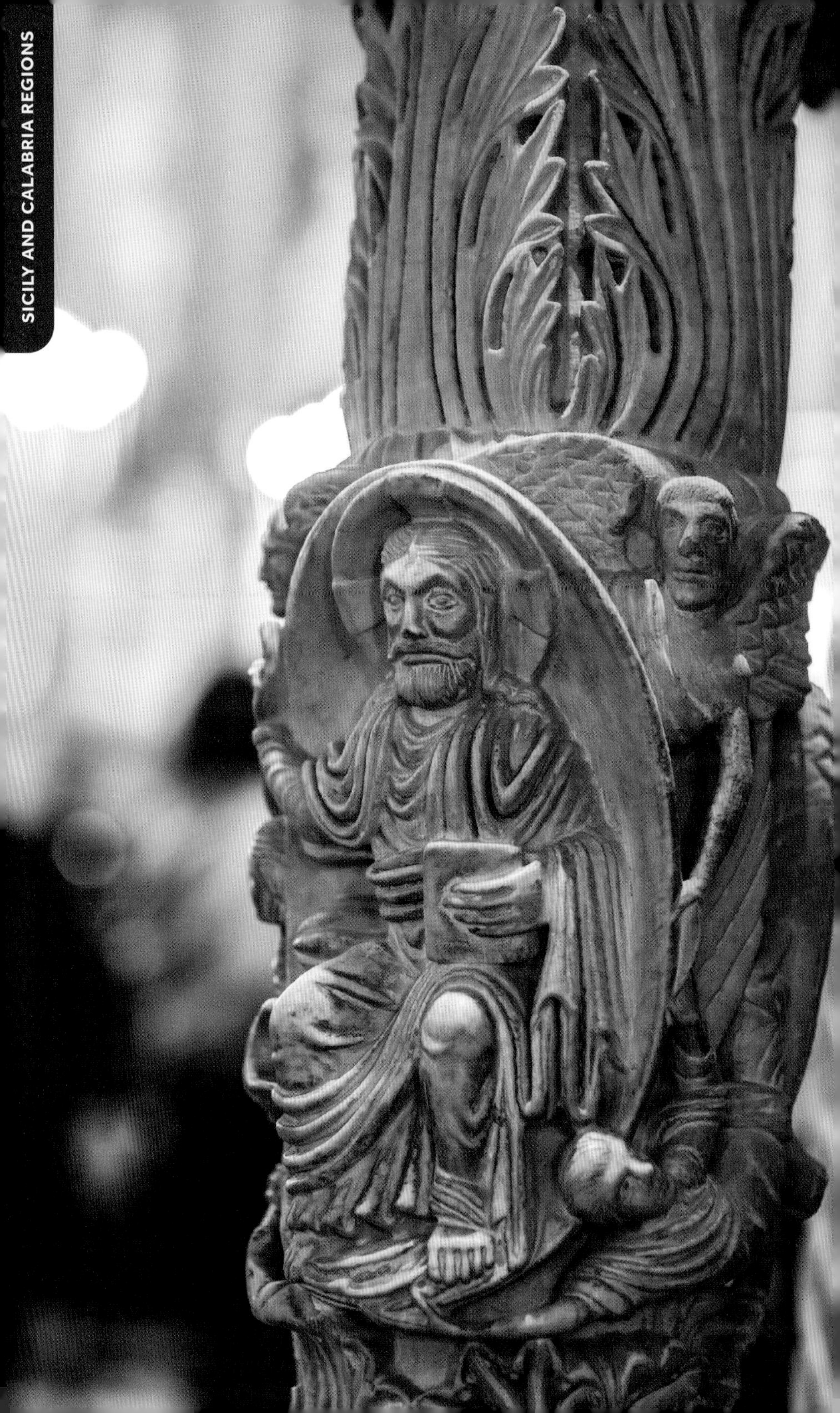

CALABRIA REGION
SACRED SPACES

- - - - - - - -

The sacred spaces in Sicily and Calabria are filled with examples of the comingling of cultures. Faith is expressed very dramatically, with the basilicas and sanctuaries built literally from the earth, or from the finest of materials imported from around the world. The desire to show the glory of God in mosaics, paintings, sculptures, and wooden carvings, and the commitment to Him takes visitors to Sicily and Calabria along a trail of timeless artistic brilliance that rivals other cities known for their cultural contributions.

ST. ROSALIA OF MONTE PELLEGRINO
A Little Saint and a Big Cure

How could such a tiny person have such a colossal impact on her native land? Even the term of endearment given to Sicily's St. Rosalia — *La Santuzza*, or "little saint" — reflects on physical frailty and size.

In 2024, Sicily celebrated the four hundredth anniversary of St. Rosalia of Monte Pellegrino (1130–1170), the patron of the city of Palermo. St. Rosalina was born in 1128 to a noble family, believed to be

Opposite: Christ Pantocrator in the Palatina Chapel, Palermo

a descendant of Charlemagne. As a young girl she had a strong desire to leave worldliness behind and to dedicate herself to Christ. Her family had arranged a marriage for her, but she managed to flee. Instead, she found her peace by living austere life as a hermit in a cave. When she died she left behind a simple declaration about her life of prayer and solitude on the walls of her cave inside Monte Pelligrino: "I, Rosalia, daughter of Sinibald, Lord of Roses and Quisquina, have chosen to dwell in this cave out of love for my Lord, Jesus Christ."

Rosalia died around 1170, yet her remains weren't discovered until hundreds of years later. In 1624, she appeared to two locals including a hunter. Tradition says that the saint directed the hunter to where her remains could be located and told him that the plague would end if her relics were processed through the city. A short time later, in 1625, a shrine was built in the cave where her body was discovered, which became the Sacred Grotto of Monte Pellegrino. The shrine stretches almost one hundred feet into the cave.[1]

Monte Pellegrino is a formidable hill outside of Palermo and is hard to miss. When we visited the church built on the spot of her cave dwelling, we were surprised about how different the outside, with its

yellow façade, was from the inside. Although dramatically extended from giant rock formations, the exterior of the church is simple and, except for the bell tower and a few religious statues and scenes, not as ornate as one might expect given the popularity of this saint.

Shrine of St. Rosalia, Monte Pellegrino

[1] "Cave Shrine on Mount Pellegrino," Atlas Obscura, accessed September 2, 2024, https://www.atlasobscura.com/places/santuario-di-santa-rosalia.

Relics of St. Rosalia

All that changes when you step inside and discover a beautiful shrine with marble pillars, images of the saint, and a beautiful grotto. You'll also notice something odd: different pieces of tin or metal that, at first glance, you could mistake for some sort of modern art, are actually custom-made gutters that collect water from the rocks. Tradition says that the water contains healing powers.

On July 15, 2024, the four hundredth anniversary of the discovery of her relics, Pope Francis said that St. Rosalia reminds us that in the modern age we suffer different types of plagues, including worldliness and loneliness. And that the call to become countercultural as St. Rosalia was can promote positive change.

> Christians are those who always love, but often in circumstances in which love is not understood or is even refused. It remains a countercultural choice today, since those who follow Christ are called to adopt the logic of the Gospel, which is hope, deciding in their hearts to make room for love in order to give it to others, to sacrifice it for the sake of their brothers and sisters, to share it with those who have not experienced it because of the "plagues" that afflict humanity.[2]

---

[2] Francis, Message of the Holy Father on the Occasion of the IV Centenary of the Discovery of the Relics of Saint Rosalia (June 29, 2024).

PALERMO
Cappella Palatina

"The twelve gates were twelve pearls, each of the gates made of a single pearl, and the street of the city was pure gold, transparent as glass."

— Revelation 21:21

Palatina Chapel in Palermo

Perhaps the artists who created the myriad mosaics inside Palermo's Cappella Palatina or Palatine Chapel were meditating upon this verse as they were working on these Byzantine masterpieces. All around you in this amazing space are images that certainly look like something one might see when they pass through those pearly gates into the heavenly realm.

The elaborate chapel, decorated with mosaics from the ceiling to the floor, was built by Roger the First of Sicily, the first grand count. It was commissioned in 1132, taking less than ten years to complete and serving as both the palace's active church and its religious center.

The view is so overwhelming that your eyes don't know where to look first. This type of reaction has been recorded down through the centuries. In 1143, at the chapel's inauguration, the Greek monk and preacher Philagathos of Cerami described how he felt upon entering.

> Brilliant with lights, shining with gold, glittering with mosaics, and bright with paintings. He who has seen it many

times, marvels when he sees it again, and is as astonished as if he were seeing it for the first time, his gaze wandering everywhere.[3]

The central mosaic is *Christ Pantocrator,* Christ Ruler of the Universe, surrounded by eight angels. Around the chapel are scenes from the Old and New Testaments and the lives of St. Peter and Paul.

It's hard to believe that a treasure like this would ever have been abandoned, but when the Normans left Sicily this treasure was left behind and began to decay. It was rediscovered by the Spanish in the mid-sixteenth century and slowly restored.

Christ Pantocrator (mosaic)

3   Dirk Booms and Peter Higgs, *Sicily: Vulture and Conquest* (Ithaca, NY: Cornell University Press, 2016), 198, quoted in Catherine Carlisle, "Palermo's Cappella Palatina: A Cross-cultural Jewel Box in Sicily," Decorative Arts Trust, accessed September 2, 2024, https://decorativeartstrust.org/capella-palatina-article/.

CHIESA DI PIEDIGROTTA DI PIZZO
Faith on the Rocks

So often as I travel through Italy I realize it's the stories of how the people came to build the many "shrines and wonders" that are almost as and sometimes more inspiring than the shrines and wonders themselves.

This could easily be said of the legend handed down since the 1600s along Calabria's western coast that surrounds the construction of Chiesa di Piedigrotta di Pizzo. This grotto church is built into the rocks about an hour north of Reggio. And while the town of Pizzo is worth visiting for its wonderful beaches and striking beauty along its narrow and steep streets, it is the church on the rocks below that garners the most attention.

The legend of the church has been passed on since the early seventeenth century. Neapolitan sailors were hit by a fierce storm as they made their way along the waters of the Tyrrhenian. The wind and the waves became treacherous, and they decided to seek shelter in Pizzo's caves. Asking for the intercession of the Blessed Mother, they promised to build a church in her honor if they survived the storm.

After they survived, they kept their promise in a very special way. The sailors attributed their safety to an image of the Virgin Mary that they had discovered on a beach and taken with them for their journey. They built a shrine inside the caves not far from where their ship crashed into the shore, carefully placing the picture at the center of the sanctuary. You'll find a copy of that original Marian image on the main altar.

The shrine is described as combining both art and nature. In the late nineteenth century, a local artist, Angelo Barone, decided to expand the property. His son continued the work after the death of his father. This is not just one cave but a series of connected caves, each with different religious sculptures by the Barones, including scenes from the Bible as well as the depiction of various saints all carved from the same tufa rock found in the caves.

There is a large nativity scene, along with an area dedicated to Our Lady of Lourdes and St. Bernadette complete with the familiar image of the saint kneeling before the Blessed Mother who appears before her in an alcove. Other carvings include medallions of Pope St. John XXIII and John F. Kennedy. Today the church is among the most popular monuments in all of Calabria.

Church of Piedigrotta di Pizzo

CALABRIA REGION
FASCINATING PLACES

- - - - - - -

The regions of Sicily and Calabria have long been favorites among Italians and Europeans in search of everything and anything under the sun, from beaches and water sports to volcanoes and national parks to ancient ruins to award-winning cuisine.

Of course, it was only a matter of time before the rest of the world (including plenty of Americans) came calling. And in so doing, we discovered an area that, much like the rest of Italy, needs to be revisited because of its never-ending appeal.

Calabria, for example, has five hundred miles of coastline and an incredible history reaching way back to the fifth century B.C. Sicily boasts two active volcanoes, Mt. Etna and Mt. Stromboli, along with incredible architecture, amphitheaters, Greek temples, and a cuisine that maintains its regional flair full of flavor and color just like its surroundings.

TROPEA
The Pearl of Calabria

Nothing beats the sunsets in the city known as the Pearl of Calabria, Tropea. About four hours south of Naples, Tropea really is a jewel that stands out along La Costa degli Dei (the Coast of the Gods). The little

Opposite: The Church of San Giuseppe in Taormina at sunset

Santa Maria dell'Isola Monastery

I knew about Tropea before traveling there was based on iconic photographs of the sun setting over a beautiful pastel chapel with its pink hues matching the colors of the sky above the Tyrrhenian Sea.

That chapel is actually a fourth-century medieval monastery, Santa Maria dell'Isola, and is perched on top of a rocky cliff. Although it is connected to Tropea, it looks as if it is an island unto itself, practically surrounded by the turquoise-blue waters of the ocean. Much of the original structure is gone, and the topography has also changed greatly (when it was first constructed it was sitting on an island). It's still a popular destination for pilgrims as it is home to a twelfth-century Marian image, a Byzantine portrait considered the protector of Tropea.

The city is known for its beaches and waterfront resorts. Also not to be missed is the nightlife as the streets are filled with wine bars, restaurants, and elegant shops, along with small lively piazzas with outdoor entertainment.

ANCIENT AND NEW
Agrigento, Mt. Etna, and Taromina

Greece in Italy? Yes, and in a very big way. Greek influence can be seen in many areas of Italy, in the southern part of the country and on the big island of Sicily. Having been to Greece more than once, I have to say that when we toured the ancient temples of Sicily's Agrigento, I felt like I had been transported to Athens.

In no time at all, this area of Italy takes you back in time with its amazing temples and ruins, but then transforms you to the present day with beautiful beaches, lovely hotels and shopping areas, and restaurants.

Valley of the Temples

AGRIGENTO

If you're looking to learn more about Sicily's incredible ancient past, head about 138 miles south on the island's southern coast, most well-known for the Valle dei Templi (the Valley of the Temples) next to the city of Agrigento. The valley is considered one of Sicily's most famous historic sites, built between 510 and 430 B.C. The tour of eight amazingly preserved temples takes under three hours.

According to the UNESCO world heritage site, the Valley of the Temples covers just over five square miles, containing some of the best representations of Doric architecture in the world. Other excavated areas provide a look into the burial practices of early Christian inhabitants.

The city of Agrigento began as a Greek colony in the sixth century B.C., quickly becoming a major Mediterranean city. Visiting Mt. Etna, Taormina, and Agrigento will give you a real flavor of the variety of art, history, culture, and cuisine that Sicily has to offer.

MT. ETNA

It's one thing to see an active volcano from a distance, as visitors to the Amalfi Coast have glimpsed Mt. Vesuvius. It's quite another to be nearly on top of one, as when we visited Mt. Etna. Although the volcano did not erupt while we were there, it certainly was exhilarating walking up paths made of compacted lava and sand, knowing that we were traversing ancient history.

Then, in July 2024, Mt. Etna erupted, giving the inhabitants of Sicily and Calabria quite a show, with geysers of bright orange lava lighting up the sky. In nearby Catania, the *New York Times* reported that the runway of the local airport couldn't be used because the volcano spewed so much ash into the air. Yes, every now and then, Etna has a way of reminding the world that it is still an active volcano.

Mt. Etna is daunting in its size, some eleven thousand feet above sea level with a circumference of ninety miles. There are a variety of tours available, including hiking up to the summit with a guide. There is also a very nice tour combining two types of transportation up the mountain, a cable car ride and a 4x4 excursion. Its first eruption was recorded in 1500 B.C., Etna was named a UNESCO world heritage site in 2013, and its smoking craters are always impressive.

TAORMINA

Taormina is an exotic place. It's ancient. It's also new and extremely elegant. Sitting high above the Strait of Messina with panoramic views of the Calabrian and Sicilian coastlines, Taormina makes you feel as if you're on a movie set. And you very well may be, as several movies, such as parts of the *Godfather* trilogy as well as TV productions, including the HBO series *White Lotus*, have been shot there.

After you've had your fill of walking along Corso Umberto, the main street lined with wonderful shops, romantic buildings, and picture-perfect balconies loaded with flowerpots and colorful ceramics, stop at one of the local sweet shops to try the famous cannoli. The delectable *dolce* originated here and they're the real thing.

Burn off those calories by heading over to Taormina's most famous landmark, Teatro Greco. The Greek theater was originally built in the third century B.C. The Romans moved in during the second century and rebuilt it. Though this theater is fascinating from an archaeological perspective, it also provides one of the best views looking out toward Mt. Etna.

T's Italy

T'S TIP!

The Sensational Sicilian Cannoli

Stop counting the calories and enjoy the cannoli! They were created in Sicily and are made the original way with ricotta cheese — a truly memorable experience!

CELEBRATIONS

Sagra della Ricotta e del Formaggio
VIZZINI, SICILY

Not all the festivals in Italy date back hundreds of years. One thing is for certain: food is always a main feature of any celebration, old or new. Such is the case with the annual Ricotta Cheese Festival in Vizzini, Sicily. Vizzini is in southern Sicily, west of Syracuse and south of Catania, with a long history of ricotta production.

The Sagra della Ricotta e del Formaggio, at only fifty-plus years old, is a baby in comparison to other Italian festivals. It's also known as the Feast of Flavors and Knowledge. The knowledge component connects the festivities to a famous Italian writer, Giovanni Verga, who has strong ties to Vizzini, allowing attendees to participate in literary walks exploring places mentioned in his short stories. You can feast on local products, many made with ricotta cheese, such as cannoli of course.

Finally, as with every Italian festival worth its weight in salt, or in this case perhaps some *ricotta salata*, (a firm salted version of the cheese), there are plenty of costumed parades, musical performances, and wine tastings.

T'S ITALY INSIDER TIP
Spicy Calabrian Sausage

Some like it hot, especially in the land of pepperoncino, Calabria. So give Nduja sausage a try. It's a delicious and spicy sausage spread great to add to sauce, on pizzas, or on crostini to spice up that appetizer tray. Available in jars of all sizes, it's a great gift to take home.

SPECIALITÀ SICILIA

SICILY AND CALABRIA REGIONS
SIGNATURE DISHES

- - - - - - - -

T's Holy Cannoli Recipe
FROM GRANDMA SQUILLACE

This popular pastry, a tubular shell made of fried dough and filled with a creamy ricotta cheese mixture, goes all the way back to the eleventh century. One of the stories about its invention connects the delicacy to a convent in central Sicily. Its popularity first spread west to Palermo and then east to Messina and on to the United States in the late nineteenth century, compliments of Italian immigrants. Wherever or whomever they came from, we're grateful.

Cannoli look complicated, but the truth is that they're one of easiest *dolce* (sweet treats) to make, especially if you use a good quality store-bought cannoli shell. You can make your own shells, of course. But why bother spending all that time rolling and frying when you can have these delectable bites done in a snap, giving you more time to spend with family and friends?

Depending on personal taste, you can use a variety of items in the cream. Chocolate chips and candied fruit are popular among traditional Italian recipes, but use your imagination and have some fun with whatever sweet ingredients you would like to add.

Here is another tip: a new hot item on store shelves for the last few years has been cannoli chips in several flavors such as lemon and cinnamon. This is another great dessert option as you can serve the cannoli cream or mixture as a dip with the chips and/or fruit.

Taken From www.travelitalyexpert.com
*(Makes two dozen miniature Cannoli
or about a dozen regular sized)*

INGREDIENTS:
- **2 pounds of Ricotta Cheese**
- **Pre-made cannoli shells (can be purchased at bulk food stores or Italian markets)**
- **1 tsp vanilla extract**
- **Pinch of nutmeg**
- **Pinch of cinnamon**
- **1/2 cup of confectioner's sugar**
- **Semi-sweet chocolate chips about 1/4 to half a cup**
- **Diced dried/candied fruit, 1/4 to half cup**
- **Chopped nuts, sprinkles, shaved chocolate for decorating**

DIRECTIONS:

1. Mix ricotta cheese with confectioner sugar, vanilla, and spices. Taste for sweetness and add a bit more sugar if necessary.

2. Divide the cannoli cream if using different items for filling.

3. Fold chocolate or fruit into cream.

4. Fill cannoli shells by using a pastry bag or long spoon.

5. Dip the shells in colored sprinkles, shaved chocolate, or crushed nuts.

6. Sprinkle confectioner sugar over the plate of cannoli for a wintery or snow effect.

7. Serve the same day as prepared as the shells will get soft if prepared too far ahead of serving time. The cannoli cream can last up to a week refrigerated.

A PILGRIM'S PERSPECTIVE
A SORRENTO STORY OF BREE SOLSTAD
BY JOHN HALE

Many of us have one or the other view of God: Some of us see Him as a taskmaster, eternally upset with our childlike self-obsession. Others imagine that He is eternally "nice" and benevolent, sanctioning and approving our every choice on a journey to an imaginary Happyland.

The Truth is that God is neither of these things. God *is* Truth and Love, both of which are demanding. But what is that love and how and where do we encounter it? We encounter His love, again, by going beyond and above ourselves, out of the places of our imaginary control, to the places where we realize that we have no control at all.

In short, we go to places "off the beaten path." Spiritually, we go beyond the rote prayers to explore the facets of God that we see and experience in each other, in nature, and, above all, in the Eucharist and in Scripture.

This demands a pause and an opening of our minds to the very idea that God is in the wounds, the deep hurts, the transcendent joys, and the whispers that come to us in quiet prayer, in Mass, and meaningful conversation with another.

I recently read about a story of a young woman, Bree Solstad, who accepted what must have been the Holy Spirit's invitation to Italy. A former pornography producer and actress who had suffered a great tragedy, her search for purpose and meaning brought her to Italy in 2023.

Profoundly touched by the beauty she saw in churches in Rome and Assisi, she experienced a profound conversion to the Catholic Faith. In Sorrento, she said, "I noticed the Virgin Mary on street corners all over the place. All of a sudden, I felt like Mary was calling me in the strangest way. Each time I entered a church, I felt compelled to seek her out."[4]

Later, at Assisi, she said, "I was impressed by St. Francis, but I was moved to tears by St. Clare. I knelt by her tomb and again asked for assistance. I felt like St. Clare was actually present with me and that she was going to take all the pain and anxiety from me and somehow give it to God."[5]

Brought up in the Lutheran tradition, Bree had a strong sense that she needed to change when she returned home, and she sought the help of a priest. In March 2024 she was received into the Church at the Easter Vigil. Like so many of the saints, this young woman had responded to the loving invitation of God. Today she supports herself by making faith-inspired jewelry and rosaries.

The story is a powerful reminder that being willing to go off the beaten path on pilgrimage is important to finding God.

---

[4] Walter Sánchez Silva, Christina Herrera, and ACI Prensa, "After Living Life of 'Countless Sins,' Actress Embraces Catholic Faith after Trip to Italy," *National Catholic Register*, April 12, 2024, https://www.ncregister.com/cna/after-living-life-of-countless-sins-actress-embraces-catholic-faith-after-trip-to-italy.

[5] Ibid.

PART FIVE

Tuscany, Liguria Regions, and Cinque Terre

DELIGHTING BY LAND AND BY SEA

TUSCANY, LIGURIA REGIONS, AND CINQUE TERRE

Liguria Region

Tuscany Region

Previous page: A Tuscan landscape at sunrise

WHAT YOU'LL EXPLORE...

TUSCANY AND LIGURIA REGION HIGHLIGHTS

- **Beyond Madison Avenue:** A Closer Look at Tuscany, Liguria and Cinque Terre
- **Beloved Saint of Italy — St. Bona of Pisa**
- T's Ultimate Must-Sees and Dos in Tuscany
- T's Ultimate Must-Sees and Dos in Liguria
- T's Ultimate Must-Sees and Dos in Cinque Terre

SACRED SPACES OF TUSCANY AND LIGURIA

- **La Verna and the Via di Francesco:** The Sacred Stigmata and the Way of St. Francis
- **Via Francigena:** All Roads Lead to Rome
- **Basilica of St. Francis, Siena:** The Miraculous Hosts
- **Marian Shrines along the Seashore:** The White Madonna and Our Lady of Montallegro

FASCINATING PLACES OF TUSCANY AND LIGURIA

- **The Renaissance City of Florence:** And Other Breathtaking Tuscan Towns Worthy of Attention
- **San Gimignano:** The Medieval Manhattan
- **Volterra:** An Inviting Tuscan Town
- **Pisa:** The Leaning Tower and Magnificent Museums

CELEBRATIONS AND SIGNATURE DISHES

- **Palio di Siena:** July and August
- **Ribollita Tuscan White Bean and Kale Soup**

A PILGRIM'S PERSPECTIVE: LORI MAHER

BEYOND MADISON AVENUE
A CLOSER LOOK AT TUSCANY, LIGURIA, AND CINQUE TERRE

Tuscany is without a doubt one of the most beautiful and probably most well-known regions of Italy. It is filled with rolling hills, golden sunsets, and endless paths lined with deep green cypress trees, vineyards, and olive groves. It even has its share of beautiful coastline — and let's not forget some of the nation's most notable cities when it comes to faith, history, art, and architecture: Florence, Siena, Pisa, Lucca, and San Gimignano.

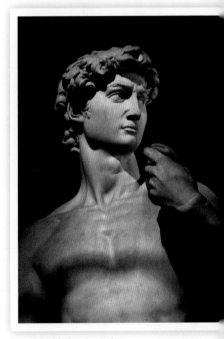

Tuscany was already popular with Americans and other travelers when Frances Mayes released her bestselling book *Under the Tuscan Sun*, the first of several about her experiences moving to Italy. Released by Random House in 1996, her book was turned into a popular film a few years later, starring Diane Lane as Frances.

Opposite: Porto Venere, Liguria

David *by Michaelangelo*

In my opinion, the movie did not do justice to the entertaining and intriguing real-life story of Mayes's journey, given that the film was true only to about 50 percent of the writer's manuscript. Nevertheless, it did help increase the attraction to all things Tuscan for those wanting to visit Italy. Recent statistics from 2023 show that some twenty-two million people chose not just to visit Tuscany but to drop the luggage and stay a while, or at least stay overnight.[1]

And although seeing the *David* and the Duomo in Florence, visiting the home of St. Catherine of Siena, and even taking that goofy but iconic photo in front of the Leaning Tower of Pisa are all must-dos in Tuscany, these sites represent a fraction of what's available to the curious traveler desiring to write their own unique Tuscan tale. Read for yourself.

Sanctuary House of St. Catherine

[1] "Number of Overnight Stays in Tourist Accommodation Establishments in the Italian Region of Tuscany from 2019 to 2022, by Nationality," Statista, July 3, 2023, https://www.statista.com/statistics/1051015/number-of-tourists-in-the-italian-region-of-tuscany-by-nationality/.

Opposite: The Leaning Tower of Pisa with the Fontana dei Putti in the foreground

BELOVED SAINT OF ITALY

St. Bona of Pisa

- **Relics:** Church of San Martino, Pisa, Italy, Province of Pisa, Tuscany Region
- **Patron Saint:** travelers, tour guides, pilgrims, flight attendants, and the city of Pisa, Italy
- **Canonized:** 1962 by Pope John XXIII
- **Feast Day:** May 29

St. Bona was born on 1156 in Pisa to an unmarried couple; she was raised by her mother after her merchant father left them when she was three. As a young child Bona experienced visions of the Child Jesus, the Blessed Mother, and St. James the Greater to whom she had a deep devotion. Her mystical gifts continued as she grew; she became an Augustinian tertiary at ten years old and fasted from a young age.

At fourteen, she traveled to Jerusalem from Pisa to find her father, whom she was told was on crusade. She found him, but on her return she was captured, wounded, and imprisoned by Islamic pirates. She was eventually ransomed and returned home. Despite ill health, she soon left for a dangerous pilgrimage to Santiago de Compostela, giving spiritual and physical aid and courage to other pilgrims. Soon after returning home to Pisa, she died in 1207.

Over her lifetime she led pilgrims nine times on the grueling thousand-mile journey to Santiago de Compostela and Spain.

TUSCANY REGION
HIGHLIGHTS

The Tuscany Region, Italy's fifth-largest region, is located in the north-west area of Italy and borders the Ligurian coastline. It's most famous for its Renaissance art and architecture. It has a diverse landscape including the rugged Apennine Mountains, the beautiful beaches on the Island of Elba along the Tyrrhenian Sea, as well as the rolling vineyards that boast of Chianti olive groves and vineyards.

There are six World Heritage Sites in this region. The most famous city (and province) is Florence, which is home to Michelangelo's David statue, Botticelli's works at the Uffizi Gallery, and the Duomo Basilica built by the Medici family. One of the most famous appetizers in Tuscany is the crostini Toscani, which is a chicken liver pâté served on a thin piece of toasted bread. This was made famous by Catherine de' Medici, the Italian noblewoman who became the Queen of France in the sixteenth century.

Basilica of Santa Croce

Right: Cathedral of San Biagio, Montepulciano
Middle: Il Porcellino *(The Little Pig) at Mercato Nuovo in Florence*
Left: Primavera *by Botticelli*

TUSCANY REGION
T'S ULTIMATE MUST-SEES AND DOS

- - - - - - -

DUOMO/CATHEDRAL OF SANTA MARIA DEL FIORE

A fourteenth-century gothic cathedral, considered the religious center of Florence.

"Gates of Paradise" by Lorenzo Ghiberti (15th century)

FLORENCE BAPTISTRY

In front of the cathedral sits one of the oldest religious monuments in the city of Florence. The baptistry is undoubtedly the most famous for its three sets of bronze doors, including the Ghiberti masterpiece, the "Gates of Paradise." Tickets are needed to enter the Duomo and to gain entrance to the baptistry.

THE BASILICA DI SANTA CROCE

Both a church and a museum. This famous Franciscan place of worship is designed in the shape of an Egyptian cross. It's located in a piazza by the same name and is southeast of the famed Duomo in Florence. People of faith, history buffs, and art lovers will want to visit this site as it is the burial place of Italians who made major contributions to culture and science: Galileo, the famous composer Rossini, and last but not least Michelangelo. It dates back to 1212, when St. Francis visited the city.

THE DAVID

One of the main reasons tourists from around the world flock to Florence is to admire Michelangelo's sculptures, with the *David* being at the top of the list. The Renaissance artist's masterpiece, along with other notable works, are housed in the Galleria dell'Accademia (the Accademia Gallery). If you have time to spare, this art gallery is worth at least a few hours. You want to have your travel agent book the tickets in advance.

UFFIZI GALLERY

The Uffizi Gallery is a prominent art museum located next to the beautiful Piazza della Signoria in Florence, housing one of the most famous art collections in the world. Famous works by Botticelli, Giotto, and others can be seen in the museum that first opened its doors way back in 1769. Here again, given the popularity and prominence of this museum it's recommended that you purchase tickets in advance.

PORCELLINO MARKET/MERCATO NUOVO

There are a number of great places to shop in Florence but among my favorite places to bargain, stroll, or grab a great deal is the Porcellino Market (new market). The Porcellino portion of the name references the wild boar statue located there. Italian tradition says you need to rub the boar's nose for good luck, fortune, and hopefully some good deals! This market is flooded with great leather products as well as scarves and other clothing items in every style and color imaginable. Even if you're not a shopper it's fun to stroll along the aisles and look all around at the variety of items. It's open from 9:00 a.m. to 7:00 p.m. Tuesday through Sunday.

THE PONTE VECCHIO

That sounds so much better than "Old Bridge," doesn't it? Stroll along this famous bridge that crosses the Arno River and is home to countess jewelry stores that line either side. Even though shopping here would break the bank for most tourists, it's still something to

T'S INSIDER'S TIP!

After you're done taking selfies with the boar, start walking across the bridge away from the tourist area toward the residential section. Make a left as you cross and you will find a number of wine bars along the Arno. If you're early enough, you can grab a table by the window and enjoy your meal and vino, watching the rowers pass by below. Nothing like it.

see and a great gathering space for those iconic photos and images that Florence is famous for.

SIENA

Birthplace and hometown of the great patron of Italy and Europe, St. Catherine, takes you back to medieval times as you stroll its quaint streets. Countless pilgrims and tourists visit here each year to venerate her relics at St. Dominic's, which is very close to her childhood home, another point of interest for pilgrims. In addition to St. Dominic's and St. Catherine's homes, there is the famous Duomo of Siena along with the Piazza del Campo, considered the most beautiful piazza in all of Italy. It's also the location for the famous horse races that take place in July and August known as the Palio di Siena (see p. 264).

Piazza del Campo, Siena

MONTALCINO

If you like red wine, **Montalcino** should definitely be on your Tuscany bucket list. Just twenty-six miles from Siena, Montalcino is a small, quaint town in the rolling hills of Tuscany famous for its Brunello di Montalcino. It has a number of winding and lovely medieval streets with great shops filled with local delicacies and has barely changed in terms of appearance since the sixteenth century. You will enjoy winding your way through the beautiful countryside and miles of vineyards. This is a great day trip from your villa or wherever you're staying in Tuscany. Several years ago my husband and I used Siena as our base and drove all over the Tuscan countryside; Montalcino was one of our favorite stops, with a number of historic treasures as well including a major fortress built in the fourteenth century.

A wine shop in Montalcino

CHIANTI

A mountainous area within the Tuscan Region of Italy best known for its namesake: Chianti wine. Breathtaking landscapes and good wine make Chianti a must if you are visiting the Tuscan wine country.

MONTEPULCIANO

A medieval hilltop town in the Tuscan Region of Italy. The entire area is surrounded by vineyards, and it is well known for producing its red wine, after the town's namesake: Montepulciano.

T'S INSIDER'S TIP!

Head to the border of Tuscany and Umbria to lovely Lake Trasimeno. It's a perfect escape from all the Tuscan tourists and close enough to the main attractions to escape for a day trip. Hop the ferry to the largest of the three islands, Maggiore, for a wonderful lakeside lunch as you watch the sailboats go by before heading back to Florence or Siena.

Lake Trasimeno and Isola Maggiore

Opposite: Street leading to the Porto Antico di Genova in Genoa

LIGURIA REGION AND CINQUE TERRE
HIGHLIGHTS

The Liguria Region is a crescent-shaped Mediterranean "Ligurian" coastline straddling the South of France and Tuscany. It is known for its mild climate and a picturesque landscape. It is often referred to as the "Italian Riviera." The city of Genoa, the capital of Italy's Liguria region, is roughly in the middle of the region. One of the most beloved places to visit in this region is Cinque Terre, which is known for its colorful homes and clifftop views. This region is covered with chestnut and oak trees and is abundant with beautiful flowers. Olive trees and wine vineyards provide much of the agricultural activity in this region, but this area is most known for its tourism as well as the trade done through the coastline ports.

Right: Monterosso al Mare, Liguria
Middle: View from the Church of San Pietro in Porto Venere
Left: Vernazza, Cinque Terre

LIGURIA REGION

T'S ULTIMATE MUST-SEES AND DOS

The Ligurian coast is so beautiful that it is referred to as the "Italian Riviera."

SHRINE OF OUR LADY OF MONTALLEGRO

This is an approved apparition sight with the focus on a picture/ icon of Mary connected to her appearance on the mountain. Take a ferry or train ride to Rapallo. You arrive via cable car, the view up the mountain is fantastic, and the shrine is beautiful. There is a wonderful restaurant near the shrine, and be sure to keep an eye out for the plaque marking the spot where Marconi first began testing radio signals, sending them down to the ships in the port of Rapallo.

Shrine of our Lady of Montallegro

We also love **Portofino**, in addition to the waterfront town of **Rapallo** (great boardwalk and shopping), and the quaint town of **Santa Margherita Ligure**, all accessible by ferry along the Ligurian coast.

Villa Bonomi, Paraggi (near Santa Margherita Ligure)

PORTOFINO

A small but quaint town, with wonderful wine bars and restaurants in the port. There is great people and yacht watching as well as shopping nearby. This little village packs a punch in terms of making you feel as if you are starring in your own episode of *Lifestyles of the Rich and Famous*. While in Portofino you also might want to visit:

Portofino's Castello Brown

- *Castello Brown* — sixteenth-century castle with gardens

- *Museo del Parco* — modern art museum and sculpted gardens

- *Church of San Giorgio* — a beautiful yellow church that was completely rebuilt after World War II.

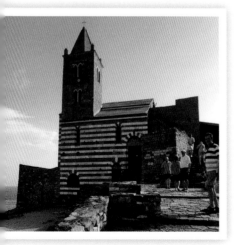

San Pietro Church, Porto Venere

PORTO VENERE

A lovely fishing village south of Cinque Terre and is the perfect place to dine and stroll seaside. Visit San Pietro Church as well as Lord Byron's grotto (Grotto Arpaia), the poet's favorite reflection spot in an area known as the Gulf of the Poets, named for all the famous writers who spent countless holidays there.

ISOLA D'ELBA AND PORTOFERRAIO

This island off the coast of Tuscany is known for its many wonderful beaches. It also is the home to many ruins, churches, Etruscan fortresses, hermitages, and the like. A beautiful place to relax in true *la dolce vita* (sweet life) style, the island is filled with large, small, and sandy beaches much different than the beaches typically found along the Ligurian coast.

PORTOFERRAIO

The largest town on the island of Elba. Here you can visit the beautiful Romanesque church of Santo Stefano alle Trane.

VOLTERRAIO CASTLE

Reopened to the public in 2016 and hosts spectacular views of Tuscany and the Archipelago.

THE ETRUSCAN FORTRESS OF CASTIGLIONE

A top tourist attraction. Take a cooking class and learn how to make delicious and authentic pesto sauce. Basil pesto originated from this beautiful Ligurian Region.

Portofino

CINQUE TERRE
T'S ULTIMATE MUST-SEES AND DOS

– – – – – – – –

CINQUE TERRE

Which means "Five Lands," comprises the five small coastal villages located in the Italian region of Liguria: Riomaggiore, Manarola, Corniglia, Monterosso al Mare and Vernazza.

THE CINQUE TERRE EXPRESS

A convenient train that runs through all of the towns and is a great way to travel through the mountains and visit all the villages.

PARCO NAZIONALE DELLE CINQUE TERRE

The towns of Cinque Terre are located in a national park famous for its hikes above the Mediterranean.

Cinque Terre Express at Manarola Station

HIKING CINQUE TERRE

If time allows, hiking between the five towns affords incredible views. The hiking trail is located in a national park. The longest section of the trail is known as the Blue Path Trail. If you just want a taste of the hike without hours on foot and want some great and romantic photo ops, make your way to "lovers' lane" between Manarola and Riomaggiore — a brief thirty-minute walk.

Take a boat ride down along the Cinque Terre coast down to beautiful, much smaller, and peaceful **Porto Venere**.

MONTEROSSA

This is the largest of the five coastal villages and is located on hills cultivated with lemons, vines, and olives. It has amazing beaches, beautiful reefs, and crystal-clear waters. This Cinque Terre village has a number of beautiful churches including:

- *Convento Monterossa* — The Capuchin convent and church with a monument to St. Francis.
- *Santuario di Soviore* — A lovely sanctuary dedicated to Our Lady of Soviore where pilgrims or tourists walk the paths between the sanctuaries of Cinque Terre. This place was built by locals bringing up each stone by hand.

T'S TRAVEL TIP

Consider staying at one of the not-so-touristy towns around the famous Cinque Terre such as Rapallo or Sestri Levante to the north or La Spezia to the south.

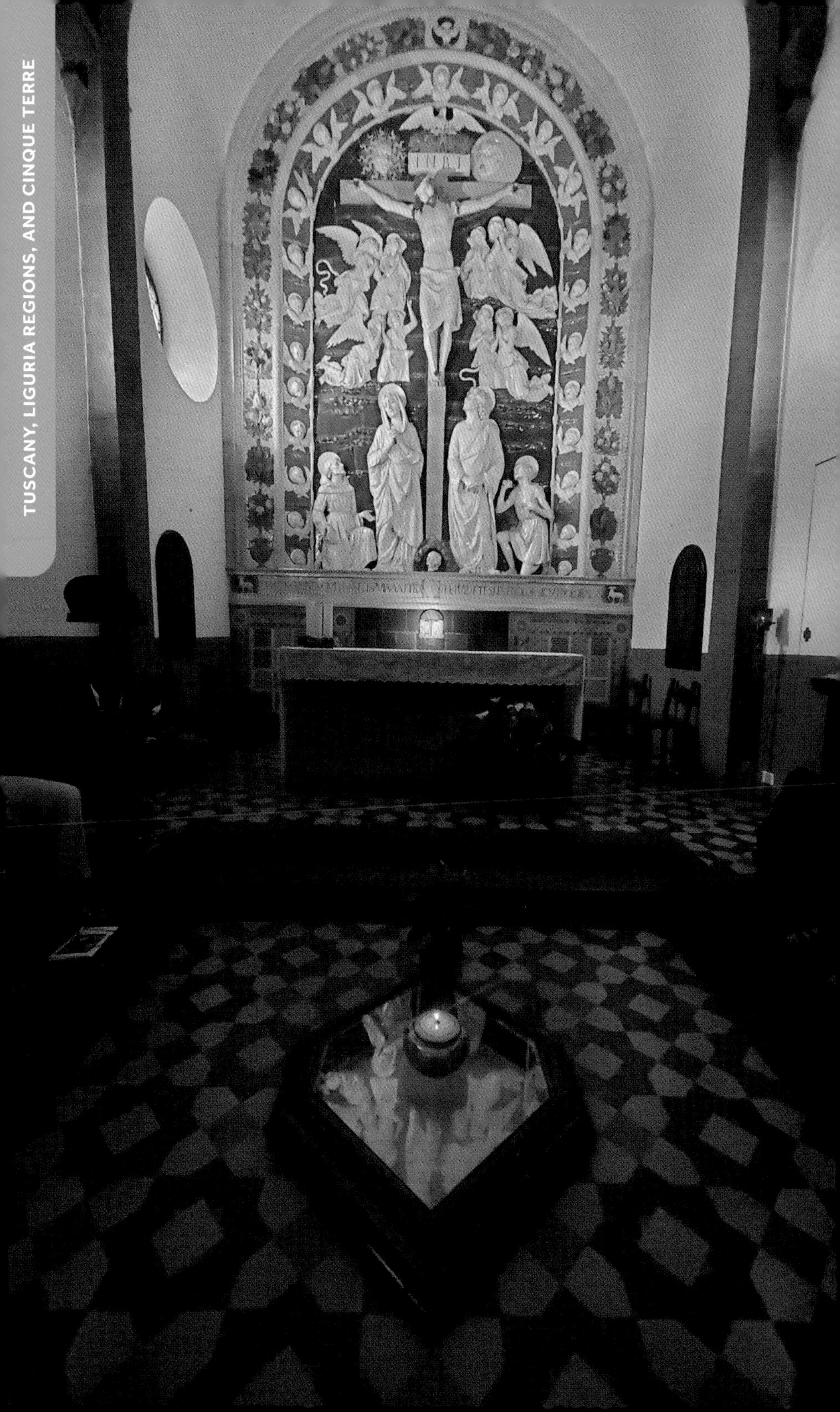

TUSCANY AND LIGURIA REGIONS

SACRED SPACES

- - - - - - -

The duomos in Florence and Siena, the home of St. Catherine of Siena, and the Basilica of St. Dominic: these are the places that come to mind when thinking of the sacred in these two regions of Italy.

And these locations are certainly attractions that need to be experienced. But visitors to Tuscany and Liguria should also consider venturing to some lesser-known sites such as St. Francis in Siena, home to a lesser-known eucharistic miracle, or a small church tucked along the backstreets of the waterfront village of Porto Venere that houses a miraculous Marian icon, along with the remote hermitage of St. Francis hidden in the Tuscan forests, if they truly wish to discover additional sacred spaces.

LA VERNA AND THE VIA DI FRANCESCO

The Sacred Stigmata and the Way of St. Francis

"Seriously, St. Francis?"

I didn't mean to blurt that question out loud, but I did. I guess I just couldn't help myself as we went around yet another steep curve up

Opposite: La Verna Sanctuary, where St. Francis received the wounds of Christ

Mt. Penna, leading to the sacred spot where St. Francis received the stigmata, the wounds of Christ's Passion.

Although La Verna, Tuscany was only ninety minutes from our Umbrian location, it felt like we were in the car forever. I'm not the motion sickness type but forever twisting, turning, and rising further and further upward was getting on my nerves. "I know St. Francis appreciated his solitude, but isn't this a bit much?" This time the question was posed to my husband who agreed and just chuckled as he drove on, and on, and on.

La Verna Sanctuary of St. Francis

Although that challenging drive up the mountain can seem endless, it is certainly very humbling when you contemplate just how far St. Francis traveled, and probably either on foot or via donkey, from his hometown of Assisi in Umbria. The site is over seventy miles north of Assisi. The Stigmata Sanctuary of La Verna, as it is formally known, is in the Casentinesi Forests National Park. The views are incredibly beautiful, and you can practically feel your blood pressure and heart rate slowing down as you look out over the lush hills that go on for miles.

St. Francis came to this area of Tuscany in 1224, two years before his death, for a period of silence and prayer. According to his biographer and close follower, St. Bonaventure, it was in this secluded location that he asked God to be able to fully share in His sufferings on the Cross. St. Bonaventure tells us in his book *Major Legend* that Jesus appeared to Francis on the mountaintop as a crucified seraph. Seraphim are described in Scripture, including in the Old Testament book of Isaiah chapter 6, as six-winged fiery angels.

> While Francis was praying on the mountainside, he saw a Seraph with six fiery and shining wings descend from the height of heaven. And when in swift flight the Seraph had reached a spot in the air near the man of God, there appeared between the wings the figure of a man crucified, with his hands and feet and extended in the form of a cross and fastened to a cross. Two of the wings were lifted above his head, two were extended for flight and two covered his whole body. When the vision disappeared, Francis was left with a "marvelous ardor" in his heart. At the same time, there "was imprinted on his body markings that were no less marvelous."

The La Verna Sanctuary allows visitors to pray at the spot where St. Francis received the signs of the crucifixion. The chapel is reached by going through a long hallway painted with vibrant scenes from the saint's life. There is also a museum and a large operating Catholic Church, a basilica, that not only houses several relics, including robes, of St. Francis, but whose walls are lined with fifteenth-century terra-cotta reliefs. In January of 2024 the Franciscans marked the eight hundredth anniversary of the saint receiving the stigmata.

A visit to this place of solitude, peace, and exquisite beauty will do wonders for body, mind, and spirit.

VIA FRANCIGENA
All Roads Lead to Rome

"Are we there yet?" Can you imagine how many times pilgrims making their way from England through Switzerland, France, and down through Italy to the Eternal City of Rome might have asked that question, hoping to get to the final point at St. Peter's tomb? And who could blame them? Even after reaching Rome, there were many who continued the road all the way south to Italy's Puglia region along the Adriatic, where it was possible to embark on the final leg of the journey to Jerusalem.

This ancient pilgrimage route, Via Francigena (in English, "Way of the Francis" or "Road That Comes from France") covers 1,200 miles of European territory. It is believed that pilgrims have been making the journey (also known as "Via Romea") as early as the late tenth century. Sigeric, archbishop of Canterbury, kept a detailed diary as he traveled home from Rome in A.D. 990. Thanks to an Italian expert in medieval history, Giovanni Caselli, Sigeric's notes were remapped and published in 1990 on the thousandth anniversary of the archbishop's European crossing.

The Via Francigena is not to be confused with the Via di Francesco ("The Way of St. Francis"). That's an entirely different path developed after the death of one of Italy's patrons, covering sites important in the ministry of the great saint and ending in his hometown of Assisi.

Some of the most picturesque stops along the Francigena take you through Tuscany, including Lucca, San Gimignano, Florence, Siena, and the famed southern Tuscany valley of Val d'Orcia (added to the list of UNESCO world heritage sites in 2004). In 2001 the European Association of the Via Francigena Ways was formed to help visitors from around the world experience, as its website explains, "the ancient footsteps of medieval pilgrims that walked toward great destinations, such as Rome, Santiago de Compostela or Jerusalem."[2]

The saying "All roads lead to Rome" was not expressed by a pilgrim who walked the ancient trails of the Via Francigena. Instead, it was a French poet, Alain de Lille, who in the late twelfth century wrote about Rome's significance as a major center of culture, history, and politics. He noted the never-ending web of roads all connecting to the metropolis. Since then it has become a very popular, even cliché phrase or idiom stressing that reaching a goal or achieving success in life can be done via many different paths. It's very apropos, when we stop and think about all the pilgrims down through the centuries who completed their Francigena expedition.

[2] European Association of the Via Francigena Ways (EAVF), accessed September 2, 2024, https://www.viefrancigene.org/en/about-us/.

BASILICA OF ST. FRANCIS, SIENA
The Miraculous Hosts

Siena is a beautiful Tuscan town with much medieval flair, most well known for being the birthplace and home to one of the female doctors of the Catholic Church, St. Catherine of Siena, a patron saint of Italy and Europe. In addition to visiting the church of St. Dominic's with her relics and her nearby childhood home, pilgrims and tourists flock here to take in the city's incredible architecture, including the famed Piazza del Campo, considered one of the loveliest piazzas in all of Italy.

Siena is also the home to the thirteenth-century Santa Maria Assunta, or the Duomo di Siena, one of Italy's top gothic structures which includes a magnificent white-and-black striped marble façade on the outside and famous frescoes and mosaic floors on the inside.

After viewing the highlights this Tuscan gem has to offer, many will move on to Florence or to another Tuscan venue without visiting another fascinating site of enormous religious significance: the Eucharistic Miracle of 1730.

On August 14, during the Catholic celebrations of the Assumption of the Virgin Mary, locals were involved in the services, leaving the Church of St. Francis in Siena empty. This gave thieves a prime

Basilica of St. Francis, Siena

opportunity to go in and steal the cherished golden ciborium, used to hold the consecrated Hosts.

When the theft was noticed the next morning, the archbishop ordered the community to pray publicly while police conducted a search for the ciborium and the precious hosts inside.

Just a few days later, at another local church, St. Mary's of Provenzano, a priest noticed something white sticking out of the collection box. A closer look revealed it to be a Host, and inside the box were 348 of them, the same number reported stolen. Since the Hosts had the same markings of the St. Francis Hosts, they were assumed to be the same consecrated Hosts. The Hosts were collected by the local Church authorities and returned to their original home. At some point some of the hosts were distributed, but since there was no way to know whether the Hosts were safe to consume, the bishop ordered the remainder of them to be set aside to decompose naturally.

The true miracle, however, was still to come. To the archbishop's amazement, those consecrated Hosts did not deteriorate. Fifty years after their recovery, an official investigation was conducted and in 1780, the minister general of the Franciscan Order consumed one of the Hosts and found it to be not only incorrupt but fresh.

Fast forward to the early twentieth century, when other tests were performed by chemistry experts at the University of Siena, confirming that the particles were made from unleavened bread and as a result should only have remained intact for a few years, but in this case they were perfectly preserved.

In 1950, another theft occurred. This time the thief left behind the Hosts but stole the container. The remaining 133 Hosts were eventually placed in an ornate ciborium, where today they are kept behind lock and key in the sacred tabernacle above a side altar in St. Francis. They are displayed for veneration several times a year, most notably on the feast of Corpus Christi, the Body and Blood of Christ. On that important feast day, they are placed in a monstrance, a transparent receptacle, and carried in procession through the city streets.

Several saints, including John XXIII and St. John Bosco, have venerated the sacred Hosts. The Catholic Church has confirmed that they were indeed consecrated in the year 1730 — but since that time they have remained whole and have not deteriorated.[3]

MARIAN SHRINES ALONG THE SEASHORE

The White Madonna and Our Lady of Montallegro

Our Lady of Montallegro, patroness of Rapallo

Sometimes we go looking for sacred spaces. Other times, surprisingly, they find us. This was the case for me with both the White Madonna of Porto Venere and Our Lady of Montallegro in Rapallo. Both shrines are in the Liguria region along Italy's northwestern coast.

3   "Eucharistic Miracle: Siena, Italy — 1730," Real Presence Eucharistic Education and Adoration Association, accessed September 2, 2024, https://www.therealpresence.org/eucharst/mir/siena.html.

THE WHITE MADONNA

I learned about the White Madonna of Porto Venere in 2022, after we had visited this small fishing village south of Cinque Terre. Porto Venere, also referred to as the Gulf of Poets (Lord Bryon and Shelley spent time there), is much less crowded than the more famous five towns to its north.

Porto Venere is a great place to dock for a few days if Cinque Terre is your destination. There are plenty of ferries to take you up and down the coast, and you can return to a more laid back but very pleasant seaside *borgo* with plenty of beach access, great fish restaurants, and even a five-star hotel overlooking the harbor, again without having to make your way through dense crowds.

After delightful cocktails along the dock, we headed up the hill to nearby San Pietro's Church. It sits high above the village overlooking the sea and thanks to its black and white stripes makes quite the impression against the deep blues of the water below.

The White Madonna of Porto Venere

Having seen so many images of San Pietro's, I thought that this was the most important religious site in Porto Venere. Then, a few months later, I was reading one of my Italian tourism magazines and realized that I had missed a real treasure: the Church of St. Lawrence, also known as the Sanctuary of the White Virgin (in Italian: Santuario della Madonna Bianca), which is tucked away behind the narrow streets and is home to an icon that prompts the annual Madonna Bianca festival filling the town with thousands of torches.

According to tradition, the White Madonna, now the town's patron, goes back to the end of the fourteenth century, when the area was hit by a plague. A faithful man was praying in his home near an image of the Blessed Mother, asking for her protection.

Suddenly the image became bright, filled with white light and colors. The man saw a second image, this time of the Blessed Virgin holding the Infant Jesus, who was holding a scroll containing words encouraging conversion. A short time later he found this second image pressed into a log near his home and he immediately brought it to the church. To this day it is kept behind glass above an ornate marble altar.

Determined to venerate the image, we headed to Porto Venere on our way down from the lake district in the spring of 2024. We were running late but were able to make it inside the church before closing and saw both the cherished image and the log on which it is said to have arrived in the area so many centuries ago.

OUR LADY OF MONTALLEGRO

"Go and tell the Rapallesi that I want to be honored here."
— The Blessed Virgin Mary

If I had passed by that tourism display in our hotel lobby I would never have seen the mountaintop shrine of Our Lady of Montallegro. And what a shame that would have been. As it was, the brochure grabbed my attention because of the amazing pictures of what to me was an unknown place of worship built around an apparition of the Blessed Mother in 1557.

The shrine sits on top of Mt. Leto, more than two thousand feet above sea level along Rapallo and the Gulf of Tigullio, part of the Italian Riviera. Visitors can drive there, but for the most dramatic experience the cable car is by far the best way to travel.

The apparition was seen in 1557 by a farmer walking his donkey in the hills above Rapallo. The Virgin Mary appeared and spoke to him, explaining that she wanted him to go to the local Church authorities and tell them that she desired a church to be built where he was standing. She then pointed to a picture of herself, a gilded icon, that was sitting on a nearby rock. She told the farmer that the image was brought from Greece to Rapallo by angels.

The farmer did as he was told. The priest took the image and brought it to the local parish for safe keeping, but the next morning it was gone from the church and was discovered back in its original spot. The following year the archbishop of Turin authorized the building of the sanctuary.

Sanctuary of Our Lady of Montallegro in Liguria

But the fascinating story of Our Lady of Montallegro doesn't end there.

Years later, in 1574, a group of sailors from Greece landed in the area. They had just survived a fierce storm at sea and had promised the Blessed Mother, in thanksgiving for keeping them safe, that they would give thanks at the nearest Marian shrine. Upon visiting the basilica, they saw the icon and recognized it as the one that had mysteriously disappeared from their area in 1557. The Greek's interest in reclaiming ownership led to legal battles, with the image ultimately being given back to them.

The Blessed Mother, however, wasn't having any part in the

move from Rapallo. The image was loaded onto the ship but disappeared, only to be found back in the shrine. Everyone then agreed the best place for the Blessed Mother's icon was in the place where she wanted to be, the Shrine of Montallegro.

According to Church tradition and records, intercession or prayers to Our Lady of Montallegro brought about deliverance from the plague in the sixteenth and seventeenth centuries.

The hill on which the shrine was built is known as the "Hill of Joy," and every July 2 in Rapallo is known as "Apparition Day" and includes a major procession, other religious celebrations, local festivities, and fantastic fireworks over the Gulf of Tigullio. Lining the walls of the church are hundreds of ex-votos or offerings of thanksgiving, mainly embroideries, paintings, and bas-reliefs that highlight graces given over the years after calling on the intercession of Our Lady of Montallegro. Our Lady of Montallegro is the patroness of Rapallo.

T's Italy

T'S TIPS

Before or during your trip look up the patron of each city you plan to visit. Learn about their lives, where they were born, and where they were buried. You will be inspired, and sometimes the saints will find you even if you weren't looking for them! Consider saving a prayer for each saint on your phone and praying that prayer as you arrive in their patron city.

TUSCANY AND LIGURIA REGIONS

FASCINATING PLACES

- - - - - - - -

THE RENAISSANCE CITY OF FLORENCE

And Other Breathtaking Tuscan Towns Worthy of Attention

Built along the Arno River in Tuscany, Florence — or "Firenze" as it is known by locals — is called the "Renaissance city" or "the birthplace of the Renaissance." The most well-known writers, painters, philosophers, mathematicians, and sculptors called Firenze home — as did their wealthy benefactors.

Florence has always been a prosperous area, filled with rich families, including the Medici family, who could easily afford to support promising new artists. The Medicis ruled Florence for sixty years and are credited with being the backbone of the Renaissance movement.

This period of rebirth, much of which took place in Florence following the Middle Ages, took place over several hundred years beginning in the fourteenth century and ending in the seventeenth century. It then spread to other parts of Italy, including Venice and Milan, and then swept through Europe. Some of the names associated with this important

Opposite: Aerial view of the Cathedral of Santa Maria del Fiore in Florence

Ponte Vecchio

period might ring a bell: da Vinci, Botticelli, Galileo, Donatello, Giotto, Dante, Raphael, Shakespeare, and of course Michelangelo.

Florence is home to Michelangelo's *David* statue, Botticelli's works at the Uffizi Gallery and the Duomo Basilica, and Santa Maria del Fiore, built by the Medici family. The Basilica di Santa Croce (Church of the Holy Cross) is both a church and a museum, and it is filled with famed frescoes of sacred scenes by Giotto and his pupils as well as Donatello sculptures. People of faith, history buffs, and art lovers will want to visit Santa Croce as it is the burial place of Italians who made major contributions to culture and science including Galileo, the famous composer Rossini, and Michelangelo.

One of my favorite places to linger in Florence is not one of the famous art galleries or another important attraction. Instead, it's the Ponte Vecchio or "Old Bridge." Originally built by the Romans in A.D. 996, it was rebuilt after a flood in 1117 and constructed again in 1345 after a second massive flood. This third bridge, known again as the "Old Bridge," does not only serve as a way to cross the River Arno — it is the only bridge on the Arno not destroyed by the German army in World War II. Hitler ordered it spared because of its grand views.

And even though I am a shopper, I love to cross over the Arno, away from the Piazza della Signoria, and wander into the more residential or local section of the city. There you will find great restaurants and wine bars, many with terraces that afford a striking view of the Ponte Vecchio. Go there for a relaxing midday meal as you watch the rowers go up and down the waterway. Or visit for the perfect *aperitivo* time, enjoying a spritz or a *vino* as you watch the sun set and paint the bridge and the other architectural masterpieces that line the water's edge in an explosion of pastel colors.

SAN GIMIGNANO
The Medieval Manhattan

If you would like to feel like royalty after spending time in the Renaissance City, head about fifty miles south to San Gimignano, a town referred to as "Medieval Manhattan."

San Gimignano earned its clever nickname thanks to its many towers. Fourteen towers (of the original seventy-two) are still standing in this small Tuscan town. When we take a look back at the city's history, we learn that San Gimignano boasted that many towers thanks to

San Gimignano Towers

rivalries between upper-crust families who erected them to show off their power and wealth, accumulated through the production of wine and costly saffron. The tallest tower, the Torre Grossa, stands 177 feet tall and dates to 1298.

The city was developed as a village by the Etruscans, and during the Middle Ages served as a popular starting point for the Via Francigena. You get a sense of strength when you buy a ticket and make your way up one of those towers overlooking the city and the Tuscan countryside.

Visit San Gimignano to stroll the ancient streets, take in its regal vibe, and enjoy award-winning gelato that can be found in Piazza della Cisterna.

VOLTERRA
An Inviting Tuscan Town

There are so many incredible hilltop villages and towns in the Tuscan region that it is hard to choose which ones to visit. In addition to Florence, Siena, and San Gimignano there is also a long list of *borgos* to visit for their famous wines: Montalcino, Montepulciano, and Greve in Chianti. That said, there is one more place that is often overshadowed by its more famous Tuscan neighbors: the mountaintop town of Volterra.

Volterra was not on our list of places to visit when my husband and I spent two weeks in Umbria and Tuscany. But it was highly suggested by our guide leading our Vespa tour. Our guide pointed it out in the distance and recommended that we put it on our to-do list. It was hard to resist, given how stunning it looked in the distance as we moved through the Tuscan countryside.

Volterra is certainly history-worthy, with its medieval wall dating back to the thirteenth century and the town going back much further to the eighth century B.C. Visitors will feel like Rod Taylor in the 1960 cult film *The Time Machine*, as a tour through Volterra's churches, archeological sites, and museums will take you from the Etruscan period to the Roman to medieval and Renaissance, all the way to the nineteenth century, with a stop at the majestic Palazzo dei Priori, the thirteenth-century palace that is Volterra's town hall.

There is the ancient Roman theater in Volterra, for example, is one of the largest and best preserved in Italy. Based on its size, experts believe it could seat thirty-five hundred people.

Santa Maria Assunta, Volterra's cathedral, is exactly as the city's tourism website describes. It is a religious center and an excellent work of medieval art. Walk through its doors and take in the thirteenth-century wooden sculptures portraying the *Deposition of Christ from the Cross*. As the Volterra tourism site explains, the figures are among the best-preserved wooden sculptures from the thirteenth century. They are made of poplar wood, are gilded with gold and silver leaf, and include images of the Blessed Mother,

T's Italy

T'S TRAVEL TIP
Take a Vespa!

A Vespa (teasingly called "mosquito") is a small motorbike. If you can take a Vespa tour, I recommend it. They are well structured, and you receive a quick but solid lesson on how to handle your bike. The tours take you on small country roads without traffic, allowing for plenty of photo ops, and go at a very easy pace. If you're still not sure about driving one, do what I did and opt for riding instead of driving so you can take in the scenery!

St. John the Evangelist, and Joseph of Arimathea, along with a cross and a ladder.[4]

The religious, historic, and archeological sites are impressive. But it is the beauty of Volterra and its key location, high above the hills in central Tuscany, that are hard to beat. It also receives high marks for another off-the-beaten-path destination. Strolling through its romantic streets you will find a more laid-back place compared to other sought-after Tuscan destinations.

PISA
The Leaning Tower and Magnificent Museums

It usually doesn't take much to convince Italy travelers to make Pisa part of their itinerary. The town in central Tuscany not far from the coast, at the end of the Arno River, is home to the world-famous Leaning Tower or Tower of Pisa. The eight-story medieval tower is made of 207 columns and is leaning at an angle of just four degrees, thanks to sandy soil and an unstable foundation. Those who don't want to wait in the long lines to get inside seem to get a kick out of taking the iconic photo in front of the freestanding bell tower, strategically leaning from a perspective that makes it seem like you're helping to keep it from toppling over.

The Leaning Tower, however, is just a small part of the religious complex of Piazza del Duomo as well as the Piazza dei Miracoli, or the square of miracles. This site has so much to offer for art aficionados. The square was named a world heritage site by UNESCO in 1987. The tower along with the baptistery, said to be the largest in Italy, are both connected to the duomo, the Cathedral of Santa Maria Assunta. Built in 1604 by the famed architect Buscheto, the church is considered an emblem of Pisan Romanesque architecture. It mixes several different

---

4   "A Romanesque Treasure in the Middle of Tuscany," Volterra, Valdicecina Toscana, accessed September 2, 2024, https://volterratur.it/en/poi/cathedral-and-baptistry-in-volterra/.

styles and cultures, reminding sailors of the many places they visited around the world.

If you don't have time to visit the Leaning Tower, the baptistery, or the church, buy a ticket for the Cathedral Museum of Pisa or the Museo dell'Opera del Duomo, as it contains original artwork from all three. The museum's twenty-five small rooms are filled with a variety of sculptures, detailed religious vestments, liturgical furnishings, and even an original twelfth-century bronze door from the cathedral, containing twenty-four panels depicting the life of Christ.

So yes, take that iconic photo when visiting Pisa, but make the effort to lean into the other incredible sites that the Square of Miracles has to offer.

Piazza dei Miracoli and the Leaning Tower of Pisa

CELEBRATIONS

Palio di Siena
(JULY AND AUGUST)

No doubt the Palio di Siena is the most famous festival in all of Tuscany. The horse race occurs twice over the summer months in July and August, taking place in the city's lovely shell-shaped square, Piazza del Campo. The Siena tradition began with the first race in 1633 and involves very serious competition among the seventeen *contrade* (districts). Each district has its own emblems, colors, and flags. And even if you can't manage to get a seat for the races themselves, other festivities go on throughout the city, including open-air dinners in each **contrade**, with historic processions and a special Mass for the jockeys.

The Palio lasts for days including warmups and six (yes, six) trial runs. The rules of the race are rather complicated. Suffice it to say, not all of the seventeen districts participate at once. The race itself only lasts about a minute, ninety seconds tops, and the horses must go around the piazza three times. At the end of the day, the competitors are vying for the coveted Drappellone or drape, created each year for the Palio by a different artist. The winning team proudly displays the fancy drape in their *contrade's* museum.

If you're interested in experiencing what is considered among the ultimate Tuscan traditions, entrance to the piazza is free, but you'll need to be there at the crack of dawn or earlier as again this is the most famous festival in the region and is also extremely popular across Italy and with tourists. Be prepared to be packed in like sardines (or maybe anchovies, since this is Italy). Look at some online videos and photos before deciding to wait all day long. Both races are smack in the middle of summer. You can email the tourist office in Siena for more on ticket information. Local shops and restaurants around the Piazza del Campo also offer seating at a price. Pack your patience and your sunscreen, as you will wait for hours under the Tuscan sun.

TUSCANY, LIGURIA REGIONS, INCLUDING CINQUE TERRE
SIGNATURE DISHES

- - - - - - -

Ribollita Tuscan White Bean and Kale Soup
FROM TERESA TOMEO'S KITCHEN

(Ribollita *simply means "re-boiled" as it was usually made from leftovers*)

The first time I tasted the Tuscan Ribollita soup, we were having a late dinner in the center of San Gimignano at the lovely Hotel Cisterna. Our table was next to a large picture window, and the moon lit up the sky, clearly revealing the gorgeous Tuscan hills below. It would have been no problem to just continue staring out the window, munching crusty Tuscan bread while sipping my *vino rosso* but then the soup came. And soon I was putting that delicious *pane* to even better use as I used it to soak up all the flavors.

Although there are vegetables in this delicious dish, it cannot be mistaken for a minestrone. It is a hearty dish including a mixture of veggies, plus delicious cannellini beans that add creaminess. The real zinger is the chunk of parm that is a must to throw in as the soup is simmering. I also like to add pancetta as it gives additional flavor.

Since my heritage is not from Tuscany, I had to go in search, after that amazing meal in San Gimignano, for a Ribollita recipe that came close to what I remembered. I looked at different recipes and made up my own very similar to flavors we experienced. You can use white cabbage as well and if you don't like bitter greens, use spinach instead of the kale. I also like to use the immersion blender for half the beans to get a really nice textured soup.

Don't be put off by the steps needed to get all those healthy veggies in the pot. And make sure you use good olive oil and provide some extra chunks of bread for dipping.

INGREDIENTS:

- 1 large onion, diced
- 1/3 cup pancetta, diced
- 2 celery stalks, diced
- 2 carrots, peeled and diced
- 2 cloves of garlic, crushed
- 1 bay leaf
- Salt and Pepper to taste
- 1–2 tablespoons of olive oil
- Parmesan rind or chunk
- ½ teaspoon red pepper flakes (optional)
- 4–5 cups of vegetable broth
- ½ white wine (optional)
- 2 cans cannellini beans (drained and rinsed)
- 1 large can of diced tomatoes
- 1 large bunch of kale and/or spinach (6–8 cups) — you can buy the prewashed and cleaned to save time.
- Crusty Italian bread sliced thick, grilled, or toasted under the broiler
- Extra grated parmesan for topping

DIRECTIONS:

1. Heat olive oil in a large saucepan.

2. Sauté the pancetta until slightly crisp.

3. Remove the pancetta and sauté onion, celery, carrots, and garlic.

4. Add the tomatoes, wine, vegetable broth, bay leaf, red pepper, pancetta, and parmesan.

5. Simmer at least 30–40 minutes so the flavors blend well.

6. For a thicker soup add torn bread pieces while simmering.

7. About 10 minutes before the soup is done add the kale or spinach.

8. Finish by service in large bowls over the toasted bread with more cheese and salt and pepper to taste.

A PILGRIM'S PERSPECTIVE

LORI MAHER
AS TOLD BY JOHN HALE

Lori had never visited Italy when she first hosted an event to benefit the first national Sistine Chapel Choir tour in 2018. Over the next several years, I extended several invitations to her. But, as life goes, we each had a series of difficult curveballs over the years that followed, and personal circumstances prevented her from making the trip until Spring 2023.

Lori Maher with John and Kristan Hale at Castel Gandolfo

Lori was hesitant to travel overseas alone, and she had difficulty deciding whether to go to Tuscany on retreat. But when her children encouraged her to go, she decided to add Rome to her itinerary. She envisioned walking into St. Peter's Basilica and saying, "Hello, God — it's Lori! I am here!"

When I heard from Lori, I asked her to come to my office so I could help her with her plans — I knew a quick trip to St. Peter's wasn't going to satisfy her for long. I also saw that the dates of her itinerary coincided almost perfectly with one of the most coveted trips on the pilgrimage market — a Patrons of the Arts in the Vatican Museums member's pilgrimage. This special trip included an evening visit, cocktail reception, and candlelit dinner in the Vatican Museums. She would also enjoy a tour with Catholic art historian Dr. Elizabeth Lev, a private concert by a quintet from the Sistine Chapel Choir, and dinner at and a tour of Castel Gandolfo, historically the pope's summer home.

Initially hesitant — she had been through some difficult family issues and was concerned she might not fit in with the others on the pilgrimage — she soon contacted us and signed up. She told us that our conversation had helped her find the courage to go. For Lori, it was a great step of faith.

The first surprise God had in store for Lori occurred on the flight to Rome, where she reconnected with friends who were on their way to attend the transitional diaconate ordination of their nephew in Rome; the following spring he would be ordained a priest in the Archdiocese of Detroit. This was just one in a series of "God-incidences" repeated over the course of her two-week trip.

Once in Rome, she encountered beauty beyond anything she could have imagined. As she walked through the galleries of the Vatican Museums she was compelled to put away her phone so she could be fully attentive and present. It was another level of letting go in faith, allowing all the beauty God had placed before her to sink in at a deeper level to her heart and mind. Tour after tour and experience after experience, she felt a quiet born of the breathtaking beauty that was transformative. Later on during the trip, she met some warm and welcoming Vatican patrons whose sincere interest in Lori made her feel most welcome. She was no longer afraid that she wouldn't connect with the others on the trip. Their "sweet, tender, and caring" conversations were a source of healing and joy, and Lori and the patrons remained friends because of that open and vulnerable dialogue on the journey.

Through a series of encounters, Lori felt that she had found a renewed place in the Church; she says her faith wasn't changed so much as it was "cemented," to give her a solid foundation even though the realities of her life had changed. At each point of the trip God continued to meet her needs with surprises and "coincidences" that assured her that she was loved and that she was always welcome.

Another consolation came after her return home, when Lori attended Mass at Holy Trinity Church in Detroit. The nephew of her friends on the plane to Rome was now a priest! During his homily he seemed to be looking directly at Lori, and once again she experienced a profound sense of welcome — and an invitation to continue her journey of faith. Had Lori not been willing to consider traveling overseas alone, she might have missed the patrons pilgrimage — a next step of faith that opened up a world of experiences. "It really is remarkable what happens when you forgive yourself, say yes to new experiences, and allow yourself to live in the present moment. Thank you for helping me see through my fog — every day is a gift!"

St. Catherine of Siena statue
at her home in Siena

PART SIX

Lombardy, Piedmont, and Veneto Regions

NORTHERN LIGHTS

EXPLORING ITALY'S SCENIC
NORTHERN REGIONS

LOMBARDY, PIEDMONT, AND VENETO REGIONS

Lombardy
Region

Veneto
Region

Piedmont
Region

Previous page: Cityscape of Turin

WHAT YOU'LL EXPLORE...

LOMBARDY, PIEDMONT, AND VENETO REGION HIGHLIGHTS

- **Lovely Lakes, Endless Acres, and Captivating Canals:** Exploring Italy's Scenic Northern Regions
- **Beloved Saint of Italy — St. Giovanni Battista Scalabrini**
- T's Ultimate Must-Sees and Dos in Milan and Lombardy
- T's Ultimate Must-Sees and Dos in the Piedmont Region
- T's Ultimate Must-Sees and Dos in the Veneto Region

SACRED SPACES

- **Madonna della Corona:** The Crown Jewel of Lake Garda's Mount Baldo
- **La Sindone:** The Shroud of Turin and the Duomo di Torino
- **Sacro Monte di Orta:** The Holy Hills and the Far Reach of St. Francis
- **The Hermitage of St. Catherine (Santa Caterina del Sasso, Lago di Maggiore):** A Stunning and Serene Lakeside Sanctuary on Lake Maggiore

FASCINATING PLACES

- **Navigating the Navigli:** The Often-Overlooked Canal District of Milan
- **Up on the Roof:** The Spectacular Roof of the Duomo in Milan
- **No Small Matter:** Piedmont and the Birth of the Big Bench Community Project
- **Murano, Burano, and Torcello:** Glass Blowing, Lace Making, and Living la Dolce Vita in Venice

CELEBRATIONS AND SIGNATURE DISHES

- **Regata Storica Venice**
- **T's Cotoletta alla Milanese:** Veal Milanese

LOVELY LAKES, ENDLESS ACRES, AND CAPTIVATING CANALS
EXPLORING ITALY'S SCENIC NORTHERN REGIONS

- - - - - - -

What I love about the northern area of Italy in these three amazing regions is the variety offered to visitors. You could easily plant yourself in one of them for a week or longer and have more than enough to do, see,

View of Lake Como from Bellagio

Opposite: Bellagio

St. Mark's Square

and enjoy — regardless of your interests. Or you could hop from region to region, by car or train, perhaps beginning in the Lake District of Lombardy, stopping for a few nights in the fabulous and peaceful wine country of Piedmont, and then head east to Veneto enjoying the mosaics of Ravenna before wrapping up your northern experiences in romantic Venice. There really is something for everyone, whether you're a hiker, biker, boater, wine connoisseur, faithful pilgrim, or foodie: these regions are diverse enough for every taste and interest and offer enormous amounts of natural and architectural beauty as well as religious and historic significance.

Who hasn't dreamed about strolling the cobblestone streets of Lake Como's stunning Bellagio, floating along the Grand Canal in Venice, or visiting Venice's St. Mark's Square and the remarkable basilica that gave the piazza its name?

In between these two major areas loaded with attractions are some of the other wonderful sites Italy has to offer including the city of Milan. "Milano" is often used as a starting point for a northern vacation to Italy, offering quick half-day tours that can be enjoyed before heading on to one of the nearby lakes. That's fine, but it is worth so much more than just a short visit.

In addition to touring the duomo, viewing the *Last Supper*, and having an Aperol Spritz in the luxurious Galleria Mall, all must-do items on any Lombardy vacation itinerary, what about an evening in some of the truly unique neighborhoods such as the incredibly hip Navigli district? This area in the southwestern part of the city is filled with boutiques, wine bars, art galleries, and great restaurants planted along two main manmade canals that were once used to transport goods and for irrigation. Navigli offers opportunity for *la dolce far niente*, the sweetness of doing nothing.

For those seeking a truly spiritual experience, the Shrine of Madonna della Corona, not far from Lake Garda, is simply glorious as well as awe inspiring as it was built into the amazingly steep cliffside of Mt. Baldo.

The city of Turin also should not be missed. Turin sits along the River Po and has a rich and royal past. In addition to important churches, such as St. John the Baptist which houses the famous Shroud

Piedmont

of Turin, and Our Lady of Help of Christians, where St. John Bosco is buried, Turin is also filled with parks and green spaces and is also home to many art galleries — not to mention forty museums. It is a former industrial hub, the birthplace of the Fiat, but it truly embraces its natural surroundings, including being part of the Sacro Monte or the Holy Hills of Piedmont and Lombardy.

The Piedmont region is also where the Big Bench Community Project was born, another favorite attraction of mine that offers visitors, residents, and Americans who've relocated to Italy a chance to truly feel like a kid again as they literally sit in a big bench looking out over spectacular scenery.

This is why the phrase "northern lights" came to mind when I sat down to plan sections of *Italy's Shrines and Wonders*. These three regions shine so very brightly from the top of the boot and the bottom of the Alps. They encourage us to take our time and taste and see God's goodness in so many ways.

Opposite: Lake Como with Bellano in the background

BELOVED SAINT OF ITALY

St. Giovanni Battista Scalabrini

- **Relics:** *Piacenza Cathedral in Piacenza (Province of Piacenza, Emilia-Romagna Region)*
- **Patron Saint:** *Italian immigrants, missionaries, catechists, and Piacenza*
- **Canonized:** *October 9, 2022 by Pope Francis*
- **Feast Day:** *June 1*

Born on July 7, 1839 in Fino Mornasco, the third of eight children, as a child Giovanni would frequently recite the Angelus and had a deep devotion to St. Joseph and Francis de Sales that lasted all his life.

Considered a "model shepherd" with the heart of a missionary, St. Giovanni Battista Scalabrini burned with zeal for God and his people. As bishop of Piacenza, he exhausted himself with spreading the catechism, love for the Eucharist, and tending the sick and poor, especially Italian emigrants who were forced to leave to other countries to survive. He started new religious orders, reformed seminaries, comforted prisoners, saved farmers and workers from famine by selling his valuables, his chalice, and his horses, and afterward walked on foot to visit the people of his diocese.

Pope Benedict XV thought of him as a "bishop beyond compare." Before his death on June 1, 1905 in Piacenza, his last words were "Lord, I am ready. Let us go."

T's Italy

LOMBARDY REGION
HIGHLIGHTS

The Lombardy or "Lombardia" Region is located in northern Italy. The north side is bordered by Switzerland. The capital of this region, **Milan**, is most notable for being a global hub of fashion and finance, with many high-end designer shops and restaurants. Its Gothic-style famous **Duomo di Milano Cathedral**, as well as the Santa Maria delle Grazie convent, where Leonardo da Vinci's painting of *The Last Supper* is hung, testify to centuries of rich history, art and culture. **Lake Como** is one of the most famous lakes and upscale alpine resort areas in northern Italy, with stunning scenery.

From north to south, Lombardy is physically divided into three geographical parts: the mountainous Alpines to the foothills of the mountains to the plains sloping gently to the Po River. The alpine

Leonardo da Vinci's The Last Supper

region reaches over thirteen thousand feet. Lombardy is also Italy's leading agricultural area — mainly on the irrigated plains of the Po River valley, producing mainly rice, wheat, corn, and sugar beets.

Right: Sunset over the River Po
Middle: Statue of Antonio Stradivari in Cremona, the birthplace of the legendary luthier
Left: La Scala opera house, Milan

MILAN AND LOMBARDY REGIONS
T'S ULTIMATE MUST-SEES AND DOS

– – – – – – – –

DUOMO DI MILANO

The most famous cathedral in Milan.

GALLERIA VITTORIO EMANUELE II

The enchanting and oldest shopping center in the world.

SANTA MARIA DELLE GRAZIE

The beautiful Milano church of Santa Maria delle Grazie houses *The Last Supper* (also called *Il Cenacolo*) by Leonardo da Vinci — one of the most recognized and appreciated artistic masterpieces in the world.

TEATRO ALLA SCALA

La Scala, one of the world's most famous opera houses, is in Milan. It was founded in 1778, and is where talented artists such as Giuseppe Verdi and Luciano Pavarotti have collaborated/performed.

CANAL DISTRICT

This favorite stop of mine is a never-ending walkway of shops, restaurants, and wine bars. Also, it's not exactly on the average tourist's sightseeing list which makes it even more attractive.

LAKE COMO

Be sure to visit the stunning lakeside cities in Lombardy along Lake Como including Como, Varenna, and Bellagio.

LAKE GARDA

Visit the largest lake in Italy: Lake Garda. Be sure to visit the sanctuary of **Madonna della Corona**. Even those who don't consider themselves very religious will marvel at the dedication of the faithful who built this place of prayer and solitude hundreds of years ago. The drive up the mountain is an experience all its own.

SIRMIONE

This is a charming castle town on the water, and one of the most picturesque villages along the Lake Garda and in the entire lake district of Italy.

MONTE BALDO

Take the cable car ride up the mountain, which rotates 360 degrees, adding to the already jaw dropping views.

CREMONA

Located about sixty miles south of Milan, this ancient "Violin Capital of the World" was awarded a place on the UNESCO world heritage list in 2012. World-renowned violin maker, Antonio Stradivari, was born here. Be sure to check out the Museo del Violino (Violin Museum), and be sure to see the magnificent Torrazzo and Vertical Museum, which is a 365-foot bell tower that is known for its breathtaking panorama views and time-measuring. The façade of this medieval bell tower boasts the largest astronomical clock in the world.

T'S TRAVEL TIP

If time allows, visit both Bellagio and Como using the picturesque town of Varenna as your base. You won't regret it, and as a matter of fact, you won't want to leave. It's that lovely and peaceful.

T's Italy

PIEDMONT REGION
HIGHLIGHTS

The Piedmont or "Piemonte" Region of Italy is known for its sophisticated cuisine and wine and for its famous gorgonzola cheeses, fall truffles, and risotto. It is the second-largest region of Italy — located in the northern part of the country, and it borders France and Switzerland. It sits at the foot of the Alps. It is so picturesque due to its surrounding mountains and stunning lakes and views. Turin is the most famous city in this region and is crossed by Italy's longest river, the Po River.

This region's name comes from the Italian word *pie* which means foot and *monte* which means mountain — because it stands at the foot of the mountains. It has four major geographic areas — the Alps, the Lake District, the plain of the Po River Valley where rice is cultivated, and the hills of Piedmonte where winemaking is predominant. Lake Maggiore is lovely to visit and is the second longest of the three main lakes in Italy.

Piedmont Region
T'S ULTIMATE MUST-SEES AND DOS

— — — — — — — —

LAKE MAGGIORE

Although it borders both the Lombardy and Piedmont regions, Lake Maggiore runs nearby the Swiss Alps, so it boasts of stunning views. With thirty miles of coastline, it is the second-largest lake in Italy. If it seems a bit crowded, head over to the lesser-known Lake Orta, tucked behind it. Then spend some time visiting beautiful cities along the coast: Stresa, Arona, Cannobio, Locarno, Baveno, and Verbania.

SAN GIULIO ISLAND

While visiting Orta, make sure to slow down and walk around Orta's San Giulio Island. This tiny island is known as the Island of Silence and has a twelfth-century basilica. There is a circular path the Italians call la Via del Silenzio (the Way of Silence). Special meditations are posted along the path meant to allow time for silent reflection.

TASTE THE WINES OF PIEDMONT

Make sure to try some of the best red wines from the Piedmont region, especially the Barbera and Nebbiolo.

CATHEDRAL OR DUOMO OF TURIN

The Cathedral of Turin is one of the great Gothic structures in northern Italy, completed in the late fifteenth century. It houses the beautiful chapel of the famous Shroud of Turin.

Right: Autumn day in Piedmont with snowcapped mountains in the backdrop
Middle: A winery in Piedmont
Left: Asti Cathedral

SHRINE OF BL. PIER GIORGIO FRASSATI

When you are in the Duomo of Turin, don't miss visiting the resting place and learn about the life of Bl. Pier Giorgio Frassati, a young amazing blessed and mountain climber from the Piedmont region that used travels up the mountain to evangelize about the Holy Eucharist and the Blessed Virgin Mary.

BASILICA OF OUR LADY HELP OF CHRISTIANS IN TURIN

The basilica where St. John Bosco, the beloved saint who founded a home for poor boys, is buried.

THE SACRED MOUNTAINS

Nine "Sacri Monti" or Holy Mountains are groups of chapels and other buildings located in Turin and built in the fifteenth century dedicated to different aspects of the Christian faith.

ALBA

Visit the hometown of the famous Nutella hazelnut chocolate spread and the famous white truffle, considered the best in the world.

ASTI

Visit the beautiful Asti Cathedral, known as the Cattedrale di Santa Maria Assunta, the Bapistery of San Pietro (twelfth-century structure with adjoining cloisters and a museum), or check out the stunning nearby agritourism winery, Moretti Adimari. If you like to hike, visit the Valle Andona, Botto or the Grande Special Nature Regional Reserve, which boasts of spectacular trails and nature walks.

T's Italy

T'S TRAVEL TIP!

Take a truffle-hunting tour in Piedmont!

Follow the truffle hunters and their truffle-hunting dogs and watch them miraculously detect where these Italian gems are buried.

Shopping for all things truffle with friend Fr. John Klockeman, Archdiocese of Minneapolis-St. Paul

VENETO REGION
HIGHLIGHTS

Located in the northeastern part of Italy along the Adriatic coastline, the Veneto Region of Italy is the fourth-largest region in Italy, bordered by Switzerland in the mountainous area of the Dolomites. Although the city of Venice, also known as "Veneto," is the most popular city in this region, Verona is the largest city in this region. Many are also familiar with the city of Padua, the resting place of one of the most popular saints, St. Anthony of Padua.

Veneto's capital city, Venice, has been called by many different names due to its unique geography: the "Queen of the Adriatic," the "City of Water," the "City of Bridges," the "City of Canals," the "City of Masks," the "Floating City," and the "City of Light." Venice is built on a chain of 118 small islands separated by canals and linked by over four hundred bridges. The islands are shallow and are enclosed by the mouth of two rivers — the Po and Piave Rivers, or more exactly between the Brenta and the Sile.

One of the most famous of the Venice sites is the Basilica of San Marco, housing the relics of St. Mark the evangelist. This city also boasts of its Venetian Gothic architecture, its beautiful hand-blown Murano glass, and its Mardi Gras Carnevale Festival. One of most famous Italian musicians is from this region: Catholic priest and baroque composer Antonio Lucio Vivaldi. Vivaldi is best known for his beloved violin concerto, *The Four Seasons.*

Popular foods in this region include polenta and risotto, as well as the Venetian pasta *bigoli,* which is like thick spaghetti made with buckwheat or whole wheat. The Venuto area in this region is most popular for its wine-making. Many also don't know that Veneto produces more bottles of DOC Wine than any other area in Italy. The Amarone della Valpolicella, a wine from the hills around Verona, is made with high-selected grapes and is among the more expensive red wines in the world.

Right: Casa di Giulietta (Juliet's House) in Verona
Middle: Glasswork in Murano
Left: Interior of St. Mark's Basilica

VENICE AND THE VENETO REGIONS
T'S ULTIMATE MUST-SEES AND DOS

- - - - - - - -

GONDOLA RIDE

Originating in Venice, the gondola is the preferred and official transportation choice in the city. The "streets" of Venice are the waterways and canals. I recommend you take at least one gondola ride.

Bridge of Sighs in Venice

ST. MARK'S BASILICA (CHURCH OF SAN MARCO) AND ST. MARK'S SQUARE

Enjoy a waterview drink or meal and practice *la dolce far niente*, soaking in the stunning view and square.

DOGE'S PALACE

A beautiful Venetian Gothic Style Palace founded in 1340.

BRIDGE OF SIGHS

A beautiful bridge that passes over the Rio di Palazzo.

MODERN ART MUSEUM

If art is your thing, you don't want to miss the modern art museum in Venice, the **Peggy Guggenheim Collection**.

VENETIAN ISLANDS OF MURANO, BURANO, AND TORCELLO

Hop on the Venice water bus to visit the lovely Venetian Islands. The Island of Murano is known for its long tradition of glassmaking. Burano is even more beautiful than Murano and is known for brightly colored fishermen's houses and famous lacemaking. The shops sell lace products like linens and clothes.

ST. ANTHONY OF PADUA

Take a forty-minute drive west for a day trip to Padua from Venice and visit the tomb of the miraculous saint, Anthony of Padua.

Basilica of St. Anthony of Padua in Padua

JULIET'S HOME IN VERONA

Take a day trip to stunning Verona, nestled between the river **Adige** and **Lake Garda** and visit Shakespeare's famous romantic setting for the moving tale of Romeo and Juliet.

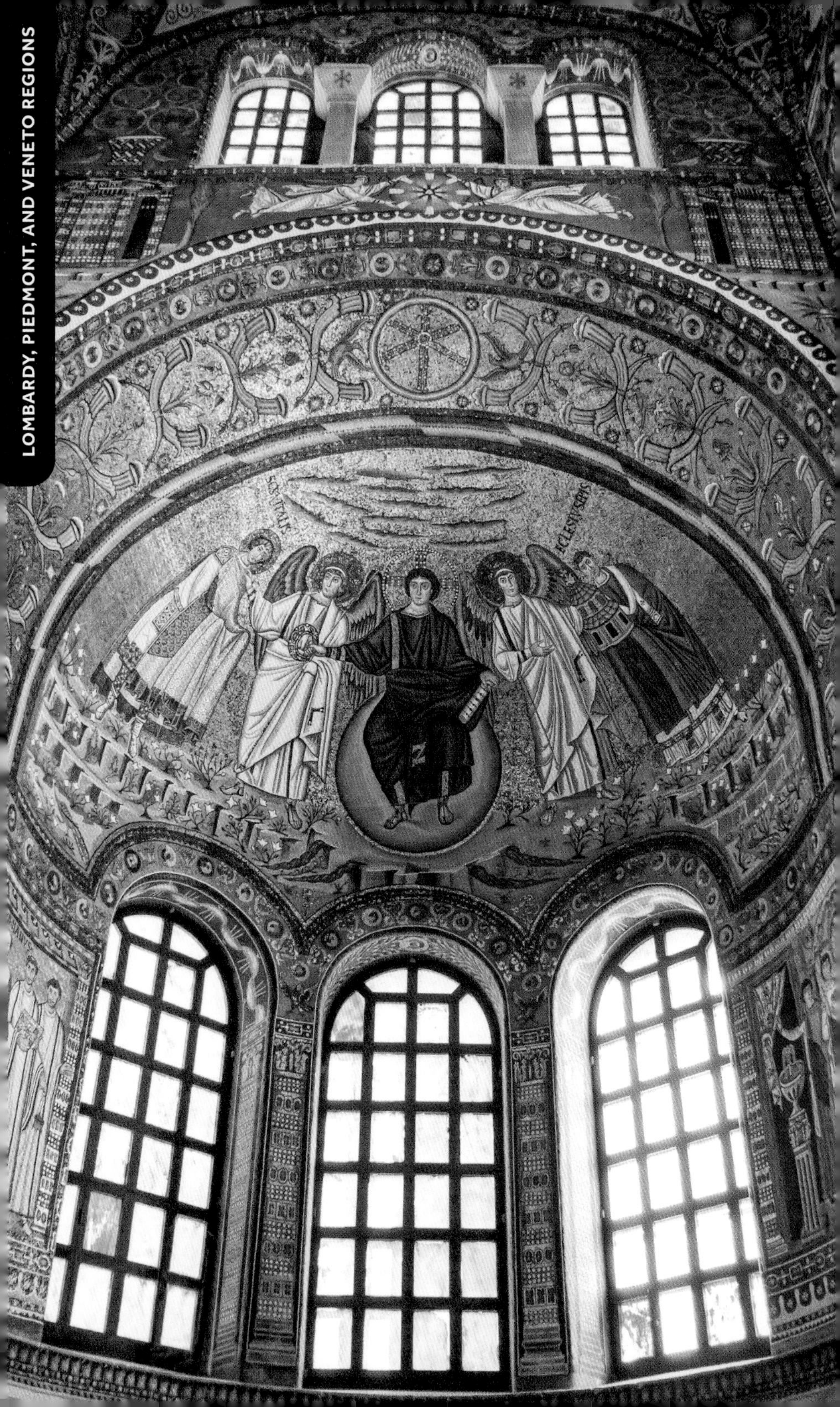
SCS VITALIS
ECLESIVS EPIS

LOMBARDY, PIEDMONT, AND VENETO REGIONS
SACRED SPACES

- - - - - - -

The northern lights of Italy offer those seeking deep spiritual experience truly transcendent opportunities. Beyond the major basilicas and religious art in magnificent museums, the sacred spaces of the north offer serenity among some of the most spectacular scenery. One location might embrace the natural surroundings while another is designed by architects and molded by the hands of sculptors. It's obvious that all those involved desired to carry on the Faith by leaving behind a legacy of love for God, His creation, and His Church.

MADONNA DELLA CORONA
The Crown Jewel of Lake Garda's Mt. Baldo

"You simply have to go to this shrine!"

Those were the words of a volunteer who was helping me at a speaking event several years ago. As we were setting up my book table in the parish hall, this dear woman, also of Italian heritage, was just bursting at the seams. She could not say enough about the Sanctuary of Madonna della Corona. She was a listener of mine and enjoyed following my Italy experiences.

Opposite: Mosaics in the Basilica of San Vitale in Ravenna

Shrine of Madonna del Corona

She then proceeded to show me jaw-dropping photos of her visit to Monte Baldo, nestled in the mountains east of Lombardy's gorgeous Lake Garda. After finally making our way there several years ago, I can say the description on the official website sums up merely some of what you will experience.

> This place is ideal for those who want to combine moments
> of prayer and inner peace to opportunities to relax and enjoy
> the silence of the shows that nature can offer in this lovely
> place.[1]

Madonna della Corona sits almost 2,600 feet above sea level, clinging to the cliffs of Mt. Baldo, suspended between Heaven and earth. The shrine's earliest religious connections date back to the year 1000, when it was occupied by local hermits from the Abbey of St. Zeno. St. Zeno

---

[1] "Presentation and History," Basilica Santuario Madonna della Corona, accessed September 3, 2024, https://www.madonnadellacorona.it/en/presentation-and-history/.

was a bishop of nearby Verona who lived and served in the fourth century.

A pilgrimage destination since the Middle Ages, the background of how the sanctuary came to be is almost as mind-blowing as the structure itself. According to one local tradition, the shrine was built in honor a statue of the Blessed Mother holding the crucified Jesus in her arms. The statue was allegedly discovered after villagers in the surrounding area noticed a bright light coming from near the top of the mountain. The light was emanating from the statue, and even though the people on several different occasions tried to keep it safe in their church, the statue kept disappearing only to be rediscovered in its original location. That's when a decision was made to build a chapel.

There is another version of the chapel's origins that dates to the mid-sixteenth century, when the statue was miraculously moved from the Island of Rhodes during a Muslim invasion. But this conflicts with the early veneration of another image of Mary and Jesus, a fourteenth-century painting, in the original chapel. We do know that it officially became a shrine in 1625. The fact that the site was so inaccessible for so long helped in its preservation.

However the shrine came to be, we can be grateful that the Madonna della Corona is with us today. In 1975, major renovation work turned the shrine into a larger complex measuring 6,500 square feet. Access routes were improved and rearranged, turning it into a popular pilgrimage site in northern Italy. Inside the shrine are amazing sculptures made of white Carrara marble of Our Lady of Sorrows, St. Mary Magdalene, St. Joseph, and St. John the Baptist. There are also several bronze pieces by the architect Raffaele Bonente from Verona. It's hard to take your eyes off his altarpiece and the bronze panels portraying the Nativity, Crucifixion, and Pentecost.

Pilgrims can certainly spend extended hours in prayer inside the shrine admiring the religious art and marveling at how such a stunning church could be built so high up and so deep into a side of a cliff. They will find great inspiration outside, simply looking out over the valley or praying along the outdoor path of the Stations of the Cross.

Although gorgeous Lake Garda is not visible from the shrine, no trip to the lake would be complete without making the trek up Mt. Baldo to visit Madonna della Corona.

LA SINDONE
The Shroud of Turin and the Duomo di Torino

*Jesus turned, and saw them following, and said to them, "What do you seek?" And they said to him, "Rabbi" (which means Teacher), "where are you staying? He said to them, "**Come and see.**" They came and saw where he was staying; and they stayed with him that day.*

— John 1:38–39

These words of Christ to His disciples ring in our ears as well as we look upon La Sidone or Sindone di Torino (the Shroud of Turin). We do not have to believe that it is the actual burial cloth of Christ, but we are invited to "come and see" as Jesus told His soon-to-be disciples in this passage.

But how can one "come and see" when the Shroud of Turin is rarely offered for public viewing? Thanks to the history and information provided by the Church, we can learn a great deal about one of the most talked about and studied artifacts in human history, which is here in Turin's beautiful gothic Cathedral of St. John the Baptist, where it has been kept for over four centuries.

The fourteen-foot-long linen cloth bears the full-sized image of a naked, crucified man. Although the Catholic Church has remained neutral about the shroud's authenticity, leaving it up to scientific research, we believe that the cloth still serves as an important symbol of Christians' Faith. And so it has been venerated by Christians for hundreds of years.

Reliquary of St. John the Baptist, Cathedral of St. John the Baptist, Turin

During the height of COVID in 2020, the archbishop of Turin organized a livestreamed exposition of the Shroud on Holy Saturday. In response, Pope Francis said that he joined in prayer turning his gaze to the one he called the "Man of the Shroud."

> In His face "we also see the faces of many sick brothers and sisters, especially those more alone and less well cared for. But also, all the victims of wars and violence, slavery and persecution."

> As Christians, and in the light of the Scriptures, continues Pope Francis, "we contemplate in this Cloth the icon of the Lord Jesus crucified, dead and risen. We entrust ourselves to Him." "Jesus gives us the strength to face every trial with faith, hope and love, in the certainty that the Father always listens to His children who cry out to Him."[2]

[2]   "Pope Expresses Gratitude for Exposition of the Shroud of Turin," Vatican News, April 10, 2020, https://www.vaticannews.va/en/pope/news/2020-04/pope-expresses-gratitude-for-exposition-of-the-shroud-of-turin.html.

The Cathedral of St. John the Baptist (Cathedral of Turin) is considered a Renaissance church, rebuilt in the late fifteenth century. On the church's façade you'll notice Renaissance-style figures depicting God the Father, God the Son, and St. John the Baptist along with musical angels. On the inside there are several exquisitely detailed chapels featuring altars adorned with paintings of several different saints who are the patrons of various trades, including artists, goldsmiths, bakers, and shoemakers.

One could spend hours admiring the religious artwork on the walls in the sacred spaces of the cathedral. But visitors will also be amazed by looking up. In 2018 the Guarini Chapel, where the Shroud is kept, including a dome that is considered a baroque masterpiece designed by Guarino Guarini, reopened following a major renovation project. The dome is admired for its intricate design with overlapping or interlocking arches which allow for an amazing display of daylight. The Shroud is kept in the Guarini Chapel, a carefully climate-controlled space especially built for safekeeping, in a "conservation case." That case is itself enclosed in a large metal box.

Christians will find themselves right outside the chest that holds the Shroud. They can "see" how reverently the Shroud is treated and can pray and contemplate the mystery that has captivated humankind for hundreds of years. Imagine being so close to what so many around the world believe is the burial cloth of God! There is also a fantastic Shroud Museum in the duomo complex and a marvelous bookstore where travelers can learn about the Shroud's amazing journey to Turin and the incredible stories of those who protected the cloth and helped find its permanent home.

The Cathedral of Turin also carries special meaning for Catholics for reasons other than the Shroud. Many faithful flock here to venerate the tomb of Bl. Pier Giorgio Frassati, known as the "saint for the youth of the third millennium." Pope St. John Paul II called him the "boy of the eight beatitudes."

Born in Turin into a wealthy family that did not embrace or regularly practice the Catholic Faith, Pier Giorgio lived to serve the poor and strongly embraced Catholicism, becoming a lay Dominican and becoming active with many Catholic charities serving the poor in his area. He died in 1925 at the age of twenty-four.

My favorite quote from Pier Giorgio is one that is suitable for much contemplation inviting all of us to respond to Jesus' call to again "come and see." And if your Italy journey takes you to the Piedmont region and the elegant city of Turin, what a wonderful opportunity to reflect on his words inside the Cathedral of St. John the Baptist.

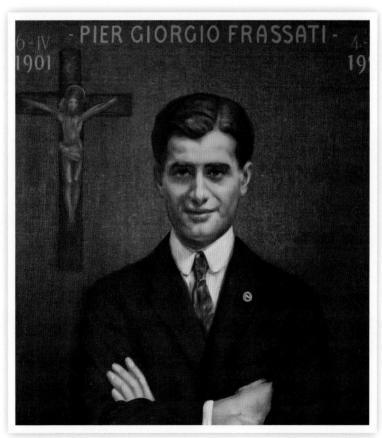

Bl. Pier Giorgio Frassati

"To live without faith, without a heritage to defend,
without battling constantly for truth, is not to live but
to 'get along'; we must never just 'get along.'"

— Bl. Pier Giorgio Frassati

SACRO MONTE DI ORTA
The Holy Hills and the Far Reach of St. Francis

The Sacro Monte (Holy Hills) of the Piedmont and Lombardy region afford pilgrims some of the most peaceful venues for prayer and contemplation. The Sacro Monte are a series of nine devotional centers scattered through the mountains of these two northern regions of Italy.

The sacred structures were built in the sixteenth and seventeenth centuries as part of the Counter-Reformation and feature scenes from Scripture interwoven with images from the lives of the saints, the life of the Blessed Mother, and the mysteries of the Rosary. The beauty of the Catholic Faith is presented in the Holy Hills through dramatic and colorful life-sized statues as well as through detailed paintings. The expressions of faith have also received great praise as superb examples of Renaissance art and are often referred to as the Great Mountain Theatre.

We visited one of the complexes during our stay in Lake Orta. Orta is a small, lovely lake nestled in the northeastern area of the Piedmont region not far from the much larger and more glamorous Lake Maggiore. Orta is one of Italy's best-kept secrets, providing great scenery, fine restaurants, a small shopping district, watersports, and hiking. And all of this without garnering the amount of attention of Maggiore and Como, translating into less congestion.

Orta also has something very special to offer those seeking a spiritual respite. Although again, Orta is not nearly as busy as its neighbors, it can get crowded with the locals in the know. That's why making a short ride or walk about the nearby San Nicolao Hill to the Sacred Mountain of Orta is such a treat.

This location is part of the Holy Hills and is named yet another site on the UNESCO world heritage list. This complex, made up of twenty chapels, is dedicated in great detail to the life of St. Francis of Assisi. Construction began in 1583, with the chapels scattered along the top of the hill above the lake offering incredible views of the water and San Guilio Island below. You could spend the entire day enjoying the natural beauty from the Holy Hill vantage point, but there is so much beauty offered by the artwork inside the chapels.

The chapels of Sacro Monte di Orta are filled with 376 statues and frescoes by Pier Francesco Mazzucchelli, known as Morazzone, an Italian artist based in northern Italy, primarily in the city of Milan. His work can be found in at least two other complexes that make up the Holy Hills.

Thanks to the realism of the sculptures inside the chapel, Sacro Monte di Orta places you back in the thirteenth century alongside Francis, his monks, and the people of Assisi, Rome, and other areas important in the life of this great saint. The Sacro Monte di Orta is the only Holy Hill across Piedmont and Lombardy that is totally dedicated to the life of a saint.

Deacon Dom and Teresa at Lago Maggiore

St. Francis welcomes you as you begin the journey by walking under an arch with a beautiful statue. You end the pilgrimage in the Romanesque church of San Nicolao, renovated in the seventeenth century and modeled after the basilica of St. Francis in Assisi. It's no surprise that this portion of the Holy Hills is also known as the Assisi of the North.

THE HERMITAGE OF ST. CATHERINE
(Santa Caterina del Sasso, Lago di Maggiore): A Stunning and Serene Lakeside Sanctuary on Lake Maggiore

Although the Lake District of Lombardy and Piedmont are certainly inviting, exciting, and bustling with activities, at some point you may want to break away. That's why I am grateful for the sacred spaces that sit among some of the most prominent tourist areas of Italy. They really help you refocus and concentrate, as a late colleague of mine, Al Kresta, used to say, "on the things that matter most."

St. Catherine del Sasso Hermitage

Santa Caterina del Sasso (St. Catherine of Stone) clings to the cliffs along the eastern coast of Lake Maggiore. Maggiore is the second-largest lake in Italy in the region of Lombardy. The most populated and popular area of the lake is the western shore in the Piedmont region. Along with Sacro Monte di Orta, this shrine is among my new favorite sacred spaces of Italy. These sanctuaries provide so much serenity as they combine the best of the spiritual, the artistic, and the natural. The stories behind them are fascinating and inspiring as it takes incredible faith, not to mention money, time, and talent to erect these magnificent places of worship on challenging terrain and often in the middle of nowhere.

Catholic tradition says that this hermitage was founded in the late twelfth century by a local merchant, Alberto Besozzi. As he was struggling to cross the lake during a storm, he called on the intercession of St. Catherine of Alexandria. After surviving the shipwreck, he decided to retreat to the mountains to live a life of prayer and solitude as a show of gratitude. This was a complete change from the wealthy man who, prior to that near-death experience, lived a life of greed and debauchery. He also decided to build a chapel in honor of the saint whom he believed helped save his life.

He became a spiritual leader to the Christians in the area, who asked for his help and guidance during a severe plague. Alberto Besozzi is now Bl. Alberto Besozzi, whose remains are still there today.

To reach the hermitage, visitors can climb down the eighty steps, or take an elevator built into the rock. The site is made up of three different buildings connected by porticos and pathways, providing amazing vistas of the lake and the surrounding countryside. You can't help but notice those approaching the hermitage from the water, some by boat, some making their way there on a warm day by jumping in the clear water and swimming from a nearby beach. However you decide to get there, just get there, as Santa Caterina del Sasso is one of the most splendid and evocative settings in the Lake District of northern Italy.

LOMBARDY, PIEDMONT, AND VENETO REGIONS
FASCINATING PLACES

Canals in the middle of a landlocked major metropolis. Something quite large that makes you feel small, and for a good reason. Italy's own Byzantium. These are just a few of the descriptions connected to some of the many fascinating places in Italy's northern lights. The places on which I decided to focus for this final section of *Italy's Shrines and Wonders* are very different but are exceptional. Some are destinations geared toward entertainment and dining. Others are more suited for taking a deep dive into art appreciation and local culture. All the sites will take you somewhere special and are places that will hopefully help you truly appreciate the incredible variety of this country and return to discover more spaces, places, and destinations that are like no other.

NAVIGATING THE NAVIGLI
The Often-Overlooked Canal District of Milan

Canals in the middle of Milan? "Wait, what?"

Our pilgrimage bus was pulling out of Milan's Malpensa Airport to begin our northern Italy tour when our guide chuckled and told us all about the Navigli, a district in the southwestern part of the city that

Opposite: A fresco in a chapel on the Sacred Mountain of Orta

developed from artificial canals built in the twelfth century. These were navigable canals, built to transport goods. The canals were even used to bring in some of the heavy materials, such as marble, used to construct Milan's iconic Duomo di Milano. Renaissance genius Leonardo da Vinci was brought to Milan by the duke in 1482 to improve the city. Of course, his *Last Supper* was considered his greatest contribution, but some local experts suspect that he may have helped with the renovation of the canals.

Only in Italy could such an amazing and eclectic area be born from something so functional and at the same time medieval. Navigli is now one of the city's most popular and treasured neighborhoods.

Once we had some free time during our stop in Milan, I hopped in a cab on my own and made my way there. Given the traffic, I could have saved a ton of hard-earned euros and made my way via a much more affordable public transportation mode such as bus, subway, or tram. However, the expensive ride certainly paid off. The neighborhood was an absolute delight to discover and explore.

The Navigli District of Milan

I walked up and down walkways along the canals, strolled across quaint bridges that reminded me of the streets of Venice, and found a place to dine alfresco. It felt like a city within a city, and I noticed that most of the people there were speaking Italian. Clearly Americans hadn't discovered the cool canals of Milan yet.

There are now two main canals, Naviglio Grande and Naviglio Pavese, and in the warmer weather you can even hop on a boat and see the area from the water. The area is filled with dining and drinking options including upscale restaurants and trendy bars, not to mention plenty of galleries and boutiques. It's a refreshing break from the big city even though you're still in the heart of the metropolis.

UP ON THE ROOF
The Spectacular Roof of the Duomo in Milan

On the roof, it's peaceful as can be
And there the world below can't bother me.
— The Drifters, 1962

When it comes to seeing Italy's second-most populated city, Milan, I concur with the Drifters and their oldie-but-goodie hit "Up on the Roof." Heading to the top or up on the roof of the famous Duomo di Milano is a chance to see the cathedral's flying buttresses, pinnacles, three thousand statues, 150 gargoyles, and some 135 spires up close in vivid detail.[3]

The Duomo, the Cathedral of the Nativity of St. Mary, is the largest Gothic church in all of Italy. Work on the cathedral began in the fourteenth century and was finally finished with the final details on the façade in 1965. Experts estimate that there are close to 3,400 statues in

---

[3] "The Terraces," Duomo di Milano, accessed September 3, 2024, https://www.duomomilano.it/en/art-and-culture/the-terraces/.

Duomo, Cathedral of Milan

and on the Duomo including those on the roof. You can buy a combination ticket to tour both the inside of the church and the roof, which I highly recommend. You can climb 250 stairs or, for a slightly more expensive ticket, take the elevator.

This Duomo tour is different than other rooftop excursions offered at many other iconic and important churches across Italy, such as St. Peter's in Rome or the Duomo in Florence, because of this roof's incredible detail. The top of the Duomo di Milano catches your attention right away even from a distance. The rooftop terraces have been referred to as the "stone forest" and are one of the most evocative places of Milan. And yes, being up on the roof of the Duomo does offer amazing panoramas of the city and the surrounding Po Valley. I guarantee, however, that despite those views, your eyes will be focused elsewhere.

The creativity stunned the great American writer Mark Twain during his visit in 1867. He chronicled his trip to the Holy Land and Europe in his 1869 publication of *Innocents Abroad*, referring to the Duomo as, among other things, "a miracle in marble."

LOMBARDY, PIEDMONT, AND VENETO REGIONS

Toward dusk, we drew near Milan and caught glimpses of the city and the blue mountain peaks beyond. But we were not caring for these things — they did not interest us in the least. We were in a fever of impatience; we were dying to see the renowned cathedral! We watched — in this direction and that — all around — everywhere. We needed no one to point it out — we did not wish anyone to point it out — we would recognize it even in the desert of the great Sahara. At last, a forest of graceful needles, shimmering in the amber sunlight, rose slowly above the pygmy housetops, as one sometimes sees, in the far horizon, a gilded and pinnacled mass of cloud lift itself above the waste of waves at sea — the Cathedral! We knew it in a moment. Half of that night, and all of the next day, this architectural autocrat was our sole object of interest. What a wonder it is! So grand, so solemn, so vast! And yet so delicate, so airy, so graceful! A very world of solid weight, and yet it seems in the soft moonlight only

Rooftop terraces of the Milan Cathedral

a fairy delusion of frost-work that might vanish with a breath!
How sharply its pinnacled angles and its wilderness of spires
were cut against the sky, and how richly their shadows fell
upon its snowy roof! It was a vision! — a miracle! — an
anthem sung in stone, a poem wrought in marble!

This attraction is extremely popular, so it is important not only to carve
out time for the experience but to make reservations ahead of time. If
you don't want to wait in line for hours at the ticket office, purchase the
tickets online through the main website, https://www.duomomilano.
it, which also offers guided tours.

Go see the "miracle in marble" inside and out, but especially up on
the roof.

NO SMALL MATTER
Piedmont and the Birth of the Big Bench Community Project

*"Truly, I say to you, whoever does not receive the
kingdom of God like a child shall not enter it."*

— Mark 10:15

Given all that there is to experience in Italy, as you've been reading in
this book; all the sacred spaces and fascinating places, why would anyone
put sitting on a park bench in this magnificent country on their "must-do"
list? It seems rather silly, given all *Bella Italia* has to offer. But as we began
to wrap up this journey through Italy, I hope you've come to agree that
if Italy is in your travel plans, then that park bench should be close to
the top of that "must-do" list.

These particular benches are hardly what you might see in your
hometown or local gathering space. They are part of what's known as
the Big Bench Project. The effort has been around for several years, the

The Big Bench Project, Piedmont

brainchild of an American couple who moved to northern Italy's Piedmont region. Chris and Catherine Bangle certainly understand the importance of downtime and reflection. They fell in love with the landscape and were trying to get more visitors to appreciate the natural beauty of Italy by simply hopping onto a big bench — and yes, looking at the world through different lenses and with childlike wonder.

Chris Bangle, a designer, came up with the plans, and shares those plans with those who share his vision on the Big Bench website: "How to become children again by rediscovering the landscape" and to have "an experience to share or a moment to rediscover ourselves."[4]

Though not coming from a religious perspective per se, the folks behind the effort so strongly believe in *la dolce far niente* that they either built or supported the building of hundreds of oversized, brightly colored benches in Italy and around Europe. There is no better time to slow down, sit down, and learn to see the world from unique and fun vantage points that not only help you catch your breath but also make

[4] Big Bench Community Project, accessed September 3, 2024, https://bigbenchcommunityproject.org/en/home.

you appreciate the Italy pilgrimage or holiday experience more deeply — and just as, if not more importantly, help you feel like a child again. And doesn't Our Lord tell us that we are to have a childlike faith?

> Truly, I say to you, unless you turn and become like children, you will not enter the kingdom of heaven. (Matt. 18:3)

So far, we've experienced looking at the world from this very different perspective from three different regions including Piedmont, Umbria, and most recently along the coast of Calabria in Tropea. These benches are so large that you automatically do indeed feel like a kid again. You'll have to climb up cement blocks or small wine barrels (only in Italy of course) to take a seat. For those of us old enough to remember, think Edith Ann, comedienne Lily Tomlin's character from the late 1960s comedy show *Laugh-In*. Tomlin portrayed a five-year-old girl who sounded off about life from a giant rocking chair.

The benches are placed in spaces that can be accessed by the public. Among the other requirements to receive the design from the Big Bench Project, the structures also must be erected in a "panoramic and contemplative" location away from large buildings and structures. In other words, off the beaten path.

Each venue requires a bit of an effort to reach, but that is part of the Big Bench adventure, searching for them again off the beaten path, following backroads that can lead you to some surprising locations including secluded medieval villages, or a lovely winery owned by locals, or the "real" Italy as I like to say. And don't worry, there is plenty of signage along the way, and the views are beyond spectacular and well worth the trek.

To make the most of your experience, I've been reminding you more than once to slow down. However, even though I am not a betting woman, I would bet that hopping on a gigantic, bright bench wasn't on your radar. But it should be.

So, as you plan that Italy dream vacation, be sure and visit the Big Bench website and coordinate your own Edith Ann experience on your way to Florence, Venice, or Turin. Take it all in much like we did as children when climbing up that tree in our backyard or sitting on the beach for hours. Feeling small again is a very big deal when it comes to truly appreciating one of the most beautiful places on God's green earth.

MURANO, BURANO, AND TORCELLO
Glass Blowing, Lace Making, and Living la Dolce Vita in Venice

"Venice, the most touristy place in the world, is still just completely magic to me."

— Frances Mayes

Venice has long been, as author Frances Mayes aptly described, the most touristy place in the world. To control crowds, in recent years the city issued a five-euro daily entry fee as well as a temporary ban on cruise

Doge Palace

ships docking in the historic quarter not far from St. Mark's Square. In 2023, Venice was warned by experts from UNESCO that it faced the possibility of being added to the list of world heritage sites in danger thanks to the impact of massive tourism.

But I also agree with Mayes's sentiment that Venice is "completely magical," with the magic extending far beyond the main sites of San Marco, the Grand Canal, Doge Place, the Bridge of Sighs, and the lovely Rialto Bridge. I mentioned earlier that when I was strolling through the canal district of Milan it reminded me so much of Venice. On our first visit in 2001, hours were spent getting lost on its enchanting little streets, watching the gondolas pass by, and stopping on quaint street corners to peek into the many shops. We got lost but as a result found parts of the real Venice in the process, including a great restaurant that we just bumped into, Ristorante Sempione. We had a window seat to the waterways and ate and drank as we watched the world float by.

We also went much further and ventured out to the islands of Venice. Half of the fun was getting there, leaving from St. Mark's Square hopping on more than one *vaporetto*, the Venice waterbus, for our own island-hopping experience.

MURANO AND BURANO

We made a full day out of visiting the glass-making island of Murano and the adorable lace-making island of Burano. You've heard of Murano glass? Well, you don't have to buy a tour or have one of the factories transfer you out to their location in a fancy water taxi, only to be pressured to ship home a pricey chandelier or a set or two or three of multicolored wine glasses. That's a racket. You can, instead, venture into any of the stores on Murano at leisure and see the glass-making in several locations. Venice had been known for its glass-making for quite some time and in the late thirteenth century, local leadership decided to move all the glass-making factories to Murano. They were concerned that the fires used to make the glass would lead to fires in the city. Murano is a

Burano – Center for fishing and lace-making

lovely place with some very good, as you might imagine, waterfront restaurants. We ate dinner at a *ristorante* with steps going right into the canal just inches away from our table.

Burano is another one of those Italian villages that seem like a setting for a Hollywood film. It's a small, colorful fishing village that just doesn't seem real. The houses are brightly colored, bright enough to burst through any fog. And that apparently was the idea behind painting the house here in such strong hues of blue, orange, green, and terra-cotta. The fishermen were concerned that they wouldn't be able to see their homes through the dense fog as they traveled along the lagoons of Venice.

Burano is also known for its lace-making. And on any day you can stroll along the canals and see the ladies carrying on the tradition. The art form dates to the sixteenth century, with the intricate Burano designs admired across Europe. Although lace-made products are now for the most part mass produced, the art has been passed on to local women. It's special to stroll along the canals here, stopping at some of the shops, and watch the older ladies crafting intricate patterns onto tablecloths, handkerchiefs, and parasols. It's a great gift item for family, friends, and yourself. Every time you admire the craftsmanship that you brought home, memories of bright Burano will be front and center.

The easiest way to get to island-hop to Murano and Burano is by the waterbus. There is a line that will take you to Burano with a first stop in Murano.

TORCELLO

Another island worth visiting, especially for those interested in taking in more religious art but in a much more peaceful setting, is the sparsely populated Torcello, a quick boat ride from Burano. The Cathedral of Santa Maria Assunta is home to spectacular Byzantine mosaics. The church was built in the seventh century. The mosaics, including the spectacular depictions of the Last Supper, are from the eleventh through the thirteenth centuries.

The Last Judgment
(mosaic, 11 century)

The journey through history here continues with a small museum that houses treasures from elaborate homes from the fourteenth century. A good portion of the island is also a nature preserve, accessible only along special walking paths.

This peaceful place also has a handful of decent restaurants and is home to an upscale venue where Hemingway wrote portions of *Across the River and into the Trees*, his novel that begins with the story of a Civil War colonel remembering his time in the Venice area and a woman he met there.

Venice and its islands — magical indeed, but also very romantic.

Opposite: Canals in Venice

CELEBRATIONS

Regata Storica Venice

Italy is full of surprises. There are so many wonderful events, celebrations, and festivals in each region year-round that you're bound to run into to one or more of them, even if you don't plan on it. Such was the case on our second trip to Venice when we literally bumped into the famous Regata Storica.

We were spending a few days in Venice at the end of a ten-day organized tour. It was an extension offered by the travel company that we jumped at because we enjoyed Venice so much the first time around. We just happened to be doing one of our favorite Italy pastimes, wandering, and as we came back out to the Grand Canal we were overcome by the elegance that was floating in front of us, a never-ending line of gondolas beautifully decorated, manned by men and women in regal medieval costumes.

What a sight to behold! We soon learned that we somehow managed to plan our trip to coincide with this historic event.

The earliest record of the Regata dates back to the thirteenth century and occurs at the beginning of September. It is a water parade and race dedicated to the sport of Venetian rowing combining ceremony, pageantry, religion, and racing. It marks the end of a series of competitions throughout the year and is spread over an entire day, with a parade early on and a series of races in the afternoon. And it is breathtaking. Even if you're not planning a trip to Venice, check out the official website, complete with a detailed history of the Regata and some wonderful photos and videos.

LOMBARDY, PIEDMONT, AND VENETO REGION
SIGNATURE DISHES

— — — — — — — —

T's Cotoletta alla Milanese
Veal Milanese
FROM TERESA TOMEO'S KITCHEN

This classic, simple dish from Milan is a mainstay of northern Italian cuisine. A little further north, in Austria, folks there use veal and call it *Wiener Schnitzel*. But I like the Italian version better: It's quick, full of flavor, and impresses guests. I like to serve these delicious, breaded veal cutlets on a large plate with slices of lemon and a fresh salad made of arugula, tomato, and onion. Green beans also go well. This same recipe is easily adaptable with chicken cutlets.

This is a family recipe that I like to tweak a bit. I love spice, so I tend to add a hefty dose of black pepper as well as Italian breadcrumbs as opposed to plain and, as far as I'm concerned, extra grated parmesan never hurt anyone or any recipe. Some recipes call for a vinaigrette on top of the veal, but I like it with just a good squeeze of lemon juice and some parsley. Leave the vinaigrette for your side salad.

You can make this an hour or two ahead of time and keep the oven on a low temperature in the oven.

INGREDIENTS:

- 8 to 10 slices of thinly sliced veal or veal cutlets (the thinner the slices the faster they will cook)
- 4–5 eggs, beaten
- 1 to 2 cups of all-purpose flour
- 2–3 cups crumbs of Italian breadcrumbs (or plain depending on taste)
- Salt and black pepper
- ¼ cup or more of grated parmesan cheese
- 4–6 tablespoons of unsalted butter
- Oil for frying (canola oil is best — start with enough to coat the pan but you may need more)
- Fresh lemon juice along with sliced lemons for serving
- ½ cup chopped parsley
- Chopped fresh parsley along with a few parsley leaves for decoration

DIRECTIONS:

1. Season the flour with salt and pepper.
2. Season the veal with salt and pepper.
3. Mix the cheese and about half the parsley with the breadcrumbs.
4. Set up your assembly line with several separate dishes/bowls for the flour, eggs, and breadcrumbs.
5. Coat a large frying pan with canola oil (I also use cooking spray first to prevent sticking).
6. Melt the butter slowly and watch so it doesn't burn.

7. Dredge the veal slices in the flour (shaking off any extra), then in the eggs, and then coat with the breadcrumbs. If any spots of the veal are missing breadcrumbs simply grab a spoonful and press onto the meat.

8. Fry the slices until golden brown, turning over after about 3 minutes. Depending on the thickness of the meat you may have to adjust the time. Scallopini slices will cook quickly, so keep an eye on them.

9. Transfer to plate and, if serving right away, serve with fresh lemon slices, fresh chopped parsley, and a squeeze of lemon juice on top.

10. Top with a salad of arugula, cherry tomatoes, and sliced red onions mixed with olive oil and vinegar.

PART SEVEN

Going Home Again

CONTINUING TO EXPLORE

ENJOYING THE REST OF ITALY

1. Abruzzo
2. Emilia-Romagna
3. Friuli-Venezia Giulia
4. Marche
5. Molise
6. Trentino-Alto Adige/ Südtirol
7. Aosta and the Aosta Valley
8. Basilicata
9. Sardinia

Previous page: The historic Torre dell'Orologio in Brisighella

WHAT YOU'LL EXPLORE...

REGION HIGHLIGHTS

- **Continuing to Explore, There's Always Something More:** Enjoying the Rest of Italy
- **Beloved Saint of Italy — St. Peter Damien, Doctor of the Church**
- **Further Regions to Explore**

  1. Abruzzo Region
  2. Emilia-Romagna Region
  3. Friuli-Venezia Giulia Region
  4. Marche Region
  5. Molise Region
  6. Trentino-Alto Adige/Südtirol Region
  7. Aosta and the Aosta Valley Region
  8. Basilicata Region
  9. Sardinia

CONTINUING TO EXPLORE, THERE'S ALWAYS SOMETHING MORE
ENJOYING THE REST OF ITALY

- - - - - - -

Perhaps you brought this book with you on your recent journey to Italy. Or perhaps *Shrines and Wonders* has been a pleasant diversion, an armchair experience to feed your dream of traveling to this incredible land. Whatever the case, in one way or another ... Wait! There's more!

Just when you think there just can't be anything else worth seeing, Italy shows us — *again* — that it is the country that keeps on giving. I hope that after reading this book you will understand why we keep going home to Italy again and again: Italy's scenery, its activities, and its history are inexhaustible. Each time, there is something new to discover: Italy's saints, her people, her food and wine. Always something more to love.

So whether you are simply settling in for a plane ride home or are so excited about your first trip that you can't wait to start planning to go back again another time or two or three, rest assured that Italy always has *more* activities, beautiful scenery, and opportunities just waiting for you.

Opposite: The Fontana Fraterna in Isernia

335

EVERYBODY LOVES . . . ITALY

Italy has a way of slowing us all down, even for those for whom the concept of *la dolce far niente* isn't exactly on the radar. One of my favorite sitcoms, *Everybody Loves Raymond*, had a two-part special in season 5 (filmed in July 2000) dedicated to the Barone family going to Italy on a big family vacation — *Italy* was filmed in Anguillara Sabazia outside of Rome.

Everyone was excited to go on the trip except Raymond. He wasn't looking forward to two weeks away from work and was even more concerned about spending time with his, how shall we say, challenging family. He went to the land of his heritage reluctantly; everyone but Raymond had a great time, fully embracing the laid-back Italian life-style. And yet, as you watch Raymond and Debra (played by Patricia Heaton) wander the cobbled streets and take in the scenery, you can't help but feel that Ray can't wait to get on the plane back to New York.

Because everybody loves ... Italy

Finally, he too, has his "aha" Italy moment where he realizes just how special the country truly is. We then see him enjoying time with his wife and children as they eat gelato, play soccer, go on bike rides, and stroll through lovely parks and along the water. He finally gets it, before it's too late. He learns to embrace what really matters in life: the true, the beautiful, and the good. He sees his family and the world differently thanks to his Italian journey.

For the Christian and Catholic Christian particularly, Italy, as you have seen through hundreds of pages in this book, offers so many places for spiritual encouragement, knowledge, and enrichment that one could spend an entire lifetime exploring the sacred places of Italy and barely scratch the surface. The same goes for history and art. Italy helps us rediscover or discover ourselves, maybe for the first time, in the nature of the human person and our dignity — through the great saints and their incredible stories of faith and endurance, and through the artists who gave us their lives along with images of times gone by through paintings, sculptures, and mosaics. Archaeologists bring forth the peoples that inhabited this land long before we set foot on the peninsula. We've looked back and more importantly looked up in awe and wonder. All of this helps us go forward in a deeper way.

There are a total of twenty regions in Italy. Here in the pages of *Italy's Shrines and Wonders* we've taken you to twelve of those regions, barely scratching the surface of what those regions have to offer with their basilicas, museums, natural beauty, and a multitude of other attractions.

As we close this book, we'll highlight briefly some of the important sites in the remaining nine regions: Abruzzo, Emilia Romagna, Friuli-Venezia Giulia, Marche, Molise, Trentino-Alto Adige/Süditrol, Aosta, Basilicata, and Sardinia. One could easily spend several weeks or more in each region of Italy, never having to leave in order to have an amazing holiday.

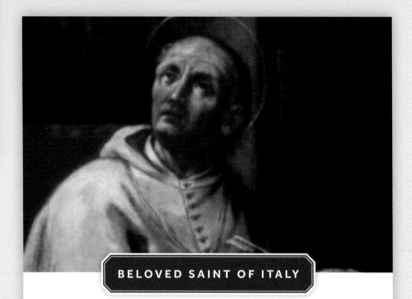

St. Peter Damian, Doctor of the Church

- **Relics:** *Chapel of St. Peter Damian in the Cathedral of Faenza in Faenza, (Province of Ravenna, Emilia-Romagna Region)*
- **Patron Saint:** *Faenza, Italy*
- **Feast Day:** *February 21*

Born in Ravenna in 1007, St. Peter Damian was orphaned at a very young age and treated poorly by his extended family. Impressed by his intelligence, a priest arranged for his education in Ravenna. Peter made rapid progress and eventually studied theology and canon law, and by age twenty-five became a teacher in Parma, Italy. In time he would become a Benedictine monk, bishop of Ostia, a papal legate, and a cardinal.

Peter Damian was famous for monastic and clerical reform after hundreds of years of poor clergy education, laxity, and sinful living. He was so highly respected that the famous author Dante placed him in one of the highest circles of Paradise.

After his death in Faenza (in the Province of Ravenna) on February 22, 1072, St. Peter's relics were moved six times until they were finally interred in the Chapel of St. Peter Damian in the Cathedral of Faenza.

In 1828, Pope Leo XII named him a Doctor of the Church and extended the observance of his feast day throughout the Western Church. *Note: "Doctor of the Church" is a special title given by the Catholic Church to saints recognized for their significant contribution to doctrine or theology through their personal research, study, or writings.*

ABRUZZO REGION
HIGHLIGHTS

Medieval village of Pacentro

With its western border only thirty-one miles west of Rome, Abruzzo enjoys a central location bordered by the Adriatic to the east, Molise to the south, and Le Marche to the north. It is a great area for outdoor enthusiasts along with those seeking to learn more about Italy's eucharistic miracles.

Abruzzo is home to the country's largest and one of the most beautiful national parks, the Gran Sasso, and several nature preserves. It is popular with hikers and nature lovers. Catholic pilgrims also have Abruzzo high on their itinerary as the town of Lanciano is the site of the earliest eucharistic miracle in Italy, dating back to the eighth century.

A Basilian monk who had doubts about the Real Presence of Jesus in the Eucharist witnessed the bread and wine turn into flesh and blood which coagulated into five globules. The Catholic Church recognizes this miracle, the relics of which are kept on the altar of St. Francis in Lanciano.

Gran Sasso National Park

Site of the Miracle of Lanciano

T's Italy

EMILIA-ROMAGNA REGION
HIGHLIGHTS

Ancient University Library, Bologna

Bologna, the capital city of this northern region of Italy, is home to and the namesake of the oldest university in the world, established in 1088. St. Dominic, originally from Spain, arrived in the city early in the thirteenth century, where he founded the Dominicans (Order of Preachers) and quickly realized the importance of having a university as part of his mission field. St. Dominic is buried in the exquisite *arca* of his chapel in the Basilica of San Domenico.

This area is also a "must-do" for the foodies of the world as it is home to the famous Parmigiano Reggiano, Prosciutto di Parma from nearby Parma, and balsamic vinegar from Modena.

Opposite: Basilica of San Domenico, Bologna

T's Italy

Friuli-Venezia Giulia Region
HIGHLIGHTS

This unique region in the far northeast of Italy offers visitors a real variety in scenery and culture, located east of Venice and bordering Slovenia and Austria. Historically it was part of Austria, and then later Yugoslavia. It became an autonomous Italian region in 1963.

The most important city is the capital city of Trieste, located in the region's southeast corner. The city is home to what is considered one of the largest and most beautiful seafront piazzas in the world. There are several important Orthodox and Catholic churches in Trieste, including San Nicolo and San Spiridione, and the Catholic Church of Sant'Antonio Nuovo. Several important and uniquely built churches were established here, including the unusual concrete triangular Marian shrine, the Sanctuary of Monte Grisa.

Sanctuary of Monte Grisa, Trieste

The city is also famous for its connection to famous authors, including James Joyce, who lived here. I like to imagine him writing or relaxing in one of the city's coffeehouses — Trieste and coffee go together like salt and pepper. The oldest coffeehouse in the city dates back some two hundred years. The region is known for its stunning Dolomite Mountains and for the white wine produced in the area.

Opposite: Trieste town hall

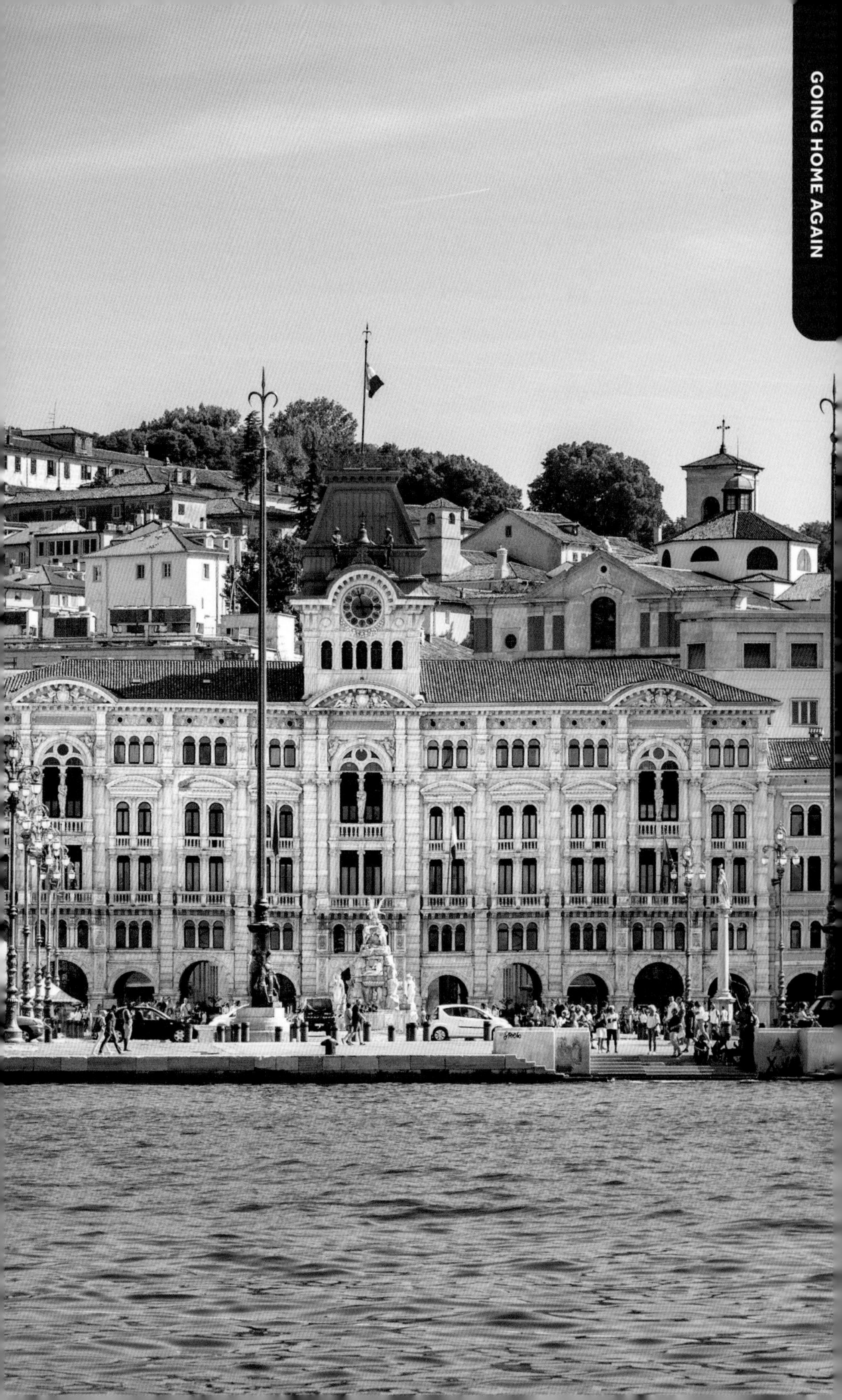

MARCHE REGION
HIGHLIGHTS

Visitors coming to Marche to worship at the Basilica Santa Casa (the Holy House of Mary) are often more familiar with the name of the city where the shrine is located — Loreto — than the actual name of the region itself.

Loreto, a hill town in the Le Marche province of Ancona, is home to one of the most important Marian pilgrimage sites in all of Italy. According to Catholic tradition, the church contains the house where the Blessed Virgin Mary was born and raised and where the archangel Gabriel appeared to Mary at the Annunciation, telling her that she would become the Mother of God (see Luke 1:30–37).

Tests done on the structure confirm that the stones used to build the house come from northern Israel, and the techniques used are like those used some two thousand years ago in the same area. There are different stories as to how the house ended up in Italy. Most likely it was moved in the thirteenth century by a wealthy family, the Angeli family, who paid to have it removed and reconstructed in Loreto.

Holy House of Mary, Loreto

Le Marche is centrally located in Italy, with the Adriatic Sea on its eastern border, the Umbrian region to the west, and the Abruzzo region to the south. In addition to the Holy House of Loreto, visitors come to Le Marche for its pleasant mix of resort towns, quaint villages, and rugged scenery.

Opposite: Piazza della Madonna, Loreto

T's Italy

MOLISE REGION
HIGHLIGHTS

Molise, Italy's newest region, was part of the Abruzzo region until 1963 (the break from Abruzzo wasn't official until 1970). Its sizeable coastline along the Adriatic, some twenty-two miles, touches four other regions including Abruzzo to the north, Apulia to the east, Lazio to the west, and Campania to the south.

Molise is rising from obscurity thanks to a quirky conspiracy due to its small size and remote location. "Molise non esiste" ("Molise doesn't exist," a.k.a. the Molise conspiracy) has prompted several articles, videos, songs, social media pages, and more.

Although Molise may not attract as many visitors as other regions due to its relatively small size and dearth of major churches and attractions, it is the location of the relics of a very important saint from early Christianity: the cathedral in the town Termoli contains the relics of St. Timothy, the evangelist who traveled with St. Paul.

The Cathedral of St. Mary of the Purification was first built in the sixth century, with the present Romanesque structure built between the twelfth and thirteenth centuries.

Cathedral of St. Mary of the Purification, Termoli

Opposite: The Sanctuary of Castelpetroso, Orfanotrofio

T's Italy

TRENTINO-ALTO ADIGE/SÜDTIROL REGION
HIGHLIGHTS

Welcome to Italy's northernmost region, an entirely mountainous area (apart from Adige Valley, which is considered hilly). The region lies between the central and eastern Alps with parts of Lake Garda on its southern border.

The region's capital city, Trento ("Trent" in English) is known for its art as well as its religious architecture including the city's duomo, the Cathedral of St. Vigilio, erected on a site that housed a temple dedicated to the saint. The name *Trent* should ring a bell with anyone interested in religious history, as this is the city and the church where the decrees of the Council of Trent (1545–1563), the nineteenth ecumenical council of the Catholic Church, were formed. The Council of Trent definitively determined the doctrines of the Church in response to the heresies of the Protestant Reformation.

Trento Cathedral

This region attracts both cultural enthusiasts and nature lovers. And if you are looking for variety, especially when it comes to food, this region is greatly influenced by its Austrian neighbor, so you can expect to find scrumptious items such as strudel and sauerkraut on the menu.

Opposite: Village of Burgeis

T's Italy

AOSTA AND THE
AOSTA VALLEY REGION
HIGHLIGHTS

Aosta is Italy's smallest region and contains some of the highest peaks of the awesome Alps including Mt. Cervino, rising more than fifteen thousand feet above sea level and defined as "the noblest rock in Europe." If enchantment and a fairy tale-like experience set in the middle of majestic nature are what you're looking for, this is the region for you to visit.

Thanks to the prevalence of ancient Roman ruins and numerous structures still standing, the city of Aosta is referred to as the "Rome of the Alps." Its most popular church, the eleventh-century Cathedral of Sant'Orso is both a symbol of worship in this northern city and the site of a religious celebration that goes back over a thousand years: The Fiera di Sant'Orso (the St. Ursus Fair) is held annually at the end of January and attracts over one hundred thousand people. It's held in honor of an Irish monk who is said to have lived in the city during the sixth century.

*The Cathedral...
and the Festival
of St. Ursus*

*Opposite: Mt.
Cervino*

T's Italy

BASILICATA REGION
HIGHLIGHTS

Basilicata, you may recall, was mentioned briefly in our section on Apulia as it is right next door and is the home to the fascinating and ancient city of Matera. Because my maternal grandmother was born in this region, I feel a particular closeness to this beautiful, sometimes rugged area of southern Italy.

Dolomite Zip Line

Basilicata (or Lucania, as it is sometimes called) forms the instep of the boot bordering Campania, Calabria, and a small area along the Tyrrhenian Sea. It is less populated than other regions of Italy, with just over six hundred thousand inhabitants. The Lucanian Dolomites provide a stunning backdrop for the picturesque mountain villages that dot the landscape. Its numerous small but lovely inland lakes make Maratea an incredible place to visit if one is looking for a beautiful beach vacation without the crowds. It is also the perfect place for peace and quiet and the opportunity to truly get back in touch with nature by hiking its many peaks and nature parks.

Adventure seekers, however, can head to Pietrapertosa and Castelmezzano, two towns in the Dolomite Mountains, where a five-thousand-foot zipline journey is stretched between them. The Vollo dell'Angelo (Flight of the Angel) promises amazing views of Basilicata's fantastic natural landscape — and it is the fastest and longest zipline in Europe. I seriously wanted to try this but when we reached one of the starting points the wind was too strong, so the flight was not available that day. (We did visit the towns, which are quite literally out of this world.)

Volare — fly!

Opposite: Castelmezzano

T's Italy

SARDINIA REGION
HIGHLIGHTS

If you're looking for more island time, head out to sea to visit the island region of Sardinia, the second-largest island in the Mediterranean (next to Sicily). It is known for its natural beauty, fabulous beaches, and busy nightlife with its many resorts and nightclubs, and it is also popular with Europe's rich and famous. It lies 120 miles west of Italy's mainland and 124 miles north of Africa's coast. The closest land is the large French island of Corsica.

Sardinia's well-known Costa Smeralda is located in the northeastern part of the island and offers a twelve-mile stretch of pristine shoreline. If sunbathing and swimming aren't your thing, Sardinia offers an abundance of activities for all types of travelers. There are castles to visit, archeological sites to discover, and the fantastic Porto Flavia built into a cliff and facing the sea. And don't forget Neptune's Grotto, one of the island's most visited natural wonders. It's a two-million-year-old cave (yes, you read correctly) that introduces visitors to a natural world of sculptures known as stalactites and stalagmites. Neptune's Grotto is also known for Lago Lamarmora, one of the largest saltwater lakes in Europe.

Wherever your Italy journey takes you, we hope you've enjoyed journeying with us through *Shrines and Wonders* and that this book inspires you to keep exploring *Bella Italia*.

Grazie, ciao for now, and *buon viaggio*!

Neptune's Grotto

Opposite: Buggerru, Sardinia

APPENDIX

T's Italy

YOUR ULTIMATE INSIDER TRAVEL TIPS

APPENDIX

T'S ITALY
YOUR ULTIMATE INSIDER TRAVEL TIPS

– – – – – – –

ULTIMATE TRAVEL TIP #1

Be Sure to Plan Ahead!
The Early Bird Catches the Cappuccino:

In real estate you often hear the phrase that it's all about "location, location, location." When it comes to traveling in Italy, it's all about "reservations, reservations, reservations." Whether it's nailing down the hotels, picking your flights, renting a car, planning your meals, or getting the tours, if you don't book ahead of time, you can quickly say *ciao* and *arrivederci* to that dream vacation.

The number of tourists in Italy keeps rising. In 2023, for example, nearly sixty million people (57.25 million) made Italy their vacation destination, spending nearly fifty-six billion in tourism dollars. You have a lot of competition when it comes to grabbing hotel space, securing guides, and getting prime seats at the many great *trattorias* and *ristorantes*. And don't forget to do your research in advance about which credit card has no or the lowest international transaction fees.

Previous page: Sanctuary of Madonna della Ceriola in Monte Isola
Opposite: Statue of an angel on the Ponte Sant'Angelo

So how far in advance should you start making those reservations? Nine months to a year is ideal — no less than six months. You might be able to hold off on the airline tickets as bargains come and go so often. If you have status on an airline there is more flexibility but again, here too, the early bird catches the cappuccino.

The only variable here will be the restaurants. It's best to reserve dinner and even lunch reservations two weeks ahead of time.

ULTIMATE TRAVEL TIP #2

Do Your Research! Know the Regions, the Seasons, and the Celebrations:

It is always a good idea to read up on the areas on your itinerary and find out about other happenings in Italy during the time you want to visit. For example, there may be a large festival, convention, or worldwide event happening in that region of Italy when you want to visit.

Register with U.S. Smart Traveler Enrollment (https://step.state.gov/) and read through the U.S. State Department Travelers "Preparing for a Trip Abroad" with tips and checklists for U.S. travelers (https://www.state.gov/travelers/).

ULTIMATE TRAVEL TIP #3

Know the Best Way to Get Around (Tips on Planes, Trains, and Automobiles):

Italy is not that difficult to navigate if you plan and don't bite off more than you can chew. (If reading this section makes you feel nervous about arranging the details yourself, don't worry! "T's Italy" is happy to arrange it all for you!)

PLANES

Rome's main airport, Leonardo da Vinci or Fiumicino (FCO), is often the starting point for most Italy travel. However, there are several other decent-sized airports that offer puddle jumpers that can easily get you from one area of the country to another. You just need to manage your time well. Every day needs to count, and you don't want to spend any more time in the airport than necessary.

- Rome's main airport (Rome Fiumicino International Airport "Leonardo da Vinci") is located about twenty miles outside Rome, near the coast, in the city of Fiumicino. It is the busiest airport in all of Italy.
- Be sure to look at the length of layovers between connections. If there is a connection from Rome, compare the layover times to help you discern whether renting a car or hiring a driver might be better alternatives.
- If you're starting your trip in Florence or Milan, for example, you might save precious time by connecting through another European airport such as Frankfurt or Amsterdam and going directly to your first destination.

TRAINS

Railways in Italy are extremely popular and prevalent, including regional trains that connect smaller towns, luxury and high-speed trains, and even an express train from Rome's main airport into the city. It all depends on how quickly you want to arrive and how much money you want to spend. It might be worth it to pay a little extra for first-class service, especially on the cross-country trips.

High-speed trains are affordable and efficient, with tickets that can be easily purchased online. Remember, when you arrive by train to your destination, you still need to get to your hotel. Most of the stations offer taxi service, but I suggest contacting your hotel concierge to check on transfers they may offer. Here are some other tips:

- Be sure to buy your tickets in advance, if possible.
- Double-check your train number and be sure to board the correct train.
- Arrive at the train station thirty minutes prior to your train time.
- Know the exact name of the train station you are leaving and going to.
- Note: *partenze* is the word for departures in Italian and *arrivi* is for arrivals.

Here are a few sites to review regarding train travel in Italy.

- **Rail Europe:** *https://www.raileurope.com/*
- **The Trainline:** *https://www.thetrainline.com/*
- **Italia Rail:** *https://www.italiarail.com/*
- **Trenitalia:** *https://www.trenitalia.com/*
- **Italo Treno:** *https://www.italotreno.it/en*

T's Italy

T'S INSIDER TRAVEL TIP
Transportation strikes

Transportation strikes are a common occurrence, especially before or after national holidays. Businesses across Italy like to hold work stoppages and use them as a ponte or a bridge to make for more time off. Keep this in mind when planning your vacation and consider alternative means of transportation as a backup.

AUTOMOBILES

Renting a car in Italy can be a bit intimidating at first, but once you understand a few of the basics it's not anything that you can't do with confidence. The good news is that you don't need a car when staying in larger cities. Most are very walkable and offer public transportation and regular taxi service. Taxis can be scheduled through your hotel and can be found at taxi stands across the metropolitan areas.

Because you'll be driving in a foreign country, you'll need to be comfortable getting lost once in a great while and to understand some different rules of the road. If not, it might not be for you. However, here are a few tips that will be important for a successful and enjoyable experience.

- Book your car reservation here in the States. Walk-up rentals are almost impossible in the large cities. Be sure to deal only with reputable companies — if a deal sounds too good to be true, it probably is.
- Most cars in Italy and throughout Europe do not have automatic transmissions, so you should be comfortable driving with a stick shift. Even reserving an automatic is not a guarantee that you will get one because of their limited supply.
- Bring your passport to rent a car. It must be good for six months after the dates of departure.
- The International Driving Permit is now required to drive in Italy. Please visit any AAA office to obtain. It is very easy to get even if you are not a member.
- Carefully read your rental agreement, including mileage limitations, drop-off charges (returning your car to a different location than your origination can be quite expensive), and other surcharges, such as for late returns.

- I recommend buying daily car insurance for several reasons. Even if your U.S. insurance companies cover you while in Italy (many do not) you will be required to pay the entire bill and then get reimbursed from your U.S. carrier. The paperwork and forms needed to do this can be intimidating. Secondly is the time or peace of mind factor — you're driving in a foreign country, as I've said, and your attention may be distracted from time to time; not to mention some of the tight spaces you might find yourself dealing with.
- Warning: Gasoline is about four times as expensive as in the United States, so just be prepared for that.

ULTIMATE TRAVEL TIP #4

Don't Be a Lone Wolf (Why a Tour Group Might Be Worth Considering):

If I've heard it once, I've heard it a thousand times: "I don't want to go on a tour. I want to see Italy my way and on my own." That may seem very adventurous or romantic. But especially for first-time travelers it's not reasonable and can also be unsafe. When all is said and done, flying solo can also waste a lot of money.

I'll never forget that as our very first Italy tour was wrapping up, we had a little bit of free time, so we went back to a great restaurant near our hotel. We sat outside admiring the dome of St. Peter's and reminiscing about our experience. We couldn't help but overhear the tired voices of a couple sitting at a nearby table.

They had several well-worn guidebooks piled high next to their wine glasses and apparently had done some homework. Yet nothing had prepared them for trying to navigate Italy by themselves. They lamented the long lines, watching tour groups go ahead of them, and watching smaller groups with guides pass them by. They had little appreciation for the sites because there was too much information that they were trying to consume. They were simply miserable and quite obviously mad at themselves for thinking they knew better.

If you go it alone, no matter how much reading you have done prior to traveling, it can be overwhelming. Going it alone means standing in line with every Tom, Dick, Harry, and Helen who are also trying to go it alone as they wait outside the Vatican Museums, for example, where the lines during high season can stretch for miles. Going it alone, even if alone means with a few relatives or friends, makes tourists much more vulnerable to pickpockets, tourist traps, and quite frankly sheer exhaustion.

Although my exclusive travel partner, Corporate Travel Service, and I would love for you to join us on one of our exceptional journeys, even if you choose another travel provider an organized tour is highly encouraged, especially on your first trip. Everything is handled for you, from your hotels to your restaurants to your guides. Most organized tours also offer free time for you to explore on your own and break away from the group. You can also plan smaller excursions before or after the main tour.

In addition to taking away the guess work and the hours of research, planning, and booking that it takes to travel on your own, a planned tour or pilgrimage is guaranteed to result in new friends. Some of our closest friendships began this way and, on each pilgrimage or tour we lead, there are new friends to encounter.

If a group tour is still not your cup of espresso, it's still important to get guidance in planning your vacation to Italy, which should include small or individual group tours. That's why I started my coaching services at T's Italy, www.travelitalyexpert.com. You can do a tailor-made trip for one, two, or for a small group that is structured enough with our suggestions for experienced guides, which are a must, yet flexible enough to do what you want when you want. In other words, you can have, in many ways, the best of both worlds.

ULTIMATE TRAVEL TIP #5

When in Italy, Do As the Italians Do:

Finally, here are a few cultural and social niceties to keep in mind to help you get the authentic Italian experience!

- Remember, dinner is going to be late. Italians eat after eight o'clock in the evening and few restaurants are open before 7:00 p.m.
- Don't forget the dinner reservations! Avoid restaurants trying to hand you menus on the street. They're tourist traps.
- If you don't want to look like a tourist, don't order cappuccino after twelve noon. It's for breakfast. Try an espresso instead.
- Please don't cut the long pasta. Ask for a tablespoon and twirl away or order shorter pasta.
- What to wear? Leave the heels home, ladies. Modest clothing is required when visiting churches — which means knees and shoulders must be covered.
- Keep your passport and valuables in your room safe and only carry a credit card and some cash for cabs.
- Italians are very friendly and most speak English. But trying to say a few words in Italian will be appreciated.
- When contacting family and friends back home via phone, I recommend using WhatsApp's free app while traveling throughout Italy. Depending on your cell phone plan, text messaging and data plans can sometimes be costly.

INDEX

A

Abruzzo, 337, 340–41

Adriatic Coast, 145, 149

Aeolian Islands, 193–94

Agnes of Foligno, Saint, 74

Agrigento (Sicily), 209–10

Alba, 292

Alberobello (Puglia), 167–68

Amalfi Coast: about, 131–32, 136, 145; Capri, 137, 168–70; Maratea, 162–65; Mount Vesuvius, 137, 210; Path of the Gods, 161–62; Santa Maria Assunta, Church of, 146–47; Sassi di Matera, 165–67; St. Andrew, Cathedral of, 138, 145, 147–48; "Walk of the Gods," 2. *See also* Positano; Praiano

Amata of Assisi, Saint, 74

Amatrice, 59

Ambrose of Milan, Saint, 37, 38

Angela of Foligno, Saint, 74, 78–79

Anne Catherine Emmerich, Blessed, 106–7

Anthony of Padua, Saint, 103, 297

Aosta, 337, 352–53

Appolonia, Saint, 56

Assisi: about, 64, 72, 219; Basilica of St. Clare, 74, 83, 100, 124; Basilica of St. Francis, 83, 96, 117, 124, 308; Calendimaggio of Assisi, 116–17; Rocca Maggiore, 84; Sacro Monte di Orta and, 307–8; San Damiano Cross, xi, 83, 95, 99, 124; St. Clare of Assisi, xi, 72–74, 83, 93, 98–100, 101, 219; St. Mary Major, 77, 83, 98, 99; St. Mary of the Angels, 83, 99; Temple Minerva, 84, 117. *See also* Francis of Assisi, Saint

Asti, 292

Atrani, 132

Augustine of Hippo, Saint, 37–38

B

Barberini gardens (Vatican), 23, 48, 49

Bari, 145

Barone, Angelo, 204

Barron, Robert, 5

Basilica of Our Lady Help of Christians (Turin), 292

Basilica of Santa Christina (Lazio Region), 34

Basilicata 162–65, 337, 354–55

Benedict of Nursia, Saint, 72, 74

Benedict XV, Pope, 285

Benedict XVI, Pope, 48

Bernadette Soubirous, Saint, 205

Bernini, Gian Lorenzo, 29, 31, 51

Bolsena, 91, 113

Bona of Pisa, Saint, 228–29

Bonaventure, Saint, 43, 47, 246

Bonente, Raffaele, 301

Boniscambi, Ugolino, 105

Borghese Gallery and Gardens (Rome), 26

Botticelli, Sandro, 257, 258

Bracciano, 34

Burano, 296–97, 320–21

C

Calabria: about, 185–86; eastern coast beaches, 197; highlights, 194–95; map, 182; Reggio, 88, 185–86, 191, 194, 196, 204; Sanctuary of Santa Maria dell'Isola, 196–97; St. Francesco di Paola, Saint, 187–88; Tropea, 101, 194, 196, 197, 207–8, 318

Calendimaggio of Assisi, 116–17

Callistus, Saint, 25, 75

Campania: Capri, 132, 136, 137, 145; Herculaneum, 159–60; highlights, 136; Ischia, 170–71; *Limoncello*, 175–76; map, 128; Mount Vesuvius, 157, 158; Paestum, 160–61; Piazza della Vittoria, 137; Pomeii, 158–59; Procida, 171; Sorrento, 132, 137, 169, 171, 175, 218–19; St. Joseph of Cupertino, 133–34. *See also* Amalfi Coast

Cappella Musicale Pantifica Sistina (Sistine Chapel Choir), 61, 270, 271

Cappella Palatina, 192

Capri, 132, 136, 137, 145

Carlo Acutis, Saint, 77, 83, 96, 97–98

Cascata delle Marmore (Marmone Falls) (Umbria), 112

Cassian of Todi, Saint, 75

Castel Gandolfo, 34, 48–49, 270, 271

Castel Sant'Angelo (Rome), 25, 30

Castello (Umbria), 75

Castello Aragonese (Reggio), 196

Castello Brown (Portofino), 240

catacombs (Rome), 25

Catania, 192

Catherine of Siena, Saint, 20, 25, 31, 73, 234, 249

Cattedrale di Monreale, 192

Cecilia, Saint, 21, 29, 55

Chapel of the Corporal (Orvieto), 91

Chapel of the Crucifix (Assisi), 100

Chianalea di Scilla (Calabria), 197

Chianti (Tuscany), 235, 260

Chiesa Piedigrotta di Pizzo (Calabria), 204–5

Chiusi (Tuscany), 106

Christmas, 39–40, 42–43

Cinque Terre Region: about, 225–26, 242; highlights, 238; hiking trails, 243; map, 222; Monterossa, 243

Civita di Bagnoregio (Lazio), 45–47

Clare of Assisi, Saint, xi, 72–74, 83, 93, 98–100, 101, 219

Clare of Montefalco, Saint, 74, 93, 100–102

Clement VII, Pope, 114

Clement VIII, Pope, 21

Colosseum (Rome), x, 19, 25

Column of the Immaculate Conception (Rome), 26

Convento Monterossa, 243

Cornaro Chapel, 31

Coronation of the Virgin (mosaic), 55

Cremona (Lombardy), 289

Cristoforo di Filippo, 108–9

Cupertino (Lecce, Umbria), 133–34

D

Deruta (Umbria), 85, 108–9

Digna of Todi, Saint, 75

Divine Mercy devotion, 30

Dominic, Saint, 172–73, 234

Duomo di Firenze (Florence Cathedral), 232, 258

Duomo di Milano (Milan Cathedral), 286, 288, 313–16

Duomo di Orivieto, 5, 90–93, 113

Duomo di Torino (Turin Cathedral), 291–92, 304

Duomo of Siena, 234

E

Elba, 230, 241

Emilia-Romagna: about, 337, 338–39, 342–43; Lake Garda, 34, 281, 289, 297, 299–300, 302, 350; St. Giovanni Battista Scalabrini, 284–85

Etruscans, 33, 46, 80, 114, 241, 260. *See also* Orvieto; Tarquinia

Eucharistic miracle of Bolsena, 91, 113

F

Facchini, 40, 41

Faenza, Cathedral of, 338, 339

Faraglioni rocks, 137

Faustina, Saint, 30

Festa dei Ceri (Gubbio), 102–3

Florence: about, 257–59; baptistry, 232; Basilica di Santa Croce, 232; Cathedral of Santa Maria del Fiore, 230, 232; *David* (Michelangelo), 230, 233; Ponte Vecchio, 233–34, 258–59; Porcellino Market, 233; St. Francis of Assisi in, 232; Uffizi Gallery, 230, 233, 258

Fontana dei Matti (Gubbio), 105

Fontana del Bicchierone (Tivoli), 51

Fortunatus of Todi, Saint, 75

Forum (Rome), ix, 19, 25

Fountain of the Organ (Tivoli), 51

Francesco di Paola, Saint, 187–88

Francis, Pope, 48, 61, 75, 77, 78, 201, 284, 303

Francis de Sales, Saint, 284

Francis of Assisi, Saint: about, 72–73, 87, 219; Assisi and, 93–94; *Convento Monterossa* monument to, 243; in Florence, 232; fresco of life of, 125; Greccio Sanctuary of St. Francis, 42–43; in Gubbio, 103–5; life of, 94–96; Maggiore Island and, 84; *Return of St. Francis* (statue), 94, 95; Sacro Monte di Orta and, 307–8; San Damiano Cross, xi, 83, 95, 99, 100, 124; St. Angela and, 78; St. Bonaventure and, 47; St. Carlo Acutis and, 77, 97, 98; St. Clare of Assisi and, 98–99; St. Mary of the Angels and, 83; stigmata of, 244, 245–47; tomb of, 83, 96;

in Tuscany, 246–47; Way of St. Francis, 43

Frascatti, 34

Frederick Barbarossa, 75

Friuli-Venezia Giulia, 337, 344–45

G

Galgano Guidotti, Saint, 177–79

Galleria Vittorio Emanuele II, 288

Gargano Peninsula, 145, 149

Genoa, 238

George, Saint, 103

Giovanni Battista Scalabrini, Saint, 284–85

Grand Canal (Venice), 2

Greccio Sanctuary of St. Francis (Lazio), 42–43

Gregory the Great, Pope, 74

Grotto Arpaia, 240

Gubbio (Umbria), 102–5

H

Hale, John, xiii–xvi, 61–65, 122–25, 177–79, 218–19, 270–72

Herculaneum, 132

Hildebrand, Saint, 47

I

Ignatius of Loyola, Saint, xi

Immaculate Conception, Column of (Rome), 26

Ionian Sea, 194

Ischia, 132, 170–71

Isola d'Elba, 241

Isola Tiberina (Rome), 27, 55

J

John Bosco, Saint, 251, 282

John Paul II, Pope Saint, 124, 125

John the Baptist, Saint, 301

John XXIII, Pope Saint, 228, 251

Joseph, Saint, 284, 301

Joseph of Cupertino, Saint, 133–34

K

Keats, John, 56

L

La Costa degli Dei (Coast of the Gods), 197, 207–8

La Spezia, 243

La Verna Sanctuary (Tuscany), 245–47

Lake Albano (Lazio), 33, 48, 49

Lake Bolsena, 34

Lake Como (Lombardy), 286, 288

Lake Garda (Emilia-Romagna), 34, 281, 289, 297, 299–300, 302, 350

Lake Garda (Lombardy), 289

Lake Maggiore, 236, 290, 291, 308–9

Lake Trasimeno (Perugia), 84, 236

Lazio Region: Basilica of Santa Christina, 34; Bracciano, 34; Castel Gandolfo, 34; Civita di Bagnoregio, 45–47; Emilia-Romagna, 34; Frascatti, 34; Greccio Sanctuary of St. Francis, 42–43; highlights, 22–23, 32–33; Lake Albano, 33, 48, 49; Lake Bolsena, 34; map, 12; Ostia Antica, 37–38; signature dishes,

58–60; Tarquinia, 52–53; Tivoli, 50–51; Villa d'Este Tivoli, 50–51; Viterbo, 34, 39–41. *See also* Rome; Vatican City

Leo X, Pope, 187

Leo XII, Pope, 339

Leonard da Vinci, 286, 288, 312

Liguria: about, 225–26; Castiglione, 241; Genoa, 238; highlights, 238; Isola d'Elba, 241; map, 222; Our Lady of Montallegro (shrine), 239, 251, 253–55; Porto Venere, 240, 251–53; Portoferraio, 241; Portofino, 239, 240; Rapallo, 239, 243, 251, 253–55; Santa Margherita Ligure, 239; Shrine of Our Lady of Montallegro, 239; Volterraio Castle, 241

Little Purgatory Museum (Museum of Holy Souls), 30

Lombardy: about, 279–82; highlights, 286–87; Lake Como, 288; map, 276; signature dishes, 327–29. *See also* Milan

Lorenzo Maiorano, Saint, 150, 151

Luminaria di San Domenico, 172–73

Lungo Il Treve festival (Rome), 56

Lungomare Falcomatà (Reggio), 196

M

Macchina di Santa Rosa (Viterbo), 41

Madonna dei Bagni, Sanctuary della (Deruta), 108–9

Madonna della Clemenza (icon), 55

Madonna della Corona, Sanctuary of (, 289, 299–302

Maher, Lori, 270–72

Maratea (Basilica), 162–65

Marche, 337, 346–47

Margaret of Castello, Saint, 75

Marina Piccola (Sorrento), 137

Mark the Evangelist, Saint, 295

Marmone Falls (Cascata delle Marmore) (Umbria), 112

Mary Magdalene, Saint, 301

Matera, 145

Mediterranean Sea: Amalfi Coast, 131, 132; Lazio Region, 33, 38; Ligurian Coast, 145, 162, 238, 242; Sardinia, 356–57; Sicily, 190–91, 356

Messina (Sicily), 185, 186, 215

Messina, Strait of, 186, 190, 192, 194, 211

Michael the Archangel, Saint, 149–51

Michelangelo, 230, 232, 233, 257, 258

Milan: canal district, 288, 311–13; Duomo di Milano (Milan Cathedral), 288, 312, 313–16; Santa Maria delle Grazie (Milan), 288; Teatro alla Scala (Milan), 288

Modugno, Domenico, 143

Molise, 337, 348–49

Monica, Saint, 37, 38

Montalcino (Tuscany), 235, 260

Monte Baldo (Lombardy), 289, 299–302

Monte Cassino, 74

Monte Gargano, 149

Monte Pellegrino, 192, 199–201

Monte Sant'Angelo, 149–51

Monte Solaro, 137

Monte Testaccio (Rome), 56

Montefalco (Umbria), 100–102

Montepulciano (Tuscany), 235, 260

Monterossa (Cinque Terre), 243

Morelli, Domenic, 148

Mount Etna (Sicily), 190, 192, 207, 210, 211

Mount Ingino (Umbria), 103

Mount Stromboli (Sicily), 191, 193, 207

Mount Subasio (Perugia), 84, 93

Mount Vesuvius (Campania), 137, 210

Murano, 296, 320, 322

Musea del Parco (Portofino), 240

Museum of Holy Souls (Little Purgatory Museum), 30

N

Naples, 136, 137, 158, 159, 169, 170

Nativity Grotto (Lazio), 43

Nativity of St. Mary, Cathedral of the (Duomo) (Milan), 288, 312, 313–16

Nera River Park (Umbria), 112

Nicholas, Saint, 145

Norcia (Umbria), 72

O

Orta, 291, 306–8

Orvieto (Umbria): about, 45, 72, 80, 84, 88; Duomo di Orivieto, 5, 90–93, 113; Orvieto Underground, 84, 114; St. Patrick's Well, 114–15

Osimo (Ancona, Marche), 133, 134

Ostia Antica (Lazio), 37

Our Lady of Help of Christians (Turin), 282

Our Lady of Lourdes, 205

Our Lady of Montallego (Rapallo) (Liguria), 239, 251, 253–55

Our Lady of Soviore, 243

Our Lady of Trastevere, Basilica of (Rome), 55, 56

P

Padua, 297

Paestrum, 132

Palatine Chapel (Palermo), 202–3

Palazzo dei Papi (Viterbo), 40

Palermo, 192, 199–201, 202–3, 215

Palio della Tonna, 47

Pantheon (Rome), 25, 31

Paul the Apostle, Saint, xi

Perugia (Umbria), 84, 106–7

Peter Damian, Saint, 338–39

Peter of Prague, 91

Peter the Apostle, Saint, x, 5, 23, 24, 125, 148

Philagathos of Cerami, 202–3

Phlegraean Islands, 136

Piacenza, 284–85

Piazza del Popolo (Rome), 29

Piazza della Liberta (Lazio), 49

Piazza della Vittoria (Sorrento), 137

Piazza di Commune (Assisi), 84, 116

Piazza di Santa Maria (Rome), 55

Piedmont: about, 279–82; Alba, 292; Asti, 292; Big Bench Project, 282, 316–19; highlights, 290; Lake Maggiore, 291; map, 276; Orta, 292; San Giulio Island, 291; truffle hunting, 293; wines of, 291. *See also* Turin

Pier Giorgio Frassati, Blessed, 292, 304–5

pilgrims' perspectives, xiii–xvi, 61–65, 122–25, 177–79, 218–19, 270–72

Pio of Pietrelcina, Saint, 145, 149, 152–53

Pisa (Tuscany): about, 262–64; Santa Maria Assunta, Cathedral, 262; St. Bona of Pisa, 228–29; Tower of Pisa, 262, 263

Pius XII, Pope, 100

Polignano a Mare, 143

Pompeii, 132

Porta San Maria, 47

Portiuncula (Assisi), 98–99

Porto Venere, 240, 245, 251–53

Portoferraio, 241

Portofino, 239, 240

Positano, 1–2, 131–32, 137, 138, 146–47

Praiano, 129, 132, 138, 161–62, 169, 172–73

Prati, 30

Preaching of the Anti-Christ (fresco) (Signorelli), 92

Procida, 132, 171

Proietti, Norberto, 94, 95

Puglia Region: Alberobello, 142, 167–68; highlights, 140–41; map, 128; Monte Sant'Angelo, 149–51; San Giovanni Rotondo, 142, 143, 145, 149, 152–53; Sassi, 142; St. Michael's Cave, 143; St. Padre Pio, 142, 145

Pugliano a Mare, 145

Pyramid of Cestius (Rome), 56

R

Rapallo, 239, 243, 251, 253–55

Raphael, 29, 257

Ravello, 132, 139

Ravenna, 338

recipes: *Bucatini all'Amatriciana*, 58–60; *Cannoli*, 215–17; *Cotoletta alla Milanese*, 327–29; *Limoncello*, 175–76; *Ribollita Tuscan White Bean and Kale Soup*, 267–69; *Tagliere*, 117–21

Regata Storica (Venice), 2, 324–25

Reggio, 88, 185–86, 191, 194, 196, 204

Reggio Calabria Museo Nazionale (Reggio), 196

Riccardo, John, ix–xii, 90, 123, 125

Rieti, 42

Rita of Cascia, Saint, 74

Ritchie, Mike, 61–65

Rocca Maggiore (Assisi), 84

Roman Empire, ix–x, xii, 23, 38, 111–12, 211

Romana of Todi, Saint, 75

Rome: architectural sites, 25–26; Borghese Gallery and Gardens,

26; Castel Sant'Angel, 25; Christmas in, 39; churches in, 28–31; Colosseum, 25; highlights, 22–23; Isola Tiberina, 27; major basilicas, 24; Pantheon, 25, 31; planning a visit, 19–20; Roman catacombs, 25; Roman Forum, ix, 19, 25; Santa Cecilia, Basilica of, 21, 28, 29, 55; Spanish Steps, 26; Testaccio neighborhood, 55–56; Trastevere neighborhood, 27, 54–55; traveling around, 16–18; Trevi Fountain, 26; Trinita dei Monti, Church of Santissima, 26

Rosalia of Monte Pellegrino, Saint, 192, 199–201

Rose of Viterbo, Saint, 41

S

Sabina Mountains, 42

Sacred Heart of Jesus, Church of (Rome), 28, 30

Sacro Monte di Orta, 282, 291, 306–8, 309

Sagra della Ricotta e del Formaggio (Vizzini), 212–13

San Brizio Chapel (Orvieto), 91

San Damiano Cross, xi, 83, 95, 99, 100, 124

San Domenico, Church of (Castello), 75

San Donato, 47

San Fortunato, Basilica of, 75

San Galgano, Abbey of (Tuscany), 177–79

San Gimignano (Tuscany), 20, 248, 259–60

San Giorgio, Church of (Portofino), 240

San Giovanni Rotondo (Puglia), 142, 143, 145, 149

San Giulio Island, 291

San Giuseppe da Copertino, Bascilica of (Osimo), 133

San Lorenzo, Church of (Perugia), 106–7

San Marzano, 59

San Pietro, Bapistery of (Asti), 292

San Pietro, Church of (Porto Venere), 240

San Terenziano, Church of, 75

Sangallo, Antonio da (the Younger), 114–15

Santa Caterina del Sasso (Lake Maggiore), 308–9

Santa Cecilia, Basilica of (Rome), 21, 28, 29, 55

Santa Christina, Church of, 91

Santa Croce, Basilica di (Florence), 258

Santa Maria Assunta. *See* Duomo di Orivieto

Santa Maria Assunta, Cathedral (Pisa), 262

Santa Maria Assunta, Cathedral (Volterra), 261

Santa Maria Assunta, Cattedrale (Asti), 292

Santa Maria Assunta, Church of, 146–47

Santa Maria, Basilica of (Rome), 28, 29

Santa Maria del Fiore, Cathedral of (Florence), 232, 258

Santa Maria del Popolo (Rome), 29

Santa Maria della Vittoria, Church of (Rome), 28, 30, 31

Santa Maria delle Grazie (Milan), 286, 287, 288

Santa Maria dell'Isola, Sanctuary of (Tropea), 196–97, 208

Santa Maria Maggiore. *See* St. Mary Major, Basilica of (Rome)

Santa Maria Sopra Minerva (Rome), 28, 31

Santa Rita da Cascia, Basilica of (Perugia), 74

Santo Anello (Mary's Ring) (Perugia), 106–7

Santo Spirito, Church of (Sassia, Rome), 28, 30

Santuario di Soviore, 243

Sardinia, 337, 356–57

Sassi di Matera (Basilicata), 165–67

Scholastica of Nursia, Saint, 72, 74

Sebastian, Saint, 25

Sestri Levante, 243

Shelley, Percy Bysshe, 56

Shroud of Turin, 291, 302–4

Sicily: about, 185–86; Aeolian Islands, 193–94; Agrigento, 209–10; Catania, 192; highlights, 190–91; map, 182; Messina, 185, 186; Monte Pellegrino, 192; Mount Etna, 193; Palermo, 192, 199–201, 202–3, 215; Sagra della Ricotta e del Formaggio, 212–13; signature dishes, 215–17; St. Rosalia of Monte Pellegrino, 192, 199–201; Taormina, 192, 210, 211; Valley of the Temples, 192

Siena (Tuscany): Basilica of St. Francis, 249–51; Palio di Siena, 234, 264–65; Piazza del Campo, 234; St. Catherine of, 20, 25, 31, 73, 234; St. Mary in Provenzano, 250

Signorelli, Luca, 92

Sirmione (Lombardy), 289

Sistine Chapel (Vatican), 23, 24, 61, 92, 270, 271

Solstad, Bree, 218–19

Sorrento, 132, 137, 169, 171, 175, 218–19

Spanish Steps (Rome), 26

Spello (Umbria), 113

St. Andrew, Cathedral of (Amalfi), 138, 145, 147–48

St. Cecilia, Basilica of (Rome), 21, 28, 29, 55

St. Clare, Basilica of (Assisi), 74, 83, 100, 124

St. Francis, Basilica of (Assisi), 83, 96, 117, 124, 308

St. Francis, Basilica of (Siena), 245, 249–51

St. Francis, Church of (Lanciano), 308

St. Francis of Peace, Church of (Gubbio), 103

St. John Lateran, Basilica of (Rome), 19, 24, 28

St. John the Baptist, Cathedral of (Turin), 304, 305

St. Mary in Provenzano (Siena), 250

St. Mary Major, Basilica of (Rome), 19, 24, 28

St. Mary Major, Church of (Assisi), 77, 83, 98, 99

St. Mary of the Angels (Assisi), 83, 99

St. Mary of the Purification, Cathedral of (Molise), 349

St. Michael's Cave (Puglia), 145

St. Patrick's Well (Orvieto), 114–15

St. Paul Outside the Walls, Basilica of (Rome), xi, 19, 24, 28

St. Peter, Basilica of (Vatican), x, 5, 19, 23, 24, 28, 48

St. Peter's Square (Vatican), 30, 124

St. Thomas of Villanova (Lazio), 49

St. Ubaldo, Basilica of, 103

Steinbeck, John, 131–32

T

Taormina, 192, 210, 211

Tarquinia, 16, 52–53

Teatro alla Scala (Milan), 288

Teatro Greco (Taormina), 211

Temple Minerva (Assisi), 84, 117

Terentian of Todi, Saint, 75

Teresa Benedicta of the Cross (Edith Stein), 5–6

Testaccio neighborhood (Rome), 55–56

Thérèse of the Child Jesus, Saint, 26, 29

Tiber River, 22, 25, 30, 38, 46, 54, 57, 80

Tiberina Island (Rome), 27, 55

Timothy, Saint, xi

Tivoli (Lazio), 50–51

Todi (Umbria), 72, 73, 75

Tomeo, Teresa, ix, xiii, xvi, 383

Torcello, 322

Train of the Pontifical Villas, 48

Trastevere neighborhood (Rome), 21, 27, 28, 29, 54–55

Trentino-Alto, 337, 350–51

Trevi Fountain (Rome), 26

Trinita dei Monti, Church of Santissima (Rome), 26

Tropea (Calabria), 101, 194, 196, 197, 207–8, 318

Turin: Basilica of Our Lady Help of Christians, 292; Cathedral of St. John the Baptist, 291–92, 304; Our Lady of Help of Christians, 282; Pier Giorgio Frassati, Blessed, 292, 304–5; Sacred Mountains, 292; Shroud of Turin, 281–82, 291, 302–4

Tuscany: about, 225–26; Chianti, 235; highlights, 230–31; map, 222; Montalcino, 235; Montepulciano, 235; Pisa, 228–29, 262–64; San Galgano, Abbey of, 177–79; San Gimignano, 259–60; signature dishes, 267–69; St. Bona of Pisa, 228–29; Via

Francigena, 247–48; Volterra, 260–62. *See also* Florence; Siena

Tyrrhenian Sea, 136, 145, 194, 196, 197, 204, 208, 230. *See also* Maratea (Basilica)

U

Ubaldo of Gubbio, Saint, 75, 103

Umbria Region: about, 71–72, 87–90; Angela of Foligno, Saint, 74, 78–79; Benedict of Nursia, Saint, 72, 74; Deruta Ceramics, 85; Eremo delle Carceri (hermitage), 83; Festa dei Ceri (Gubbio), 102–5; highlights, 80–81; Lake Bolsena, 34; map, 68; Marmore Falls, 112; Nera River Park, 112; Orvieto, 72; saints of, 72–77; Sanctuary of Madonna dei Bagni (Deruta), 108–9; Santo Anello (Mary's Ring) (Perugia), 106–7; Scholastica of Nursia, Saint, 72, 74; signature dishes, 117–21; Spello, 113; St. Mary of the Angels (Assisi), 83; Via Flaminia, 111–12; wine spas, 85. *See also* Assisi; Orvieto

Urban VIII, Pope, 49

V

Valley of the Temples (Agrigento), 192, 209–10

Vatican City: Basilica of St. Peter, x, 5, 19, 23, 24, 28, 48; Castel Gandolfo, 34, 48–49, 270, 271; highlights, 22–23; Lake Albano, 33, 48, 49; Sistine Chapel, 23, 24, 61, 92, 270, 271; St. Peter's Square, 30, 124; Vatican Gardens (Barberini), 23, 48, 49; Vatican Museums, 19, 23, 24, 48, 271, 367

Veneto Region: about, 279–82; highlights, 294–95; map, 276

Venice: Basilica of San Marco, 295, 296, 320; Bridge of Sighs, 296, 320; Doge's Palace, 296, 320; gondola rides, 296, 320; Grand Canal, 2; names for, 294; Regata Storica, 2, 324–25; Rialto Bridge, 320; St. Mark's Square, 296, 319–20; Venetian Islands, 296

Verga, Giovanni, 212

Verona, 297

Veronica Giuliani of Castello, Saint, 75

Via Flaminia (Umbria), 111–12

Via Francigena (Tuscany), 247–48

Villa d'Este Tivoli, 50–51

Villa Rufolo (Ravello), 139

Viterbo (Lazio), 34, 39–41

Vizzini (Sicily), 212–13

Volterra (Tuscany), 260–62

Volterraio Castle, 241

W

Wagner, Richard, 139

"Walk of the Gods," 2

Way of St. Francis, 43

White Madonna of Porto Venere (Liguria), 251–53

Wolf of Gubbio, 103–5

Y

Yoches, Annie, 122–25

ACKNOWLEDGEMENTS

To Gail Coniglio and the fabulous T's Italy Team: I can't thank you all enough for your daily dedication, tireless dedication, and creativity. Gail, you, Marcy, and Palma have not only been a major force in helping me develop my dream of T's Italy, but continue to be significant in my overall ministry especially with our online outreach. And Gail, this book would not have happened without your expertise, talents, daily support, and creative input.

To Fr. John Riccardo and Msgr. Michael Bugarin: No priests have been more influential in the lives of me and Deacon Dom than you two amazing men of God. Fr. John, (Padre), for taking the time out of your extremely busy ministry to write such a heartfelt foreword and for years of guidance and friendship, we are eternally grateful. And Msgr., for your direction and support over the years, including encouraging us in our decision to spend so much time overseas, *grazie*! You are both such a gift to the Church.

To Ave Maria Radio, EWTN, and Sophia Institute Press: I am beyond grateful for the opportunity to have a platform on-air, online, and in print. Thank you also for supporting our long-running radio program, *Catholic Connection*, as I take the show on the road throughout Italy and for embracing *Italy's Shrines and Wonders* as it took a real team effort to make this book a reality. To my producer Andrew Kruczek, for your daily wisdom and input for Catholic Connection, and extreme patience with my busy travel schedule. With the wisdom of the late Al Kresta always in our minds and hearts, may we, with the Lord's blessing, continue to bring His light to a world in such need.

To Adrian, Adriana, and Charlize Boncu, our neighbors in Umbria, who have been our "guardian angels" support system and are now like family. You have been so significant in helping us adjust to life in Italy.

To my husband, Deacon Dominick Pastore: As I always say, you're the best thing that happened to me, next to coming back to Christ and the Church. And of course, coming back home never would have happened without your love and prayers. Thank you for embracing this, God willing, continuing journey getting to know our Motherland. *Ti amo!*

IMAGE CREDITS
(Images given in order of appearance)

FOREWORD

1. St. Paul Outside the Walls (exterior view). Teresa Tomeo, all rights reserved.

PREFACE

2. Deacon Dominick and Teresa with John and Kristen Hale at Il Pellicano. Teresa Tomeo, all rights reserved.

INTRODUCTION

3. Positano village, AMALFI, ITALY, (1159784716) © Javen / shutterstock.com

4. Display of Various Flavors of Gelato, (241030088) (c) EdNurg / stock.adobe.com

PART 1: *ROME AND THE LAZIO REGION:* MARVELS OF THE VATICAN AND BEYOND

5. River Tiber, ROME, ITALY, Christian Nordmark, Unsplash.com

6. Region of Lazio (map)

7. Colosseum, ROME, ITALY, (1552896293) © LI SEN / shutterstock.com

8. St. Peter's Basilica, ROME, ITALY, (648140494) © ecstk22 / shutterstock.com

9. "St. Cecilia" by Il Sassoferrato, Museo Poldi Pezzoli, public domain image provided by Google Arts and Culture / commons.wikimedia.org

10. Romulus and Remus with the Wolf, ROME, ITALY, (32464399) © Bill Perry / shutterstock.com

11. "The Chair of St. Peter," Teresa Tomeo, all rights reserved.

12. The Elephant and the Obelisk, ROME, ITALY, (2389267063) © Ivo Antonie de Rooij / shutterstock.com

13. Sistine Chapel in the Vatican Museum, VATICAN CITY, (2C0RH2W) © Sorin Colac / stock.adobe.com

14. Basilica of St. John Lateran (interior). Teresa Tomeo, all rights reserved.

15. Catherine of Siena statue, Castel Sant'Angelo, ROME, ITALY, (439386504) © from_south / stock.adobe.com

16. The Roman Forum, ROME, ITALY, Fabio Fistarol, Unsplash.com

17. Column of the Immaculate Conception, Piazza della Trinita dei Monti, ROME, ITALY, (371124139) © BRIAN_KINNEY / stock.adobe.com

18. Trevi Fountain, ROME, ITALY, Christina Gottardi, Unsplash.com

19. Isola Tiberina. Tiber Island, ROME, ITALY, (214437729) © Vladimir Sazonov / stock.adobe.com

20. Mosaics of Maria Trastevere, ROME, ITALY, (307809668) © dddoria / stock.adobe.com

21. Statue of St. Cecilia, Basilica of St. Cecilia, Trastevere, ROME, ITALY, (94930214) © t0m15 / stock.adobe.com

22. Church of Santo Spirito. Church of the Holy Spirit, home of the Sanctuary of Divine Mercy, ROME, ITALY, (1783982696) © Marek Poplawski / shutterstock.com

23. Church of Sacred Heart. The Church of the Sacred Heart of Suffrage, ROME, ITALY, (1241631181) © Annalucia / shutterstock.com

24. Ecstasy of St. Teresa (Maria Della Vitorria), ROME, ITALY, (145435614) © Steve Kuttig / stock.adobe.com

25. Tomb of Catherine of Siena. Teresa Tomeo, all rights reserved.

26. Etruscan Tombs, CERVETERI, ITALY (1546470467) © Massimo Salesi / shutterstock.com

27. Lake Bracciano, LAZIO, ITALY, (2198607085) © Vlas Telino studio / shutterstock.com

28. Lake Albano, Teresa Tomeo, all rights reserved.

29. Basilica di Santa Christina, BOLSENA, ITALY (2349689795) © Uellue / shutterstock

30. The Pontifical Gardens at Castel Gandolfo, CASTEL GANDOLFO, ITALY, (2375705235) © Maria_Usp / shutterstock.com

31. Archaeological park of Ostia Antica, ROME, ITALY, (1184267932) © Fabianodp / shutterstock.com

32. Ostia Antica, ROME ITALY, Elena Golubeva, Unsplash.com

33. Palazzo dei Papi, home of the first papal enclave. Teresa Tomeo, all rights reserved.

34. Traditional garb of Faccini of Santa Rosa. Teresa Tomeo, all rights reserved.

35. Greccio Sanctuary. Teresa Tomeo, all rights reserved.

36. Castel Gandolfo, CASTEL GANDOLFO, ITALY, (2417457733) © Hope Writing Light / shutterstock.com

37. Civita Bagnoregio: The Dying City. Teresa Tomeo, all rights reserved.

38. Civita di Bagnoregio, LAZIO, ITALY, (327458390) © canadastock / shutterstock.com

39. Castel Gandolfo/Barbarini Gardens. Teresa Tomeo, all rights reserved.

40. Villa d'Este, Fountain of the Organ, TIVOLI, ITALY (606998739) © Kelly Cheng / stock.adobe.com

41. Tarquinia Winged Horses (4th Cent BC). Teresa Tomeo, all rights reserved.

42. Mosaic in the apse of Sancta Maria in Trastevere, ROME, ITALY © Krzysztof Golik / commons.wikimedia.org

43. Grave of John Keats, ROME, ITALY, (1910562187) © Alex_Mastro / shutterstock.com

44. Lungo il Tevere. "Lungo il Tevere" for the summer program "Estate Romana", ROME, ITALY (2KBNBG8) © Fabrizio Troiani / alamy.com

45. Bucatini all/Amatriciana. "Bucatini all'amatriciana" Pasta with bacon and tomato sauce, (F9RB1R) © Simon Reddy / alamy.com

46. Mike Ritchie, first trip to Rome. Mike Ritchie, all rights reserved.

47. Mike Ritchie and family. Mike Ritchie, all rights reserved.

48. Orvieto, ITALY, (2474402491) © ectsk22 / shutterstock.com

PART 2: *UMBRIA*: THE "GREEN HEART" *(CUORE VERDE)* OF ITALY

49. Region of Umbria (map)

50. Orvieto, UMBRIA, ITALY, (2278669833) © lincegialla / shutterstock.com

51. "Sunset in Umbria." Teresa Tomeo, all rights reserved.

52. Medieval town of Todi. Teresa Tomeo, all rights reserved.

53. "Madonna with St. Francis of Assisi and St. Clare," Chiesa di Santa Chiara. St. Clare and St. Francis, Santa Chiara, Assisi. MATERA, ITALY, (2J77DJD) © jozef sedmak / alamy.com

54. Amata of Assisi, (2366431911) © godongphoto / shutterstock.com

55. St. Benedict and St. Scholastica. (22952142) © zatletic / stock. adobe.com

56. Ubaldo of Saint Ubaldo XVIII. GUBBIO, ITALY, (527339399) © jeeweevh / stock.adobe.com

57. Blessed Jacopone. Monument to Jacopone da Todi, PERUGIA, ITALY, (533453519) © Marco Taliani / stock.adobe.com

58. St. Valentine. St. Joseph, St. Anthony the Abbot, and St. Valentine, MALCESINE, ITALY, (1609224958) © Renata Sedmakova / shutterstock.com

59. Tomb of Blessed Carlo Acutis. Teresa Tomeo, all rights reserved.

60. St. Angela of Foligno, public domain image.

61. Orvieto Cathedral, UMBRIA, ITALY (2465045957) © Andrei Nekrassov / shutterstock.com

62. Perugia, Umbria, Teresa Tomeo, all rights reserved.

63. Gubbio, Umbria, Teresa Tomeo, all rights reserved.

64. Todi, Umbria, Teresa Tomeo, all rights reserved.

65. Assisi, PERUGIA, ITALY, (1041837658) © Zdenek Matyas Photography / shutterstock.com

66. "Deruta, the ceramics capital." Teresa Tomeo, all rights reserved.

67. Basilica of St. Francis of Assisi, PERUGIA, ITALY (1548843110) © Elena Cavallin / shutterstock. com

68. View from Balcony, Teresa Tomeo, all rights reserved.

69. "Orvieto Duomo." Teresa Tomeo, all rights reserved.

70. "Preaching of the Anti-Christ by Luca Signorelli. Teresa Tomeo, all rights reserved.

71. "Return of St. Francis" (statue). Teresa Tomeo, all rights reserved.

72. Tomb of Blessed Carlo Acutis. Teresa Tomeo, all rights reserved.

73. St. Mary of the Angels, Portiuncula Church. Teresa Tomeo, all rights reserved.

74. Clare of Montefalco, artist unknown, (HY9N3N) © Art Collection 3 / alamy.com

75. Festa Dei Ceri (Gubbio) – Giant Ceri candles. Teresa Tomeo, all rights reserved.

76. "Francis and the Wolf of Gubbio" Teresa Tomeo, all rights reserved.

77. Santo Anello, Cathedral of San Lorenzo, PERUGIA, ITALY, © Nicoletta De Matthaeis / reliquiosamente.com

78. Madonna Bagni Shrine, Umbria, Teresa Tomeo, all rights reserved.

79. Mamore Falls, Nera River Park. La castcate delle Marmore, UMBRIA, ITALY, (651196101) © Claudio Quacquarelli / stock.adobe.com

80. Carsulae. Scavi di Carsulae, UMBRIA, ITALY, (504130174) © anghifoto / stock.adobe.com

81. Infiorate Flower Festival. Teresa Tomeo, all rights reserved.

82. St. Patrick's Well. Ancient Well of St. Patrick, ORVIETO, ITALY, (44545175) © ChiccoDodiFC / stock.adobe.com

83. Calendimaggio Festival of Assisi. Teresa Tomeo, all rights reserved.

84. (Tagliere), kaltes buffet (384629502) © lotharnahler / stock.adobe.com,

85. Speck and salami meat platter, (2424564593) © Kuvona / shutterstock.com

86. Annie Yoches and mother. Sr. Rita Clare Yoches, all rights reserved.

87. Sr. Rita Clare. Sr. Rita Clare Yoches, all rights reserved.

PART 3: *CAMPANIA AND PUGLIA: ITALY COAST TO COAST*

88. Amalfi, Italy, (1882132951) © Antonina Tadeush / shutterstock.com

89. Regions of Campania and Puglia (map)

90. Dome of the Church of Santa Maria Assunta, Positano, Campania, Gail Coniglio, all rights reserved.

91. Praiano Coastline, Campania, Gail Coniglio, all rights reserved.

92. "St. Joseph Cupertino" by Ludovico Mazzanti, Church of Saint Joseph of Cupertino, OSIMO, ITALY, (MNX2E3) © The Picture Art Collection / alamy.com

93. Path of the Gods, CAMPAGNIA, ITALY, (420694474) © Josef Skacel / shutterstock.com

94. Capri, NAPLES, ITALY, (683203579) © Darios / shutterstock.com

95. Fountain of the Giant, NAPLES, ITALY, (2330138469) © Ruslan Harutyunov / shutterstock.com

96. Tomato sauce, (2459323197) © New Africa / shutterstock.com

97. Faraglioni di Mezzo, NAPLES, ITALY, (2007067154) © Wierzchu / shutterstock.com

98. Traditional Ceramics, POSITANO, ITALY, (2535754597) © Alina Mosinyan / shutterstock.com

99. Villa Rufolo, RAVELLO, ITALY, (778829911) © Anna Dunlop / shutterstock.com

100. Summer Lido di Portonuovo, ADRIATIC SEA, ITALY (2473238299) © Yuriy Brykaylo / shutterstock.com

101. White Village Locorotondo, PUGLIA, ITALY, (1688967661) © camis.fc / shutterstock.com

102. Olive Grove in Salento, PUGLIA, ITALY, (1552603622) © Anna Fedorova_it / shutterstock.com

103. Gravina, PUGLIA, ITALY, (2490929891) © Rene Holtslag / shutterstock.com

104. Alberobello, PUGLIA, ITALY, (2458924671) © pixelshop / shutterstock.com

105. The Lama Monachile Bay, POLIGNANO A MARE, ITALY, (2478061857) © Nejdet Duzen / shutterstock.com

106. Cathedral of St. Andrew, AMALFI, ITALY, (352409726) © BAHDANOVICH ALENA / shutterstock.com

107. Relics of St. Andrew, Amalfi. St. Andrew, AMALFI, ITALY, (2416568555) © DyziO / shutterstock.com

108. Cave of St. Michael. Cave of St. Michael, APULIA, ITALY, (203916053) © Francesco Bonino / stock.adobe.com

109. San Giovanni Rotondo. Interior of Sanctuary of San Pio da Pietrelcina, San Giovanni Rotondo, FROGGIA, ITALY, (496900398) © angelo chiariello / stock.adobe.com

110. Church of St. Nicholas, BARI, ITALY, (726753442) © Flaviu Boerescu / stock.adobe.com

111. House of the Large Fountain, POMPEII, ITALY, (2155582405) © Lev Levin / shutterstock.com

112. Villa of Papyri, Herculaneum. Villa Papyri, ERCOLANO, ITALY, (526298399) © Matthias / stock. adobe.com

113. Cliff in Maratea MARATEA ITALY, (274913721) © Andriy Bezuglov / stock.adobe.com.

114. Christ the Redeemer (Maratea). Statue of Christ the Redeemer at MARATEA, ITALY, (447344698) © ValerioMei / stock.adobe.com

115. City of Sassi. — Sassi di Matera, MATERA, ITALY, (208435467) © davidionut / stock.adobe.com

116. Trulli homes. Trulli, homes in Alberobello, ALBERBELLO, ITALY, (257407064) © Giancarlo / stock.adobe.com

117. Ischia, the "Other Capri" Aragonese Castle, ISCHIA ISLAND, ITALY, (282296130) © Tomasz Czajkowski / stock.adobe. com

118. Festival of Luminaria. The Luminaria in Pisa, PISA, ITALY (RPK0HW) © Dyrj Taksma / alamy.com

119. Limoncello, (2412995877) © New Africa / shutterstock.com

120. Limoncello. Joan Lewis, all rights reserved.

121. Sword of Galgano. Sword in the rock in San Galgano, TUSCANY, ITALY (2447817099) © Tomasz Czajkowski / shutterstock.com

122. John Hale with son on Vespa. John Hale, all rights reserved.

**PART 4: *SICILY AND CALABRIA:*
NAUTICAL NEIGHBORS**

123. Cefalu, PALERMO, ITALY,
(1223871763) © Balate.Dorin /
shutterstock.com

124. Regions of Sicily and Calabria
(map)

125. Boats on Levanzo island, SICILY,
ITALY, (175001060) © Evgeniya L
/ shutterstock.com

126. Lungomare. Lungomare Coast
Walkway, OPATIJA, ITALY,
(151871226) © xbrchx / stock.
adobe.com

127. St. Francesco di Paola by Bartolomé
Esteban Murillo, Museo del Pardo,
MADRID, SPAIN, (MNX2B5) ©
The Picture Art Collection / alamy.
com

128. The Valley of the Temples of
Agrigento, AGRIGENTO ITALY,
(1065155945) © Gimas /
shutterstock.com

129. Mount Etna, SICILY, ITALY,
(1373396795) © kavalenkava /
shutterstock.com

130. Catalina, SICILY, ITALY,
(2205707141) © Pandora Pictures
/ shutterstock.com

131. Pretoria Fountain in Piazza
Pretoria, PALERMO, ITALY,
(2166067383) © ecstk22 /
shutterstock.com

132. Sicily – Isle of Stromboli. Teresa
Tomeo, all rights reserved.

133. Bronzes of Riace, Il Vecchio,
RIACE, ITALY, (263516681) ©
s.pellicciotti / shutterstock.com

134. Vespa, CALABRIA, ITALY, Teresa
Tomeo, all rights reserved.

135. Tropea city in CALABRIA, ITALY,
(1389390689) © Polonio Video /
shutterstock.com

136. Calabrian red pepper in Tropea
street market, TROPEA, ITALY,
(2210200893) © RasaBasa /
shutterstock.com

137. Chianalea di Scilla, CALABRIA,
ITALY, (1161360664) ©
Aliaksandr Antanovich /
shutterstock.com

138. Imperial Chapel, Palace of Palermo,
PALERMO, ITALY, (374708719)
© Andreas Zerndl / shutterstock.
com

139. Shrine of St. Rosalia (Monte
Pellegrino), PALERMO, ITALY,
(325190867) © Stefano Piazza /
stock.adobe.com

140. St. Rosalia. Santuario di Santa
Rosalia sul Monte Pellegrino,
PALERMO, ITALY, (2459252929)
© faber1893 / shutterstock.com

141. Imperial Chapel, Palace of
PALERMO, ITALY, (374708710)
© Andreas Zerndl / shutterstock.
com

142. Christ Pantocrator (mosaic).
Mosaic of Christ, Pantocreator,
Cefalu Cathedral, SICILY, ITALY,
(226392029) © e55evu / stock.
adobe.com

143. Church of Piedigrotta, Calabria,
Teresa Tomeo, all rights reserved.

144. Taormina, Sicily, Italy,
(2248501723) © Rudy Balasko /
shutterstock.com

145. Santa Maria Isola Monastery.
Monastery on Santa Maria Isola,
TROPEA, ITALY, (162235835) ©
jovannig / stock.adobe.com

146. Valley of Temples. Valle dei Templi, Agrigento, Island in Sicily, SICILY, ITALY, (188278747) © crocicascino / stock.adobe.com

147. Cannoli. Cannoli, (83385840) © arinahabich / stock.adobe.com

148. Toma and Ricotta, (1294939762) © Alessandro Cristiano / shutterstock.com

149. Salted Ricotta, (571650514) © anna.q / shutterstock.com

150. Mixed Sicilian Cannoli, (111821231) © Luca Santilli / shutterstock.com

151. Creamy Filled Ricotta Cannoli, (1896418030) © Toasted Pictures / shutterstock.com

PART 5: *TUSCANY AND LIGURIA REGIONS, AND CINQUE TERRE: DELIGHTING BY LAND AND BY SEA*

152. Tuscany Sunrise. TUSCANY, (323659901) © Photocreo Michal Bednarek / shutterstock.com

153. Regions of Tuscany, Liguria, and Cinque Terre (map)

154. Porto Venere, LIGURIA, ITALY, (GGD27X (RM) © INTERFOTO / alamy.com

155. "David" by Michelangelo, FLORENCE, ITALY, (AF1DP1) © Derek Croucher / alamy.com

156. St. Catherine's house. Teresa Tomeo, all rights reserved.

157. Leaning Tower of Pisa. Leaning Tower of Pisa, PISA, ITALY, (H3N2WD) © Steve Allen Travel Photography / alamy.com

158. "St. Bona of Pisa," San Martino Church, PISA, ITALY, public domain image provided by Samuele / alamy.com

159. Primavera by Botticelli, Uffizi Gallery, Florence, public domain image provided by Google Arts and Culture / via

160. "The Little Pig" Mercato Nuovo in FLORENCE, ITALY, (477953773) © berm_teerawat / shutterstock.com

161. San Biagio Cathedral, MONTEPULCIANO, ITALY, (95270554) © Martin M303 / shutterstock.com

162. Basilica Santa Croce. Basilica di Santa Croce, FLORENCE, ITALY (92490939) © efired / stock.adobe.com

163. "Gates of Paradise" by Lorenzo Ghiberti. Gates of Paradise, Florence Baptistery, FLORENCE, ITALY. (411153221) © Artem / stock.adobe.com

164. Piazza del Campo (Siena). Teresa Tomeo, all rights reserved.

165. Traditional Wine Shop in Montal Cino, TUSCANY, ITALY, (1024598011) © InnaFelker / shutterstock.com

166. Lake Trasimeno and Maggiore. Lake Trasimeno and Isola Maggiore, PASSIGNANO, ITALY, (F03ED3) © Frank Bach / alamy.com

167. Street in Genova Port, GENOA, ITALY, (1465348361) © Roman Sigaev / shutterstock.com

168. Vernazza (Cinque Terre). Teresa Tomeo, all rights reserved.

169. Liguria, Porto Venere. Teresa Tomeo, all rights reserved.

170. Monterosso al Mare village, CINQUE TERRE, ITALY, (2226789205) © Federica Ravettino / shutterstock.com

171. Sanctuary of Our Lady of Montallegro, MONTALLEGRO, ITALY, (1671168772) © Hubert Gemmert / stock.adobe.com

172. Santa Margherita (Ligure). Bay of Paraggi in Santa Margherita Ligure, LIGURIA, ITALY, (276422298) © katatonia / stock.adobe.com

173. Portofino's Castello Brown. Castello Brown, San Giorgio Castle, PORTFINO, ITALY, (162835434) © zigres / stock.adobe.com

174. San Pietro Church (Liguria). Teresa Tomeo, all rights reserved.

175. Marina of Portofino, CINQUE TERRE, ITALY, (2459776631) © Sina Ettmer Photography / shutterstock.com

176. Cinque Terre Express Train, MANAROLA, ITALY, (2389360805) © Chris Lawrence Images / shutterstock.com

177. Laverna, where St. Francis received wounds of Christ. Teresa Tomeo, all rights reserved.

178. Laverna Sanctuary. Teresa Tomeo, all rights reserved

179. Basilica of St. Francis (Siena). Basilica of St. Francis, SIENA, ITALY, (126974379) © Valery Rokhin / stock.adobe.com

180. Our Lady of Montallegro. Our Lady of Montallegro, RAPALLO, ITALY, (2358457185) © Simona Sirio / shutterstock.com

181. Madonna Bianca, Liguria, Italy. Teresa Tomeo, all rights reserved.

182. Sanctuary of our Lady of Montallegro, RAPALLO, ITALY, (2355206391) © Wirestock Creators / shutterstock.com

183. Duomo in Florence, FLORENCE, ITALY, (2429942587) © EyesTravelling / shutterstock.com

184. Ponte Vecchio. Ponte Vecchio over River Arno, FLORENCE, ITALY (EAMA2W) © Brian Jannsen / alamy.com

185. San Gimignano Towers. Piazza del Duomo in San Gimignano, TUSCANY, ITALY, (195783169) © Feel good studio / stock.adobe.com

186. Vespa, ITALY, (77797149) © Alessandro Calzolaro / stock.adobe.com

187. Piazza dei Miracoli complex, PISA, ITALY (84489133) © Robert Hoetink / shutterstock.com

188. Palio di Siena. Flag Waving after the Palio di Siena, SIENA, ITALY, (2279871299) © Dietmar Rauscher / shutterstock.com

189. Ribollita, (488510182) © Olga / stock.adobe.com

190. Lori Maher with John and Kristen Hale. John Hale, all rights reserved.

191. Catherine of Siena, Siena, Teresa Tomeo, all rights reserved.

PART 6: *LOMBARDY, PIEDMONT, AND VENETO:* NORTHERN LIGHTS

192. Torino Skyline, TURIN, ITALY (544205710) © Fabio Lamanna / shutterstock.com

193. Regions of Lombardy, Piedmont, and Veneto (map)

194. Lake Como, view in Bellagio, BELLAGIO, ITALY, (129674174) © Anna-Mari West / shutterstock.com

195. Lake Como, BELLAGIO, ITALY (2454134475) © Robert Harding Video / shutterstock.com

196. St. Mark's Square. St. Mark's Square, VENICE, ITALY, (259366432) © fottoo / stock.adobe.com

197. Piedmont. Teresa Tomeo, all rights reserved.

198. Lake Como, LAKE COMO, ITALY, (2503266123) © Viltvart / shutterstock.com

199. St. Giovanni Scalabrini, (2K5MWJP (RM)) © Abaca press / alamy.com

200. Scala Opera House, MILAN, ITALY, (2117656442) © posztos / shutterstock.com

201. Statue of Antonio Stradivari, CREMONA, ITALY, (452749768) © Renata Sedmakova / shutterstock.com

202. The River Po, CREMONA, ITALY, (1422347996) © D-Visions / shutterstock.com

203. "The Last Supper" (Milan). The Last Supper, MILAN, ITALY, (1150529321) © Ungvari Attila / shutterstock.com

204. Cathedral of the Assumption, ASTI, ITALY, (2046600272) © milosk50 / shutterstock.com

205. Piedmont Winery, Teresa Tomeo, all rights reserved.

206. Mountains in Piedmont, PIEDMONT, ITALY, (2048353115) © Rostislav Glinsky / shutterstock.com

207. Truffle hunting in Piedmont. Truffle, PIEDMONT, ITALY, (355691569) © Cosca / stock.adobe.com

208. Teresa and Fr. John hunt for truffles. Teresa Tomeo, all rights reserved.

209. Cathedral of St. Mark, VENICE, ITALY, (2344156941) © Florin Cnejevici / shutterstock.com

210. Lagoon of Venice, Glasswork, VENICE, ITALY, (1123005824) © Gimas / shutterstock.com

211. Romeo and Juliet Balcony in VERONA, ITALY, (493112500) © Alena 11 / shutterstock.com

212. Bridge of Sighs, VENICE, ITALY, (1999120385) © Maykova Galina / shutterstock.com

213. Basilica of St. Anthony of Padua, PADUA, ITALY, (2158539593) © Wirestock Creators / shutterstock.com

214. Mosaics of the Basilica of San Vitale, RAVENNA, ITALY, (666390586) © Gimas / shutterstock.com

215. Shrine of Madonna del Corona. The Sanctuary of Madonna della Corona, SPIAZZI, ITALY, (358050561) © Electric Egg Ltd. / stock.adobe.com

216. Cathedral of St. John the Baptist, Relics of Saint John the Baptist, TURIN, ITALY, (2397514027) © Mltz / shutterstock.com

217. Blessed Pier Giorgio Frassati. Pier Giorgio Frassati by Alberto Falchetti, CANTANIA, ITALY, (1427632292) © Renata Sedmakova / shutterstock.com

218. Deacon Dom and Teresa at Lago Maggiore. Teresa Tomeo, all rights reserved.

219. St. Catherine del Sasso Hermitage. Hermitage of Santa Caterina del Sasso, LEGGIUNO, ITALY, (248481408) © afinocchiaro / stock.adobe.com

220. Frescoes of Chapel in Sacro Monte di Orta, ORTA SAN GUILIO, ITALY, (1459998398) © Isogood_patrick / shutterstock.com

221. Navigli District (Milan). Navigli District in MILAN, ITALY, (DB6KXP) © tony french / alamy.com

222. Duomo di Milano. Milan Cathedral, MILAN, ITALY, (FN8JM1) © Boris Stroujko / alamy.com

223. Roof terraces of the Milan Cathedral, MILAN, ITALY, (499527193) © javarman / shutterstock.com

224. Big Bench Project (Piedmont). Teresa Tomeo, all rights reserved.

225. Doge Palace. Castle of Govone, PIEDMONT, ITALY, (1756010147) © kavram / shutterstock.com

226. Burano. Burano, an Island in the Venetian Lagoon, VENICE, ITALY, (251132039) © Luis / stock.adobe.com

227. "Last Judgment" (mosaic, 11th century). 12th Century mosaic of the Last Judgement, Cathedral of Santa Maria Assunta, VENICE, ITALY, (EC89DJ) © B.O'Kane / stock.adobe.com

228. Canals in Venice, Teresa Tomeo, all rights reserved.

229. Regata Storica, VENICE, ITALY, (2446141187) © Robert Harding Video / shutterstock.com

230. Veal Milanese. Veal Milanese, (1055477606) © AS Foodstudio / shutterstock.com

PART 7: "GOING HOME AGAIN": CONTINUING TO EXPLORE, THERE'S ALWAYS SOMETHING MORE

231. Brisighella Clock Tower, RAVENNA, ITALY, (2243563979) © StevanZZ / shutterstock.com

232. The Fontana Fraterna, Molise, (1522166093) © SerFeo / shutterstock.com

233. Anguillara Sabazia — Anguillara Sabazia, ROME, ITALY, (530845127) © Equatore / stock.adobe.com

234. St. Peter Damian by Andrea Barbiani, Library Classense, RAVENNA, ITALY, (MWNAWG) © The Picture Art Collection / alamy.com

235. Pacentro, ABURZZO, ITALY, (2484034861) © Cedant / shutterstock.com

236. Gran Sasso National Park. Gran Sasso Church, ABRUZZO, ITALY, (369239380) © ronnybas / stock.adobe.com

237. Miracle of Lanciano. Miracle of Lanciano, Sanctuary Church of San Francesco, LANCIANO, ITALY, (559843595) © serfeo / stock.adobe.com

238. Ancient University Library (Bologna). Library of the University of Bologna, BOLOGNA, ITALY, (J7BENP) © Roger Cracknell 01/classic / alamy.com

239. Cloister of Basilica di San Domenico, BOLOGNA, ITALY, (733438510) © Joaquin Ossorio Castillo / shutterstock.com

240. Sanctuary of Monte Grisa (Trieste). Santuario di Monte Grisa Church, TRIESTE ITALY, photo by Andreas Manessinger / Wikipedia.com

241. Town Hall, TRIESTE, ITALY (2053208399) © berni0004 / shutterstock.com

242. House of Mary. Holy House of Loreto, LORETO, ITALY, (1210414567) © Tatiana Diuvbanova / shutterstock.com

243. The Holy House of Loreto, Piazza della Madonna, LORETO, ITALY, (2333280303) © trabantos / shutterstock.com

244. Cathedral of St. Mary of the Purification, TERMOLI, ITALY, (593074709) © Shoot74 / shutterstock.com

245. Sanctuary of Castelpetroso, MOLISE, ITALY, (492875845) © Alex Photofootage / shutterstock.com

246. Site of Council of Trent. TRENTO, ITALY, (402554901) © Claudio / stock.adobe.com

247. Village of Burgeis and Abbey of Monte Maria, TRENTINO ALTO, ITALY, (2273850599) © xbrchx / shutterstock.com

248. Cathedral of Sant'Orso. Sant'Orso Cathedral, AOSTA VALLEY, ITALY, (704675341) © Simone / stock.adobe.com

249. Fiera di Sant'Orso. Sant'Orso Fair, AOSTA VALLEY, ITALY, (1566325156) © Simone Migliaro / shutterstock.com

250. Mt. Cervino, BREUIL-CERVINIA, ITALY, (19571197) © Mihai-Bogdan Lazar / shutterstock.com

251. Dolomite zip line. -Dolomite Zipline, PIETRAPERTOSA, ITALY, (617527293) © Mattia / stock.adobe.com

252. Castelmezzano, BASILICATA, ITALY, (2231125725) © Sean Pavone / shutterstock.com

253. Neptune's Grotto. Cave of Neptune, SARDINIA, ITALY, (2B4BKCR) © Hemis / alamy.com

254. Buggerru, SARDINIA, ITALY, (2452942495) © Maslowski Marcin / shutterstock.com

255. Iseo Lake, LOMBARDY, ITALY, (2189207091) © leoks / shutterstock.com

256. Angel on Ponte Sant'Angelo, ROME, ITALY (2537254291) © Maykova Galina / shutterstock.com

257. Castel Gandolfo/Barbarini Gardens (cropped). Teresa Tomeo, all rights reserved.

Adapted from Map of Rome (619370629) stock.adobe.com

ABOUT THE AUTHOR

Teresa Tomeo is a syndicated Catholic talk-show host, and motivational speaker with over 40 years of experience in TV, radio, and newspaper. She spent almost 20 of those years working in front of a camera as a reporter and anchor in the Detroit market. In 2000, Teresa left the secular media to start her own speaking and communications company, Teresa Tomeo Communications, LLC, (TeresaTomeo.com). Her daily morning radio program, Catholic Connection, is produced by Ave Maria Radio and EWTN's Global Catholic Radio Network and can be heard on more than 600 domestic and international AM and FM radio affiliates worldwide, including SiriusXM Satellite Radio. Over the past two decades, Teresa has traveled extensively throughout Italy and has led numerous pilgrimages and tours there. In 2019, she founded T's Italy, a travel consultation company, along with its website, TravelItalyExpert.com, where she shares insider tips for where to eat, stay, shop, play, and pray. As a journalist, Teresa has covered numerous Italy assignments, including the canonization of several new saints in Rome including John Paul II and Mother Teresa of Calcutta. This gave her a unique understanding of how to navigate the Eternal City, whether one is traveling there as a tourist, or a pilgrim interested in a Papal audience. Every time she goes to Italy, she uncovers something new, and explores the roots and history behind the beautiful Italian culture. After exploring almost every region in Italy, Teresa and her husband purchased a home there in 2023, and they now live in central Italy half of the year. This allows her to continue to travel extensively throughout all of the regions and provinces of Italy.